D0945271

The History of Reading, Volume 2

Brycchan Carey et al. (eds.), *Discourses of Slavery and Abolition: Britain and Its Colonies, 1760–1838*

Gail Marshall and Adrian Poole (eds.) *Victorian Shakespeare*, Vol. 1: *Theatre, Drama and Performance*, Vol. 2: *Literature and Culture*

Andrew Nash (ed.), *The Culture of Collected Editions*

Jerome McGann, *Radiant Textuality: Literary Study after the World Wide Web*

Elizabeth James (ed.), *Macmillan: A Publishing Tradition*

Elizabeth Maslen, *Political and Social Issues in British Women's Fiction, 1928–1968*

Angelique Richardson and Chris Willis (eds.), *The New Woman in Fiction and Fact: Fin-de-Siècle Feminisms*

Warren Chernaik, Martin Swales and Robert Vilain (eds.), *The Art of Detective Fiction*

Rebecca D'Monte and Nicole Pohl (eds.), *Female Communities 1600–1800*

Isobel Armstrong and Virginia Blain (eds.), *Women's Poetry in the Enlightenment: The Making of a Canon, 1730–1820*

Isobel Armstrong and Virginia Blain (eds.), *Women's Poetry, Late Romantic to Late Victorian: Gender and Genre, 1830–1900*

Warren Chernaik and Martin Dzelzainis (eds.), *Marvell and Liberty* (July 1999)

Andy Leak and George Paizis (eds.), *The Holocaust and the Text: Speaking the Unspeakable*

Warwick Gould and Thomas F. Staley (eds.), *Writing the Lives of Writers*

Ian Willison, Warwick Gould and Warren Chernaik (eds.), *Modernist Writers and the Marketplace* (1996)

John Spiers (ed.), *George Gissing and the City: Cultural Crisis and the Making of Books in Late Victorian England*

Mary Hammond and Shafquat Towheed (eds.), *Publishing in the First World War* (2007)

Mary Hammond and Robert Fraser (eds.), *Books without Borders, Volume 1: The Cross-National Dimension in Print Culture* (2008), *Books without Borders, Volume 2: Perspectives from South Asia* (2008)

Gina Potts and Lisa Shahriari (eds.), *Virginia Woolf's Bloomsbury, Volume 1: Aesthetic Theory and Literary Practice* (2010), *Virginia Woolf's Bloomsbury, Volume 2: International Influence and Politics* (2010)

Robert J. Balfour (ed.), *Culture, Capital and Representation* (2010)

John Spiers (ed.), *The Culture of the Publisher's Series, Volume 1: Authors, Publishers and the Shaping of Taste* (2011), *The Culture of the Publisher's Series, Volume 2:* (2011)

Shafquat Towheed and W. R. Owens (eds.), *The History of Reading, Volume 1: International Perspectives, c.1500–1990*. Katie Halsey and W. R. Owens (eds.), *The History of Reading, Volume 2: Evidence from the British Isles, c.1750–1950*. Rosalind Crone and Shafquat Towheed (eds.), *The History of Reading, Volume 3: Methods, Strategies, Tactics*

Also by Katie Halsey

THE HISTORY OF READING: A Reader (*co-editor with Rosalind Crone and Shafquat Towheed*)

THE CONCEPT AND PRACTICE OF CONVERSATION IN THE LONG EIGHTEENTH CENTURY (*co-editor with Jane Slinn*)

THE COMPLETE WORKS OF JANE AUSTEN IN EIGHT VOLUMES: Jane Austen and her Readers (*editor*)

Also by W. R. Owens

THE GOSPELS: Authorized King James Version (*editor*)

DANIEL DEFOE: The Life and Strange Surprising Adventures of Robinson Crusoe (*editor*)

A POLITICAL BIOGRAPHY OF DANIEL DEFOE (*with P. N. Furbank*)

DANIEL DEFOE: The True-born Englishman and Other Poems (*editor*)

JOHN BUNYAN: The Pilgrim's Progress (*editor*)

A CRITICAL BIOGRAPHY OF DANIEL DEFOE (*with P. N. Furbank*)

DEFOE DEATTRIBUTIONS: A Critique of J. R. Moore's Checklist (*with P. N. Furbank*)

THE MISCELLANEOUS WORKS OF JOHN BUNYAN, VOLS XII and XIII (*editor*)

THE CANONISATION OF DANIEL DEFOE (*with P. N. Furbank*)

The History of Reading, Volume 2

Evidence from the British Isles, c.1750–1950

Edited by

Katie Halsey
University of Stirling

and

W. R. Owens
The Open University

Foreword by
Simon Eliot

 In association with the Institute of English Studies, School of Advanced Study, University of London

First published 2011 by
PALGRAVE MACMILLAN

Palgrave Macmillan in the UK is an imprint of Macmillan Publishers Limited,
registered in England, company number 785998, of Houndmills, Basingstoke,
Hampshire RG21 6XS.

Palgrave Macmillan in the US is a division of St Martin's Press LLC,
175 Fifth Avenue, New York, NY 10010.

Palgrave Macmillan is the global academic imprint of the above companies
and has companies and representatives throughout the world.

Palgrave® and Macmillan® are registered trademarks in the United States,
the United Kingdom, Europe and other countries.

ISBN 978–0–230–24755–0

This book is printed on paper suitable for recycling and made from fully
managed and sustained forest sources. Logging, pulping and manufacturing
processes are expected to conform to the environmental regulations of the
country of origin.

A catalogue record for this book is available from the British Library.

A catalog record for this book is available from the Library of Congress.

10   9   8   7   6   5   4   3   2   1
20 19 18 17 16 15 14 13 12 11

Printed and bound in the United States of America

For Stephen Colclough

Contents

List of Figures

List of Tables

Foreword

Simon Eliot

> People say that life is the thing, but I prefer
> reading.
> (Logan Pearsall Smith, 1865–1946)

> To pass her time 'twixt reading and Bohea,
> To muse, and spill her solitary tea,
> Or o'er cold coffee trifle with the spoon,
> Count the slow clock, and dine exact at noon.
> (Alexander Pope, 1688–1744)

> Laudant illa sed ista legunt.
> (They praise those works, but read these.)
> (Martial, *c*.AD 40–104)

Little that is commonplace registers in history. Until relatively recently most history has been a record of the exceptional, of change, of difference, or of contrast. To reverse the cliché, it's always been about the elephant in the room, and never about how the room was furnished or its other, less striking occupants. Essential commonplaces such as eating, casual conversations in the street, and the street itself, fudge into a fuzzy background against which sharp change or notable differences are brought into focus. In most history the ordinary is at best out of focus or, more commonly, invisible. The quotidian is never quoted, the common place is uncommon, and 'the same old, same old' is worn out before it is ever recorded.

In most literate societies, reading is usually this sort of prosaic activity. Most of us do it most of the time. It is not necessarily a matter of settling down to spend a few hours with *On the Origin of Species* or catching up with the latest vogue novel, it is more often a matter of reading a cornflakes packet for want of anything better, or reading a 'use by' date on something dubious from the fridge, or a timetable, or a free newspaper, or an email, or an advertisement, or a street name, or a menu, or the instructions on a bottle of aspirin.

However, the reading that we tend to remember, and the reading that much more frequently gets recorded, is of the exceptional sort: the book, the chapter, perhaps even just the sentence, which strikes home, which affects us in some profound way, which sometimes even transforms us. One should never underestimate the power of reading to surprise with joy, shock with facts or reason, or force us to see things from a disturbingly different point of view, and doing so commonly against our will and inclination. Samuel Johnson's experience, while he was an undergraduate at Oxford, of taking up Law's *Serious Call to a Holy Life* on the assumption that he might laugh at it, only to find Law 'an overmatch for me' is an example of such unexpected and sometimes unwelcome power. Reading, as so many other human experiences do, often relies for its impact on the law of unintended consequences.

Now, there is a natural and understandable tendency of those, particularly in literary studies, to prioritize this exceptional form of reading. After all, what is the use of studying something if it does not have a huge potential power to change and to convert? To study something that merely entertained, or diverted, or allowed escape or, worst of all, simply passed the time, is somehow demeaning. What we want are roads to Damascus: the flash, the crash, the conversion.

But if most, or even a significant minority, of reading experiences were of this transformational sort, we as readers would soon be exhausted by it or, like Mr Brooke in George Eliot's *Middlemarch*, endlessly buffeted from one set of opinions to the next as he read one pamphlet and then another.

There is, of course, a middle type of reading between the entirely functional and the disconcertingly transcendental. This consists of reading for entertainment (escapist or otherwise), for instruction and information – and for confirmation. The first two are self-explanatory, but the third may need some unpacking. Although we are occasionally subject, often accidentally, to a reading experience that is transformational, we do spend a lot of our reading time trying to avoid such experiences. For instance, we usually choose for our newspaper one that tends to parallel our own views, and we naturally gravitate to other texts that are disposed to assure us that our opinions are the correct ones, and to provide us with further examples to back up our own prejudices. To provide the 'And I am right, and you are right' reassurance is one of the necessary and comforting functions of reading. Much of the content of even the most modern forms of communication, the text and the tweet, are devoted to variations on the theme of 'I'm OK, and you're OK'. It was ever thus: many of the clay tablets exchanged between Assyrian monarchs and their civil servants performed a similar function.

We must not forget that the act of reading or, at least, the act of appearing to read, is also an invaluable social tool. For those wishing to promote themselves as studious, for those wanting to avoid social contact or (even worse) eye contact, for those wishing to create space around themselves in a crowded place, reading is a godsend. How many of us, in dining alone in a restaurant, have taken a book or a newspaper not merely for entertainment, but in order to indicate that we are certainly not sad and lonely people?

Finally, there is the history of implied reading; that is, of reading we have not done but either implicitly or explicitly claimed to have done. The unread books borrowed from libraries, the un-perused books on our tables and bookshelves, all those monuments to our good intentions. Or, equally common, the books we bluff about, the allusion to a text that we hope will impress without being picked up by someone who has actually read the book to which we have casually referred. That this is both not new and all too human is attested by the quotation from Martial at the beginning of this foreword.

The history of reading is as much about the reader as it is about what is read. It is about the cocktail of motives and circumstances that leads us to select one text rather than another, and about the texture of our personalities and the nature of our predicament that determine how we react to that text. In our various attempts to recreate the humanity of the world we have lost, the study of the reading experiences of those in earlier centuries is an important and worthwhile endeavour. The essays that follow are part of a heroic project to explore one of the most significant of the intellectual experiences that we share with the literate past.

Acknowledgements

The editors would like to thank the Arts and Humanities Research Council for funding The Reading Experience Database, 1450–1945 (RED) project, established at The Open University in collaboration with the Institute of English Studies, University of London. Among the outcomes of the RED project was an international conference, 'Evidence of Reading, Reading the Evidence', held at the Institute of English Studies in July 2008, from which many of the essays in these three volumes emerged. Thanks are also due to Adam Mathew Digital, the Bibliographical Society, the British Academy, *History Today*, The Open University and the Royal Historical Society, who provided additional financial support for the conference, and to all the colleagues who helped with its organization, in particular Dr Karen Attar (Rare Books Librarian, Senate House Library), curator of the accompanying exhibition. We would like to thank colleagues and students at the University of Cambridge, The Open University, the University of Stirling, and the Institute of English Studies, School of Advanced Study, University of London, for helpful comments and suggestions. In addition, we gratefully acknowledge the work of all the contributors to The Reading Experience Database project. Permission to reproduce *The Tube Train* by Cyril Edward Power (linocut *c*.1934, Private Collection) on the cover of this volume was kindly granted by Bridgeman Education. We would also like to thank the following for permission to quote or reproduce material in individual chapters: Hilary Adams and Shirley Gould-Smith (Chapter 5); The Harris Museum and Art Gallery, Preston, and Mr William Smith, (Chapter 7); The National Portrait Gallery (Chapter 9); May Reid, George Rountree, Janet Murphy, Ebie Moncrieff, Bob Todd and Margot Alexander (Chapter 11). Every effort has been made to trace all copyright holders, but if any have been inadvertently overlooked, the publisher will be pleased to make the necessary arrangements at the first opportunity.

Notes on Contributors

Sophie Bankes is a doctoral student at The Open University, UK researching the reading life of the eighteenth-century autodidact and bookseller, James Lackington.

Adrian Bingham is Senior Lecturer in Modern History at the University of Sheffield, UK. He is the author *of Gender, Modernity, and the Popular Press in Inter-War Britain* (2004) and *Family Newspapers? Sex, Private Life, and the British Popular Press 1918–1978* (2009).

Rosalind Crone is Lecturer in History at The Open University, UK and Co-Investigator on The Reading Experience Database project. She has published widely on popular culture, crime and literacy in the nineteenth century and is author of the forthcoming *Violent Victorians: Popular Entertainment in Nineteenth-Century London* (forthcoming 2012).

Simon Eliot is Professor of the History of the Book in the Institute of English Studies, School of Advanced Study, University of London. He has published on quantitative book history, publishing history, the history of lighting and library history. He is general editor of the new multi-volume *History of Oxford University Press*.

David Finkelstein is Research Professor of Media and Print Culture at Queen Margaret University, Edinburgh, Scotland. His publications include *The House of Blackwood: Author–Publisher Relations in the Victorian Era* (2002), *An Introduction to Book History* (co-author with Alistair McCleery, 2005), and the edited *Print Culture and the Blackwood Tradition, 1805–1930* (2006).

Linda Fleming is a postdoctoral researcher for the *Scottish Readers Remember* project at Edinburgh Napier University, Scotland. Her published work includes a contribution on the life of Ralph Glasser in the *Edinburgh History of the Book in Scotland* (Vol. 4) (2007), and a chapter for Vol. 4 of the *Everyday Life in Scotland* series (2009).

Clare Gill is a Graduate Teaching Fellow at Queen's University Belfast, where she teaches Victorian and modernist literature. She has recently completed a PhD thesis that situates Olive Schreiner's texts in the context of the late-nineteenth century literary marketplace.

Katie Halsey is Lecturer in Eighteenth-Century Literature at the University of Stirling, Scotland. Her publications include *Jane Austen and her Readers* (forthcoming 2011), numerous articles on literature and print culture, *The Concept and Practice of Conversation in the Long Eighteenth Century* (co-editor with Jane Slinn, 2007) and *The History of Reading* (co-editor with Rosalind Crone and Shafquat Towheed, 2010).

Andrew Hobbs is a postdoctoral research assistant in the School of Journalism, Media and Communication at the University of Central Lancashire, UK, and is an associate editor of the *Dictionary of Nineteenth-Century Journalism*. His publications include 'When the provincial press was the national press (*c*.1836–*c*.1900)', *International Journal of Regional and Local Studies*, Series 2, 5:1 (2009).

Stephen Jacyna is Reader in the History of Medicine at University College London. He is the author of *Medicine and Modernism: A Biography of Sir Henry Head* (2008); *Lost Words: Narratives of Language and the Brain, 1825–1926* (2000), and *Philosophic Whigs: Medicine, Science, and Citizenship in Edinburgh, 1789–1848* (1994).

Michael Ledger-Lomas is a Fellow of Peterhouse, Cambridge, UK. He is interested in religion and Anglo-German relations in nineteenth-century Britain. He is the co-editor (with David Gange) of *Cities of God: Archaeology and the Bible in Nineteenth-century Britain* (forthcoming 2012), and co-editor (with Scott Mandelbrote) of *Dissent and the Bible in Britain, 1650–1950* (forthcoming 2012).

Alistair McCleery is Professor and Director of the Scottish Centre for the Book at Edinburgh Napier University, Scotland. Recent books include two editions of Neil Gunn's essays, *Landscape to Light* (2009) and *Belief in Ourselves* (2010), and *An Honest Trade: Bookselling in Scotland* (2009).

W. R. Owens is Professor of English Literature at The Open University, UK. He has published widely on John Bunyan and Daniel Defoe, and is Director of The Reading Experience Database, 1450–1945 (RED) project. His most recent publication is an edition of the 1611 text of *The Gospels* for Oxford World's Classics (2011).

Mark Towsey is Lecturer in Modern British History at the University of Liverpool, UK. He has previously held fellowships at Harvard, Yale and London, and has published extensively on eighteenth-century libraries and reading habits, including *Reading the Scottish Enlightenment: Books and their Readers in Provincial Scotland, 1750– 1820* (2010).

Anna Vaninskaya is Lecturer in Victorian Literature at the University of Edinburgh, Scotland. She is the author of *William Morris and the Idea of Community: Romance, History and Propaganda, 1880–1914* (2010), and numerous articles and book chapters on Morris, Chesterton and Orwell, socialism, popular reading, historical cultures and education.

Introduction

Katie Halsey and W. R. Owens

'Reading has a history. But how can we recover it?' The answer Robert Darnton gives to his own question – 'by searching the record for readers' – gives rise to a series of other questions.[1] What is the record? Where is it? How should we search it? What do we do with the readers when we find them? What is the status of the different kinds of evidence that we might find? And how might we put that evidence together to create a 'history' of reading? The very nature of the practice of reading – a practice that has often been internal, private, unremarked – makes tracking down surviving evidence very difficult indeed. Most records that survive have done so either because they relate to famous or notable historical characters, or only through serendipity or chance, and are thus not necessarily representative. They may also be only partial, or difficult to interpret. It is thus necessary to try to combine as many different kinds of evidence as possible before coming to any sorts of conclusions.

Darnton's own work on Rousseau's readers exemplifies what we might call the 'case study' method. Scholars had previously tended to focus on perceptions or representations of reading as manifested in fiction, prescriptive literature such as conduct books, articles and reviews, or on theoretical models of 'implied', 'intended', 'inscribed', 'ideal' or 'hypothetical' readers.[2] Darnton's generation of researchers, by contrast, began to try to find evidence left by actual historical readers, in the hope that a large enough collection of case studies would eventually allow the identification of broader patterns and trends across history, and therefore enable scholars eventually to write a more comprehensive history of reading. Their focus was on the first-hand accounts of reading found in letters, diaries, journals, autobiographies, annotations and marginalia. 'Anecdotal' evidence of this kind, as Darnton pointed out, itself requires interpretation, and is neither transparent nor even necessarily accurate on the level of fact. Nonetheless, the records left by real historical readers were and remain our best (perhaps our only) insight into what Darnton called the 'whys' and 'hows' of historical reading: the emotional responses and cognitive processes of readers in the past.

For some thirty years now, scholars in the field have been collecting and analysing new kinds of evidence, and considering the insights this evidence might afford into the practice of reading in history. This volume collects together eleven chapters which bring to the fore the question of evidence, focusing on the history of reading in the British Isles over a period of approximately two hundred years. Many different kinds of evidence are surveyed and analysed here. Private lending library record books function as evidence for the dispersal and reading of books in rural Scotland. Crime advertisements and court records are utilized to interrogate the links between reading and action in eighteenth-century London. Biblical commentaries are considered as evidence of attempts to direct readers towards a particular kind of reading, as well as, in themselves, evidence of religious reading practices in Victorian Britain. Letters pages and correspondence class reports reveal the construction of a particular kind of reading community in socialist circles in the 1890s. The often-neglected category of place is explored in an account of the role of the news room and the newsagent's shop in the reading life of nineteenth-century Preston. Developments in the style, format and content of newspapers pioneered by Lord Northcliffe in the early twentieth century are discussed as evidence of how what readers were believed to want from their reading matter influenced what they were given to read. Mass Observation surveys are used to show reading patterns in wartime Britain in the 1940s.

Some chapters use more traditional sources for the history of reading, such as autobiographies, private letters, articles and reviews and personal diaries. Almost all of the chapters make some use of first-hand evidence, either to corroborate or contradict evidence found in other sources. They are all characterized by an explicit or implicit epistemological agenda, exploring such issues as the reliability of individual testimony, the legitimacy of conclusions drawn from statistical evidence, the gap between representations of reading and records of historical practice, and, more broadly, the status and value of different kinds of evidence. The overall aim of the volume is to consider how these different kinds of evidence can be used to further our knowledge of the practice of reading in the past. As Rosalind Crone helpfully warns us, however, it is sometimes the 'gaps and silences' (p. 106) in the available evidence that speak to us most eloquently, reminding us that the pursuit of knowledge in this field must take account not only of the wealth of evidence available to us, but also of the many lacunae in the historical record.

In addition to the variety of different kinds of evidence discussed, the chapters deal with a very wide range of readers and the texts that they read. Readers of almost every socio-economic class, of both genders, and from significantly different geographical regions, are examined. A great diversity of texts is considered, with proper attention paid to texts often considered by traditional literary history to be unimportant, without influence, or ephemeral, such as newspapers, popular and penny fiction, and religious tracts. This approach reveals the extent to which a history of reading differs from traditional literary history in attempting to discover the texts which were *actually* read as opposed to those which were (or are) considered to be of literary importance and merit. This more reader-focused approach suggests some places where the map of literary 'influence' might need to be redrawn in the light of the texts which were commonly read and remembered.

Many of the chapters here deal with the complex relationships between reading habits and the market. They all pay attention to both the habits and the *habitus* of readers, demonstrating the ways in which individual reading is influenced (even sometimes defined) by factors such as social class, political affiliation, the place of reading, the availability of books and changes in publishing practices.[3] As Jonathan Rose has persuasively argued, books and texts have many and unpredictable uses, and this is a theme that frequently reoccurs throughout the chapters in this book.[4] The different motivations of readers – pleasure, escapism, self-improvement, community-building, to name only a few – are also described and analysed in some detail, and the importance of communal reading and reading communities emerges clearly in many chapters.

Part 1 comprises three chapters dealing specifically with the formation of reading communities. Mark Towsey's analysis of the borrowing records of a small group of castle libraries in the north-east of Scotland highlights the importance of establishing the availability or otherwise of both particular books and books in general to individuals or communities. His chapter shows how, in this corner of Scotland at least, private collections of books were made available to a much larger number of individual readers than might have been expected. The Scottish landed gentry discussed here allowed, even encouraged, borrowing from their private collections by a variety of different readers, from shepherds and factors to neighbouring lairds, with the result that 'privy borrowing from private collections expanded the reading nation dramatically' (p. 27). This kind of borrowing also encouraged the formation of informal reading communities who met to read and discuss books together. In the eighteenth century, the family library was, as Towsey says, 'one of the main focuses of genteel sociability in rural Scotland' (p. 20). In teasing out the links between the various families and individuals mentioned in the castles' borrowing registers, and by describing the role that reading together played in the lives of these families and individuals, Towsey reminds us that a history of reading is often also a history of the other uses to which books can be put. In this case, he describes the ideological implications of book exchanges in the reading community cultivated by Elizabeth Rose, the Lady Laird of Kilravock. They were, he writes, 'a crucial means by which the book-lender as moral guardian could help cultivate the virtuous domesticity that was expected of younger women readers in her social circle' (p. 27).

The extent to which books can be put to use in the service of particular ideologies, and the degree to which readers recognize, yield to, or resist ideological pressures is also the focus of both Clare Gill's examination of socialist reading communities in the 1890s and Michael Ledger-Lomas's account of Victorian commentaries on the Bible. Gill's chapter discusses the deliberate attempts of left-wing labour leaders to construct an active socialist reading community. Through an analysis of the letters pages and correspondence class reports of John Trevor's periodical, the *Labour Prophet*, Gill suggests that the periodical both directed and modelled readers' responses to socialist texts and that at least some of its readers welcomed this. The *Labour Prophet* deliberately perpetuated a 'sense of kinship among readers', and was 'a truly interactive site where readers, along with editors and writers, could participate in the formation of [Olive] Schreiner's reputation and the establishment of wider reading patterns within their own reading community' (p. 59). The journal also developed a number of new methods of book distribution, and, through direct buying and selling arrangements, Gill argues, it 'effectively fostered a community of readers by the means of an entire "communication circuit" . . . which both made use of and bypassed mainstream modes of book distribution and circulation' (pp. 58–9). Gill's discussion, like Towsey's, again points us towards a sense of reading as a 'communal activity', here directed towards 'socialist solidarity' rather than 'virtuous domesticity', but nonetheless an activity devoted to encouraging an agreed response to shared texts.

Similarly, Michael Ledger-Lomas argues that Victorian commentaries on Saint Paul's epistles were designed both to model particular kinds of reading practices and to manoeuvre readers into certain theological positions, but suggests that readers were in fact frequently resistant to the authority claimed by Biblical commentators. 'Victorian readers were not left to their own devices in interpreting authoritative texts' (pp. 43–4), but the very practices of minute scrutiny and exact attention to the Biblical text that the commentaries demonstrated and encouraged could lead to alternative interpretations. Female readers, in particular, resisted the ideological imperatives of conservative male commentators and produced their own interpretations of Paul's laws and recommendations. In this case, we see clearly that a history of reading must also take account of the history of interpretation.

One of the many uses to which books and reading are put is, of course, the pursuit of pleasure or gratification. The chapters by Anna Vaninskaya and Katie Halsey in Part 2 discuss the relationship between reading and gratification in two historical periods: the late nineteenth century and the Second World War. Vaninskaya compares the testimony of historical readers of 'penny dreadfuls' with the depictions of such readers in the late-Victorian periodical press. Late-Victorian cultural commentators commonly considered the consumption of 'penny dreadfuls' to be a mindless activity, akin to spiritual and intellectual self-poisoning on the part of the working classes. They frequently inveighed against an educational system that taught working-class children to read, but did not teach them to discriminate between literary trash and literary treasure. The accounts of the actual readers of 'penny dreadfuls', on the other hand, suggest that they in fact tended to have a much more sophisticated response to these texts, finding them pleasurable but forgettable. The readers surveyed by Vaninskaya often began by reading the 'beloved "bloods"' but swiftly moved on to other, more canonical books (p. 68). Vaninskaya also raises another important issue that runs through a number of the chapters in the volume: the relationship between reading practices and the market. She notes that both publishers and educationalists believed that providing cheap literature of a more morally uplifting kind would wean working-class readers off the 'penny dreadfuls' and set them on a path towards reading the classics. Such thinkers, she writes, 'pinned [their] hopes primarily on the market' (p. 73), and relied on a conviction that enlightened publishing practices would solve the problems of the British educational system.

Katie Halsey also pays close attention to the economic factors that affected British subjects' reading habits during the Second World War. She discusses the motivations, choices and attitudes towards reading matter of 'ordinary' British readers on the home front, in the context of the limitations on books and newspapers resulting from wartime economic, political and social conditions. The evidence used is derived from the Mass Observation surveys and diaries, individual responses accumulated in The Reading Experience Database, and the diaries and oral testimony of a living reader. The collected evidence overwhelmingly suggests a preference for reading fiction and newspapers over other genres during the war years, and a clear trend towards escapist reading: 'light books and escapist stuff', as one Mass Observation participant called it (p. 93). In his chapter, Adrian Bingham similarly identifies a desire for 'escapism and excitement' in newspaper readers of the same period (p. 147), and this desire is of course also implicit in the love of 'penny dreadfuls' described by Vaninskaya. In all three chapters, readers' accounts of their escapist reading practices are frequently characterized by mixed feelings of guilt and pleasure. Gratification in reading clearly had its costs.

In Part 3, on reading and the press, Rosalind Crone, Andrew Hobbs and Adrian Bingham discuss newspaper reading practices in three distinct periods: 1740–1820, 1855–1900 and 1890–1950. While Crone and Bingham focus on the 'what' and 'how' of reading, to use Robert Darnton's now-famous terms, discussing the relationships between the content and layout of specific newspapers and how they were read, Hobbs considers the 'where' of the reading experience, describing and analysing two locations of reading in Preston, Lancashire in the late nineteenth century.[5] Through close analysis of textual evidence from within the newspaper, and testimony from readers found in court records, Crone's chapter concentrates on the question of the extent to which the reading and readership of crime advertisements placed in the eighteenth-century *Public Advertiser* can be ascertained. Although shedding considerable light on the general reading practices of eighteenth-century Londoners, Crone points out that the two kinds of evidence for the reading of crime advertisements do not always match up: 'for reasons of expense, inconvenience or even potential criminal prosecution, many readers of crime advertisements may have wished to erase any evidence of their reading, something that the victims of crime (or the producers of crime adverts) recognized and then exploited to their own advantage' (p. 119). Crone here sounds a valuable note of caution, warning that the serendipitous survival of evidence of particular kinds of reading in the historical records 'may blind us to more widespread practices' (p. 119).

Andrew Hobbs's chapter is a contribution not only to the history of reading, but also to what Leah Price and others have called a 'geography of reading', providing another helpful prompt to historians of reading in reminding us of the insights afforded by a careful attention to the location of reading experiences.[6] Hobbs also makes the point that 'the literary roots of the discipline' have tended to skew scholarship 'towards the historical reading of high-status literary texts' (p. 121), and he calls for a closer attention to ephemeral texts such as newspapers and periodicals. Emphasis on the reader, rather than the text, he suggests, reveals new facts about nineteenth-century reading. This chapter focuses on two locations in which newspapers were read in nineteenth-century Preston, the news room and the newsagent's shop. It also pays close attention to the economics of newspaper-reading in this period, arguing that Preston's reading institutions provided the cheapest access to newspapers and periodicals for its patrons. Hobbs demonstrates that communal reading rooms flourished at this period, and that newspapers had a much longer life than has hitherto been supposed through a 'recirculation system' in which newspapers were frequently sold on. Newspapers, he concludes, 'were central to the reading world of a provincial town' (pp. 124, 135).

Adrian Bingham concurs, suggesting that in the twentieth century, for ordinary Britons, 'reading meant, above all, the consumption of newspapers' (p. 139). In his chapter, he traces the developments in newspaper format and layout pioneered by Alfred Harmsworth (later Lord Northcliffe) in the *Daily Mail*. Northcliffe 'thought deeply about the actual reading experience of readers, and tried to shape his newspapers around it' (p. 141), recognizing that many readers lacked the time, opportunity or concentration to read the newspaper cover-to-cover. In fact, as Bingham writes, most readers 'simply grabbed the opportunity to read when they had a spare moment' (p. 146). Northcliffe encouraged feedback from his readers, and structured his papers according to what he learned from letters to the editor, survey results and informal observation. The material investigated in this chapter provides evidence both of people's attitudes to their newspapers and the newspapers' attempts to give the public what it wanted. It thus usefully illuminates the dynamic two-way relationship between readers and the market touched on in earlier chapters by Vaninskaya and Gill.

Part 4 contains three studies of autodidacts. Sophie Bankes discusses accounts by the eighteenth-century bookseller James Lackington of his own reading in the light of his personal religious affiliations and his professional motivations. Bankes suggests that Lackington's autobiographies present what may be 'an idealized record of reading experience', one designed to inspire new readers (p. 157). She interrogates the evidence of reading provided by quotations in Lackington's two volumes of autobiography, showing how, in certain cases, it is possible to trace evidence of his reading through the specific typographical presentation of the quotations included. Misattributions and minor misquotations also furnish valuable evidence for his use of particular anthologies and poetical dictionaries. Bankes explores the influence of Lackington's three wives on his separate phases of development as a reader, and analyses the religious and cultural implications of his reading choices on his self-presentation as a reader. In Lackington's case, books are put to use to construct a series of personal identities: first, as a devout and hard-working Methodist; second, as a freethinking intellectual and prosperous bookseller; and lastly, as a repentant prodigal, who returns to his Methodist beginnings and promotes the cause of religion again.

As with Lackington, the scientist Henry Head (1861–1940) saw reading as part of a process of self-formation, and, also like Lackington, Head's reading life was strongly influenced by his wife. Where Lackington read predominantly for insight into religious and intellectual matters, however, Head was primarily interested in reading fiction for the insights it provided into the mind of man. Stephen Jacyna's account reveals a reader who was, throughout his life, closely attuned to the psychological and emotional benefits of reading fiction. He and his wife, Ruth Mayhew, read 'as much to gain insight into their own personalities as to analyse the works under discussion' (p. 179). Head believed that analytical skills and psychological insights could be 'honed to a higher degree of perfection through reading authors who were themselves accomplished "psychologists"' (p. 180). As a neurologist, Head had a keen professional interest in the working of the mind, and he judged novels on the basis of how accurately they described and explained the mental processes of their characters. Jacyna also suggests that literature played a therapeutic role in Head's own 'long twilight as an invalid' (p. 186). Case studies of readers such as Head and Lackington not only provide us with insight into individual readers, but illuminate also the wider uses of reading over a long historical period as we identify the patterns and themes that emerge from the analysis of the available evidence.

The final chapter focuses on working-class readers in twentieth-century Scotland. In a remote corner of eighteenth-century Scotland, as Mark Towsey shows in the opening chapter, knowledge was disseminated by the efforts of enlightened lairds who lent their books to a wide variety of readers from different social classes. In the twentieth century, this Enlightenment project bore hybrid fruit, as Linda Fleming, Alistair McCleery and David Finkelstein argue. They explore the implications of 'Scotland's historical traditions of intellectualism' for the working-class autodidacts of the twentieth century (p. 189). Using evidence drawn from an oral history research project, *Scottish Readers Remember*, the authors discuss the relationship between working-class identity and reading practices in the context of the economic and societal changes in Scotland since the turn of the nineteenth century. They present research findings on three major topics – reading, learning and libraries; reading choices; and the love of reading – concluding that Scotland differs from the general British experience described by Jonathan Rose in which love of learning declines among the working classes in the twentieth century.[7] They suggest that 'the autodidact tradition is not lost in Scotland, but has assumed new guises' (p. 200), and that mass culture and the autodidact impulse do not function in opposition, but in tandem. Working-class Scots continue to perceive themselves as the proud bearers of a tradition of autodidact reading going back to the Scottish Enlightenment, which is profoundly related to their own class identity.

What can the evidence surveyed, analysed and interpreted in these chapters, taken cumulatively and as a whole, tell us about the history of reading in the British Isles from 1750 to 1950? Because of the nature of the historical record of reading, any conclusions that we draw must remain tentative and provisional, but the essays collected in these volumes suggest some fruitful ways in which we might put this evidence to use, alongside some valuable caveats about doing so. Above all, as these chapters show, reading the evidence of reading demands a careful consideration of context – not only what Hans Robert Jauss called 'the horizon of expectations' of the reader, but also the physical and material conditions surrounding the act of reading.[8] It is impossible to ignore the part that reading plays in the complex process of fashioning an image of the self, but although the activity of reading is most often now an individual one, we see here that the communities within which a person reads can have an important influence on reading matter, opinions of texts, and personal and intellectual development. And although we may often think of the relationship between author and reader as a deeply personal one, it is evident that even the most determined and isolated of autodidacts is in fact influenced by external factors. The chapters collected in this volume remind us of the political or ideological imperatives that governed the reading of different classes, regions and individuals in the past, and they reveal something of the complicated relationship between guilt and gratification in the reading of fiction. If the past is a foreign country, as L. P. Hartley memorably claimed, these chapters, in interrogating the worth and validity of this evidence of reading practices, and deploying it to come to their own conclusions, simultaneously chart some of the territory of that 'foreign country' and mark out paths for future explorers to follow.[9]

Notes and references

1. Robert Darnton, 'First steps towards a history of reading', *Australian Journal of French Studies*, 23 (1986), 5–30 (p. 5).
2. The terms 'implied' and 'inscribed' readers are used by Wolfgang Iser, in *The Implied Reader: Patterns of Communication in Prose Fiction from Bunyan to Beckett* (Baltimore and London: The Johns Hopkins University Press, 1974). The description 'intended reader' is coined by Wayne C. Booth,

The Rhetoric of Fiction (Chicago: University of Chicago Press, 1961). The term 'ideal reader' is preferred by Gérard Genette and M. M. Bakhtin, in *Figures III* (Paris: Seuil, 1972) and *Speech Genres and Other Late Essays*, ed. C. Emerson and M. Holquist, trans. V. W. McGee (Austin, TX: University of Texas Press, 1986) respectively. The 'hypothetical' reader is discussed by Stanley Fish, in *Surprised by Sin: The Reader in 'Paradise Lost'* (London: Macmillan; New York: St. Martin's Press, 1967) and in his later collection of essays, *Is there a Text in this Class: The Authority of Interpretive Communities* (Cambridge, MA: Harvard University Press, 1980). Other theorists followed these writers in using a variety of these terms to discuss the responses of readers to texts in the field of literary theory now known as reader-response theory.

3. See Pierre Bourdieu, *La distinction: critique sociale du jugement* (Paris: Minuit, 1979), pp. 170–5, for a full discussion of *habitus*.
4. Jonathan Rose, 'Rereading the English Common Reader: a preface to a history of audiences', *Journal of History of Ideas*, 53 (1992), 47–70 (esp. pp. 60–70).
5. Robert Darnton, *The Great Cat Massacre and Other Episodes in French Cultural History* (London: Penguin Books, 1985), p. 216.
6. See, for example, Leah Price, 'Reading: the state of the discipline', *Book History*, 7 (2004), 303–20 (p. 308); James Secord, 'Geographies of reading', in his *Victorian Sensation: The Extraordinary Publication, Reception, and Secret Authorship of 'Vestiges of the Natural History of Creation'* (Chicago and London: University of Chicago Press, 2000), pp. 153–296; David N. Livingstone, 'Science, religion and the geography of reading: Sir William Whitla and the editorial staging of Isaac Newton's writings on biblical prophecy', *British Journal for the History of Science*, 36 (2003), 27–42; Richard Hornsey, 'The sexual geographies of reading in post-war London', *Gender, Place & Culture: A Journal of Feminist Geography*, 9 (2002), 371–84.
7. Jonathan Rose, *The Intellectual Life of the British Working Classes* (New Haven: Yale University Press, 2001).
8. Hans Robert Jauss, 'Literary history as a challenge to literary theory', *New Literary History*, 2 (1970), 7–37 (p. 12).
9. L. P. Hartley, *The Go-Between* (London: Hamish Hamilton, 1953), p. 1.

Part 1
Reading Communities

1
'The Talent Hid in a Napkin': Castle Libraries in Eighteenth-Century Scotland

Mark Towsey

Paul Kaufman argued forcefully in 1969 that library borrowing records can make a valuable contribution to the history of reading.[1] Though such evidence does not usually allow us to access the 'hows' and 'whys' of individual reading practices and experiences, in Robert Darnton's famous phraseology, borrowing records do allow us to get one step closer to reading encounters in the past.[2] Rather than relying on counting titles in library catalogues to estimate the circulation of books, borrowing records show which books were actually taken off the shelves, how often, for how long, and, above all, by whom. Kaufman's conclusions about what he termed 'reading vogues' have been widely cited by social and cultural historians in the decades since his work appeared,[3] while his work has been expanded in recent years by a number of scholars exploiting modern database software to construct much more detailed analyses of borrowing data than Kaufman was able to execute.[4] This chapter aims, however, to introduce evidence of book borrowing from a type of library that Kaufman himself never discussed in detail, using evidence relating to a small group of family libraries in north-eastern Scotland to illuminate the role of inter-personal book lending in the history of reading.

Although the long eighteenth century can be considered the first great age of library expansion, with enterprising booksellers, public-spirited benefactors and eager self-improvers founding book-lending institutions across the British Isles on a variety of organizational models, few scholars have considered seriously the more informal opportunities provided to Georgian readers by ostensibly 'private'

family libraries and personal book collections.[5] This neglect continues despite detailed research demonstrating that 'borrowing was
common' in earlier periods, with Elizabeth Boucier explaining that
'even a fairly modest farmer like Adam Eyre lent books, keeping
a record of loans so as to preserve his collection'.[6] Such evidence
for inter-personal book lending has been seized on by Renaissance
scholars who argue that informal book exchanges not only allowed
extremely rare or prohibitively expensive books to circulate in the
early centuries of print, but served much broader social, cultural and
political purposes in the early modern era.[7] Most pointedly for British
historians, Kevin Sharpe suggests that 'scholars interested in the constitution of a public sphere in early modern England will need to
follow carefully the investigations into those "private libraries" that
were semi-public collections, in London and in the province'.[8]

It has long been assumed that informal lending between friends, relatives, neighbours and associates remained rife in the eighteenth century. In his influential account of early modern literacy, Rab Houston
insists that such informal borrowing 'existed on an extensive and
unquantifiable scale' from the Renaissance through to the turn of the
nineteenth century.[9] Mark Girouard writes that by the 1730s, country
house libraries 'were no longer the personal equipment of the owner
of the house; they had become the common property of the family and his guests',[10] while John Brewer observes that 'among the
professional classes and minor gentry of provincial towns and rural
villages, there was always a bibliophile or two who would lend out his
books'.[11] Indeed, it may well be more appropriate to follow William
Sherman's lead in talking of 'privy libraries' rather than strictly private libraries in this period,[12] especially as the country house library
came increasingly to be regarded as a public venue explicitly intended
for the reception of guests, to encourage polite sociability and even to
facilitate a degree of chaperoned courtship.[13] As the author of a recent
seminal study of *The Lending Library in Georgian England* observes,
however, it is one thing to acknowledge that 'privy' lending occurred
in the eighteenth century but quite another to assess its impact on
the reading nation, since it depended on

essentially private exchanges of books, virtually impossible for
the historian to study systematically. They rested upon personal
intimacy between owner and borrower. And they involved texts,

often individually or in very small numbers, which belonged to collections that were neither properly institutionalised in organisation nor operated primarily for the purposes of lending.[14]

As both Houston and Allan admit, the problem is largely source-based. Off the cuff remarks about books borrowed from friends, relatives, neighbours, colleagues, lovers and employers abound in Georgian correspondence, diaries and autobiographies. Although this kind of material readily reinforces our impression that such practices were widespread, it would be a large task indeed to gather together stray hints from so-called 'anecdotal' sources into a more systematic study of book borrowing from private libraries.[15] After all, few contemporary memoirists were as perceptive in describing the cultural significance of inter-personal book lending as the celebrated 'Highland Lady', Elizabeth Grant of Rothiemurchus. She recalled that her father's 'books were a blessing, far and near' during her childhood at The Doune in Aviemore, since he 'thought a library kept for self was only the talent hid in a napkin, and that any loss or damage, rarely occurring, was to be balanced against the amount of good distributed'.[16]

Less subjective evidence that informal borrowing from private collections was widespread occasionally survives in family papers relating to the libraries themselves, often in the form of notes explicitly giving permission for borrowing. The laird of Grant drafted a memorandum on 6 December 1765, for instance, that empowered his clerk 'to lend out of the Library to any of the Gentlemen of this Country what books they may want for their amusement', although he insisted:

> You are to let no one what-ever go into the Library, only let them tell you the books they want & you will give them out. And as I would not chuse to have too many out at a time, never give out above six at once in whole.[17]

Grant was no doubt wise in seeking to control readers' physical access to his books, since the loss of even a single volume could represent a considerable loss to the integrity and value of the collection.[18] Elsewhere, it is obvious that the bond of trust that underpinned 'privy' borrowing had broken down entirely – giving further proof that such borrowing was commonplace, even if it was not always administered according to best practice. Lists of missing books from eighteenth-century libraries are a common occurrence in the archival collections of Scotland's landed families. More revealingly, desperate library owners frequently called for the return of books, not having recorded precisely who had borrowed what. This was clearly the case when the laird of Monymusk (a noted agricultural improver and public-spirited man of Enlightenment whose apparent partiality for 'privy' lending comes as no surprise) asked for the following printed circular to be distributed at churches, inns and bookshops across the region:

> Whereas many Books have been borrowed from the library of Monymusk, and have not been Returned, which renders many sets incomplete, it is entreated that those possessed of such would return them immediately to Monymusk house or to the Publisher of this paper – and if any by accident should appear at sales with the ffamilys [*sic*] <u>Arms</u> or Sir Archibald Grants Name in them – beg that they may be retained or that the family or Publisher may be acquainted which will be Gratefully acknowledged.[19]

No record has yet been traced to indicate Grant's success in reclaiming books so dishonourably (or absent-mindedly) borrowed from the Monymusk Library, though a small number of volumes bearing his bookplate did eventually end up in the collections of Aberdeen University – including some that reflect his patronage of two more formal institutions of reading in Georgian Aberdeenshire, the circulating libraries of Alexander Brown and John Burnett.[20] In exceptional circumstances, inter-personal book lending does appear to have been more effectively organized, with formal borrowing registers constituting the most detailed evidence for how it functioned. A fragmentary register survives for the Castle Grant Library between 1707 and 1744, for instance, while another survives for the collection at Glamis Castle between 1740 and 1754.[21] More importantly, complete borrowing registers have been discovered for three castle libraries in the same region of north-eastern Scotland, belonging to families of similar social status with overlapping networks of friends and associates, and covering roughly the same period – namely the 1760s through to the first decades of the nineteenth century. For these reasons, the three library ledgers allow us to look more systematically at the impact made by 'privy' borrowing on one specific reading community.

The most immaculate borrowing register survives for the library at Craigston Castle, about forty miles north of Aberdeen near the small town of Turriff. The library was kept in the traditional location for Scottish castles, in a small gallery right at the top of the castle. In spite of its relative inaccessibility and apparent marginality to the core social functions of the household, the surviving ledger shows that the library was relatively well used, with around 700 loans in all between 1768 and 1829 – most densely concentrated in the last two decades of the eighteenth century.[22] The other two libraries were located at Brodie Castle near Nairn, now in the hands of the National Trust for Scotland, and Ballindalloch Castle on Speyside. As was increasingly the case in Scottish country houses of the time, both collections were afforded pride of place within the principal apartments, reflecting Robert Adam's advice that:

> In the Country there ought to be another room upon the principal floor which I call a loitering room and it ought to be a library and large. There people spend their time with pleasure who neither like to drink or be with the Ladies. There they may take up one book and then another and read a page of each; others may like the children look at a picture book or read the title page and afterwards with importance talk of the book and the goodness of the ad[d]ition.[23]

Adam's insinuation that books constituted a form of diverting wallpaper in the polite reformulation of country house libraries receives ready endorsement in the record of book use at Brodie and Ballindaloch Castles, with the two more elegant 'drawing-room' libraries loaning books much less frequently than the Craigston Library. Just 145 loans were recorded in the Ballindalloch ledger between summer 1797 and winter 1820, and though the condition of the Brodie ledger does not allow us to quantify loans with such accuracy, around 300 loans were made over forty years from 1780.[24] These are, of course, disappointingly low totals, particularly in comparison with other types of library in Scotland for which we have borrowing registers – most famously, the Innerpeffray Library in Perthshire, which registered 1,483 loans between 1747 and 1800.[25] Although the low totals may be explained by the intense seasonality of 'privy' borrowing (necessitated, one suspects, by the fact that the library owners themselves spent large parts of the year away from their country estates), they immediately reflect the relative informality of book exchanges, even when official records were kept. Indeed, since none of the families appear to have employed a specialist librarian to manage their collections, there is no guarantee that the ledgers record every book that was ever borrowed from them.[26]

Nevertheless, the ledgers do provide some sparkling insights into informal book borrowing – not least in the broad range of individuals who were borrowing books from these families. Above all, the borrowing registers confirm that the family library was one of the main focuses of genteel sociability in rural Scotland, with 'privy' borrowing readily extending to other neighbouring families. The Urquhart lairds of Craigston Castle lent books to many of the major landed families in Aberdeenshire, including representatives of the Fergusons of Kinmudie, the Frasers of Philorth, the Gordons of Fyvie, the Menzies of Pitfoddles, the Ogilvies of Auchiries and the Turners of Turnerhall. The Brodie Castle register features an even more bewildering range of lairdly families, reflecting the greater prestige of the Brodie family: borrowers included the Gordon Cummings baronets of Altyre; the Rose lairds of Kilravock; the Brander lairds of Pitgavney; Sir Thomas Dick Lauder, baronet and novelist of Relugas; William McIntosh Esq. of Millbank, near Nairn; Lewis Brodie Dunbar of Lethen and Burgie; Alexander Falconar, laird of Blackhills; Sir James Dunbar of Boath; Norman McLeod of Dalvey; and the Russell family of Earlsmill. Three of these families, the Brodies of Lethen and Burgie, the Gordon Cummings of Altyre and the Lauders of Relugas, also borrowed books from the Ballindalloch Castle library in the early nineteenth century, as did a later laird of Monymusk. Clearly, books were one of the ways by which such individuals and families in this isolated, necessarily tight knit, though geographically-diffuse community, engaged with each other, allowing them to impress neighbours with their impeccable taste, as well as providing ample materials on which to base their polite conversation and sociable interaction.[27]

That seems to have been particularly the case for gentlewomen in provincial Scotland, despite Adam's confidence in the inherent masculinity of the country house library.[28] The Brodie sisters of Lethen, the Russell sisters of Earlsmill and Elizabeth Rose of Kilravock all used the

Brodie Library in the 1780s and 1790s, almost certainly on the invitation of young women in the Brodie household. They were joined in using that library by at least ten other ladies, even though the dangers inherent in female reading had been shockingly illustrated by the fatal accident that befell Lady Margaret Brodie in February 1786, burned alive at Brodie as she read a volume of Dodd's *Works* by firelight after the household had retired.[29] Female borrowers accounted for around a third of all registered loans from the Craigston Library, with Mary Urquhart perhaps inviting them to Craigston in part to use the library, initiating an informal reading club for likeminded genteel ladies in the area between Turriff, Banff and Peterhead. This certainly seems the implication of the extensive book exchange networks cultivated by the lady laird of Kilravock, Elizabeth Rose, who not only borrowed books from many other landed families in the area (including from the libraries at Castle Grant, Altyre and Lethen) but also regularly lent her own books to friends and neighbours, especially the Brodie sisters of Brodie Castle, the Brodie sisters of Lethen, Helen Dunbar of Boath and the Russell sisters of Earlsmill. Indeed, as we shall see, Elizabeth's book-lending strategy served to disseminate her own highly moralistic reading strategies, picking out books to send to friends that served explicitly pedagogical purposes.[30]

As the generosity displayed to daughters of the estate factor James Russell of Earlsmill by neighbouring landed families makes clear, borrowing from private libraries was not confined to the landed classes in provincial Scotland. In fact, benevolent landed families could also extend their largesse to members of the professional classes and even further down the social scale. The advocate John Erskine of Cambus lent books kept at his Edinburgh townhouse to Charles Hope, advocate and future Lord Granton, Lord Napier, soon to win celebrity as an army officer, and William Greenfield, a future Moderate minister and ultimately Hugh Blair's hapless successor at the University of Edinburgh.[31] In the north east, the Brodies lent books to physicians, surgeons and lawyers from nearby Nairn, Elgin and Inverness, enjoying particularly close links with medical men charged with the care of the army garrison at Fort George, not to mention many of the officers stationed there. Church of Scotland ministers were equally welcome to borrow books from Brodie Castle, as they were at Craigston, with the Revd Alexander Rose of Auchterless and the Revd Robert Duff of King Edward's being particularly frequent visitors. Another minister, the Revd Andrew Skene of Banff was joined in using the Craigston library by his daughter (who borrowed *Ossian's Poems* in 1788), while the two 'Misses Abernethies' (daughters of a physician from Banff) were regular borrowers in the 1790s – evidently granted ready admission to Mary Urquhart's reading circle despite their relatively humble origins.

The lairds of Ballindalloch went even further to ameliorate the scarcity of books in the wilds of north-eastern Scotland, habitually sending books to clergymen in relatively isolated Speyside parishes for the winter. For instance, the Revd John Grant of Elgin was sent the complete *Biographica Britannica* for the winter of 1802, while the Revd William Spence received *Don Quixote*, MacLaurin's *Account of Newton* and Campbell's *Lives of the Admirals* in a packet of books dispatched to his parish of Inveravon for the season in November 1801. Spence then requested *Gil Blas*, *Sir Charles Grandison*, *Clarissa* and *Tom Jones* the following winter, while his successor received Robertson's *Charles V* and three historical works by James 'Ossian' Macpherson from Ballindalloch Castle in October 1815. Such was their commitment to the local presbytery, that the widow of William Peterkin, minister of Elgin, was still receiving books from the lairds of Ballindalloch twenty years after her husband's death.

Though there is little evidence that the families at Brodie, Craigston or Ballindalloch lent books beyond the landed and professional elites – except to gardeners and other workers on their own estates – others in late eighteenth-century Scotland did allow their books to circulate further down the social scale. Thomas Crawford, baronet of Cartsburn, lent books to the usual motley collection of magistrates, clergymen, writers and physicians in nearby Greenock, but he was also happy to share them with more lowly members of the community such as John Wilson, a schoolmaster who borrowed Innes's *Critical Essay* in 1773, the carpenter Archibald Lang, the wigmaker James Stewart and the barber John McLeod.[32] Indeed, 'privy' borrowing was often a major source of books for the underprivileged who could not otherwise afford them in rural Scotland. The Lochend poet and shepherd Alexander Bethune enthused that 'after it became known that we were readers, the whole of our acquaintants, far and near, and even some people whom we could hardly number as such, appeared eager to lend us books'.[33] In his well-known *Literary History of Galloway* (1822), Thomas Murray recalled his reliance on 'privy' borrowing to make his early entrance in the literature of the Scottish Enlightenment when a student in the Stewartry of Kirkcudbright:

> My schoolfellow, George Mure, had lent me, in 1791, an edition of Ossian's *Fingal*, which is in many passages a sublime and pathetic performance. I copied *Fingal*, as the book was lent only for a few days, and carried the MS about with me ... In spring 1794, I got a reading of Blair's *Lectures*. The book was lent by Mr. Strang, a Relief clergyman, to William Hume, and *sublent* to me.[34]

Both Murray and Bethune evidently attracted book loans because they were well known to be avid readers, but such practices often facilitated a reader's first encounter with books of any kind. The son of John Forrest, a Forfarshire artisan, first became a reader when 'an old shoemaker in Trottick lent me *Robinson Crusoe* and *Roderick Random*', although he recalled with touching naivety that he was 'grievously disappointed when I afterwards learned that they were both creations of imaginative genius'.[35] More famously, the 'Ettrick Shepherd' James Hogg was given freedom to roam his landlord's 'considerable library', 'but better than any booklore was the intimacy he formed with his master's son, who directed his studies, criticised his rude literary attempts' and became a lifelong companion in reading.[36]

Hogg's example reveals that informal book borrowing could ultimately lead to the formation of discrete reading communities, the books at stake often becoming the subject of shared tastes, strategies and priorities rather than simply the object of pragmatic necessity. Nevertheless, 'privy' borrowing often meant simply the loan of specialist material to professional researchers. George III led the way in this regard, his impressive bibliophilia underpinned by the desire to stimulate the improvement of learning in the country at large. From the outset, the royal library was made available for the use of scholars, with the king's librarian, Frederick Augusta Barnard, boasting that it encompassed 'all the Learning and Wisdom which the mind of man has hitherto communicated to the world'.[37] Many noble collectors rushed to emulate their sovereign's benevolence, with the Duke of Roxburghe making his celebrated library at Floors open to 'bona fide scholars'. Joseph Ritson and Sir Walter Scott were both well qualified and made full use of the extensive collection in their researches into Scottish Border ballads.[38]

On a less exalted level, private libraries proved particularly valuable to the wider professional community in providing access to scientific and medical literature. George Sinclair, a surgeon newly arrived in Thurso, borrowed six anatomical books from his kinsman William Sinclair Esq. of Lochend on 12 April 1794, while medical men who visited Brodie Castle borrowed such works as the *Edinburgh Medical Essays* and Duncan's *Medical Commentaries*.[39] George Ridpath, a clergyman in the Scottish borders, borrowed Cleghorn's *Epidemical Diseases* from a surgeon in Kelso, while he sourced agricultural manuals like Home's *Principles of Agriculture and Vegetation* and Miller's *Gardeners' and Florists' Dictionary* from neighbouring landowners.[40] A member of the farming Pierson family of Balmadies in Angus sublet a series of works on agricultural improvement 'from Mr Brown which belong to David Cowper',[41] while William Dick, presumably a tenant farmer living in or around Blairgowrie in Perthshire, thanked General Mcintyre for the loan of an unnamed book of the same persuasion – 'I hope to improve by it in the *farming* way'.[42] The Urquharts of Craigston were also happy to lend out books like Anderson's *Essays on Agriculture* and Dickson's *Treatise on Agriculture* to local workers, including John Marr, an estate worker from nearby Turriff, and Alexander Reid, the Craigston gardener, while Monymusk – ever the benevolent improver – queried whether some books missing from his collection in 1759 (including Miller's *Dictionary*) had been lent to the head gardener, William Lunny.[43]

Importantly for the contemporary impact of the Scottish Enlightenment, 'privy' borrowing seemingly secured a much broader readership for technical works of philosophy and history that were not as widely available as bestselling books like Hume's *History of England*, Smith's *The Wealth of Nations* or the works of Hugh Blair.[44] The Revd Ridpath was again typical in this regard borrowing rare, ephemeral or prohibitively expensive works like Ferguson's attributed *History of Peg*, Fordyce's *Dialogues Concerning Education* and Logan's *Treatise on Government* from friends in Edinburgh and neighbouring Roxburghshire landowners.[45] Robert Innes of Leuchars, who would no doubt have owned his own library, borrowed Millar's *English Constitution* from Brodie Castle, while Ferguson's *Essay* and *History of the Roman Republic* were both borrowed by various interested parties. At Craigston, Ferguson's *Essay* was borrowed three times as was Montesquieu's *Spirit of the Laws*, while much rarer material like Lord Hailes's *Memorials and Letters* and Steuart's *Principles of Political Oeconomy* were also loaned out. Three local clergymen borrowed Ballindaloch's richly bound, quarto edition of Colin Maclaurin's popularization of Newton, which presumably had proved beyond their own purchasing power. Even in the 'Athens of the North', works that are generally considered important components of the Scottish Enlightenment were borrowed from private book collectors presumably because they were not readily available elsewhere. Thus Ferguson's *Essay on the History of Civil Society*, Millar's *Distinction of Ranks*, Hutcheson's *Essay* and *Inquiry* and Lord Monboddo's *Origin and Progress of Language* were all amongst the more technical works lent out by Erskine of Cambus, achieving a much wider circulation than they would have done otherwise. At the same time, 'privy' borrowing records also reflect the sheer popularity of the polite history and moral philosophy of the Scottish Enlightenment, with Hume, Robertson, Beattie, Blair and Kames flying off the shelves at Craigston, Brodie and Ballindalloch. Indeed, such practices also allowed provincial book owners to make their own contribution to the dissemination of Enlightenment, with the Revd David Cruden of Nigg lending out his own copies of Robertson, Reid, Beattie and Campbell to fellow ministers and professionals in and around Aberdeen.[46]

If private libraries therefore cast light on the social penetration of books associated with agricultural improvement and the Scottish Enlightenment,[47] they also inform recent debates surrounding the reading of women in Britain.[48] Some Scotswomen did indeed borrow the stereotypical fare – not least the widow Peterkin, who borrowed *Sir Charles Grandison* and *Roderick Random* from Ballindalloch – but by and large, the private borrowing records corroborate Jan Fergus's contention that men rather than women were the main consumers of novels.[49] Though they could always have acquired novels by other means, Mary Urquhart and her friends borrowed a much broader range of literature from Craigston than the contemporary stereotype would allow, including some of the more challenging works of the Enlightenment – such as Smith's *Wealth of Nations*, Ferguson's *Essay on the History of Civil Society*, Buffon's *Natural History* and works by Rousseau, Voltaire, Hume, Montesquieu and Robertson. Travel books by the likes of John Moore, Thomas Pennant and Tobias Smollett probably served to broaden their intellectual horizons, while they also borrowed conduct books explicitly written for the guidance of young women by the likes of Lady Sarah Pennington, Hester Chapone, Elizabeth Hamilton and Lord Kames. Most intriguingly, Elizabeth Hamilton's remarkable biography of *Agrippina* was borrowed by groups of ladies at both Craigston and Brodie, an intriguing endorsement for an unusual work that not only reinforced the idea that the classics – and history in general – were an acceptable part of a female domestic education, but that also argued that women's domestic virtue could be 'explicitly political and patriotic' in protecting Britain from the moral dangers of imperial overreach.[50]

Inter-personal book lending had unmistakably ideological implications for the younger members of Elizabeth Rose's reading group. Amongst the very many books Elizabeth lent her closest friends the Russell sisters of Earlsmill in the 1770s and 1780s are many of the most influential educational manuals of the eighteenth century, including Fordyce's *Sermons to Young Women* ('I have dotted with my pencil the passages I liked'), Fontenelle's 'admired' *Plurality of Worlds* and Bolingbroke's *Letters on the Study and Use of History* ('the last letter of vol 1st would be useful to you as the book is mine you can have it when you like'). But it is in Elizabeth's protracted commentary on Rousseau's *Emile* that her self-imposed role in fostering the Russell girls' moral education comes most to the fore. She acknowledges the book's well-known shortcomings ('there is really very queer things . . . I hardly know if I should send it you, & yet it contains as far as I have gone some admirable strokes'), advising firmly that this was a book that 'ought not to migrate beyond the little back room'. She also informs the girls that there are parts of the book that will not interest them, including passages on 'travelling & government' which are 'very good I believe – but neither of 'em much our concern'. Despite these reservations, Elizabeth felt obliged to send *Emile* to Earlsmill, happy in the knowledge that she had sufficiently prepared the sisters for the pitfalls awaiting them in one of the most controversial books of the age:

> What relates to Sophia's Education is so much adapted for your improvement & the prescription of the lovers in many parts so pathetic & so suited to your tastes that I can't resist sending you the book. Tho' remember I am led to do this from a desire of your being acquainted with its beauties, not from an approbation of the whole. I wish I had time & genius to sift it for your sakes, in several parts of his description of Sophia I thought on you – the neatness of her person, her extreme temperance, her sempulous cleanliness etc put me in my mind of the Earlsmill Taties whom I must now leave. Mama is stirring & breakfast near ready.[51]

It may not be entirely coincidental that inter-personal book lending is better documented for the north-east of Scotland than for any other part of eighteenth-century Scotland. Formal book-lending institutions arrived late in northern Scotland, so the genteel and professional readers who borrowed books from Craigston, Brodie and Ballindalloch may have had trouble accessing them elsewhere. Nevertheless, this chapter has presented some of the potentialities of this kind of evidence for the wider history of reading. As we have seen, books in private hands often reached many individual readers. 'Privy' borrowing from private collections expanded the reading nation dramatically, allowing rare and prohibitively expensive books to circulate much more extensively than would have been the case if they had been hoarded jealously by book collectors. In the reading encounters they facilitated, and perhaps too in the opportunities they no doubt provided for the sociable discussion of books, country house libraries played a vital part in the broader reading community until well into the nineteenth century. More importantly, inter-personal book lending often had serious cultural and intellectual implications for those involved. For the reading community cultivated by Elizabeth Rose, book exchanges reinforced shared reading priorities, becoming a crucial means by which the book-lender as moral guardian could help cultivate the virtuous domesticity that was expected of younger women readers in her social circle. This was certainly Elizabeth's hope as she lay awake one evening imagining the girls at Earlsmill poring over her latest recommendation: 'With Pleasure indeed would I "teach my lovely pupil all I know". At this hour, this day, tonight, perhaps she'll be receiving a lesson from her own El: Rose.'[52]

Notes and references

The research on which this chapter is based was supported by the Bibliographical Society, the Past and Present Society and the Leverhulme Trust. The author wishes to thank the National Trust for Scotland at Brodie Castle, Mr William Pratesi Urquhart of Craigston Castle and Claire Macpherson-Grant Russell, Lady Laird of Ballindalloch Castle, for permission to use manuscripts in their possession.

1. Paul Kaufman, *Libraries and their Users: Collected Papers in Library History* (London: The Library Association, 1969); idem, *Reading Vogues at English Cathedral Libraries of the Eighteenth Century* (New York: New York Public Library, 1964); idem, *Borrowings from the Bristol Library 1773–1784: A Unique*

Record of Reading Vogues (Charlottesville: Bibliographical Society of Virginia, 1960).

2. Robert Darnton, 'First steps toward a history of reading', *Australian Journal of French Studies*, 23 (1986), 5–30.

3. For instance, Robert A. Houston, *Scottish Literacy and the Scottish Identity: Illiteracy and Society in Scotland and Northern England 1600–1800* (Cambridge: Cambridge University Press, 1985); Thomas Munck, *The Enlightenment: A Comparative Social History 1721–1794* (London: Arnold, 2000).

4. Jan Fergus, *Provincial Readers in Eighteenth-Century England* (Oxford: Oxford University Press, 2006); idem, 'Eighteenth-century readers in provincial England: the customers of Samuel Clay's circulating library and bookshop in Warwick, 1770–2', *PBSA*, 78 (1984), 155–213; Vivienne S. Dunstan, 'Glimpses into a town's reading habits in Enlightenment Scotland: analysing the borrowings of Gray Library, Haddington, 1732–1816', *Journal of Scottish Historical Studies*, 26 (2006), 42–59; Mark Towsey, 'First steps in associational reading: the foundation and early use of the Wigtown Subscription Library, 1790–1815', *PBSA*, 103 (2009), 455–95.

5. For exceptions, see Giles Mandelbrote, 'Personal owners of books', in *The Cambridge History of Libraries in Britain and Ireland Volume II 1640–1850*, ed. Giles Mandelbrote and Keith A. Manley (Cambridge: Cambridge University Press, 2006), pp. 173–89; David Allan, *'A Nation of Readers': The Lending Library in Georgian England, c.1720–c.1830* (London: British Library, 2008), pp. 211–14.

6. Cited by Kevin Sharpe, *Reading Revolutions: The Politics of Reading in Early Modern England* (New Haven and London: Yale University Press, 2000), p. 283.

7. Ibid., pp. 125–6, 295; Natalie Z. Davis, *Society and Culture in Early Modern France* (Stanford: Stanford University Press, 1975), p. 213; William H. Sherman, 'The place of reading in the English Renaissance: John Dee revisited', in *The Practice and Representation of Reading in England*, ed. by James Raven, Helen Small and Naomi Tadmor (Cambridge: Cambridge University Press, 1996), pp. 62–76; Daniel R. Woolf, *Reading History in Early Modern England* (Cambridge: Cambridge University Press, 2000), pp. 168–72.

8. Sharpe, *Reading Revolutions*, p. 312.

9. Robert A. Houston, *Literacy in Early Modern Europe: Culture and Education, 1500–1800* (London: Longman, 1988), p. 210; Woolf, *Reading History*, Ch. 4.

10. Mark Girouard, *Life in the English Country House: A Social and Architectural History* (New Haven and London: Yale University Press, 1978), p. 180.

11. John Brewer, *The Pleasures of the Imagination* (London: HarperCollins, 1997), p. 186.

12. Sherman, 'The place of reading', p. 75.

13. Girouard, *English Country House*, pp. 178–80, 234; Clive Wainwright, 'The library as living room', in *Property of a Gentleman: The Formation, Organisation and Dispersal of the Private Library 1620–1920*, ed. Robin Myers

and Michael Harris (Winchester: St Paul's Bibliographies, 1991), pp. 15–24; Ian Gow, '"The most learned drawing room in Europe?": Newhailes and the classical Scottish library', in *Visions of Scotland's Past*, ed. Deborah C. Myers, Michael S. Moss and Miles K. Oglethorpe (East Linton: Tuckwell Press, 2000), pp. 81–96.

14. Allan, *'Nation of Readers'*, p. 214.
15. William St Clair, *The Reading Nation in the Romantic Period* (Cambridge: Cambridge University Press, 2004), pp. 397–9.
16. Elizabeth Grant, *Memoirs of a Highland Lady*, 2 vols (Edinburgh: Canongate Classics, 1998), I, pp. 303–4.
17. NAS GD248/25/2/20, Order by James Grant of Grant anent loan of books from Castle Grant Library, 6 December 1765.
18. Woolf, *Reading History*, p. 169.
19. NAS GD345/800/10, Library Notes at Monymusk House; *ODNB*.
20. William McDonald, 'Circulating libraries in the north-east of Scotland in the eighteenth century', *Bibliotheck*, 5 (1968), 137.
21. NAS GD248/485/8, Catalogue of Books at Castle Grant; NRAS 885 Box 67, Glamis Castle Library Borrowing Register.
22. Craigston Castle, Library Register (all subsequent citations in the text refer to this document).
23. Robert Adam to Sir James Clerk of Penicuik (1758), cited by James Macaulay, *The Classical Country House in Scotland, 1600–1800* (London: Faber, 1987), p. 170.
24. NRAS 771 Bundle 1002, Lists of Books in the Library, 1797–1820; Brodie Castle, unmarked library register (all subsequent citations in the text refer to these documents). When a volume was returned to the Brodie library, the entry was cancelled in the loan book by a series of cross-hatchings drawn through it; cf., Chester L. Shaver and Alice C. Shaver, *Wordsworth's Library: A Catalogue* (New York: Garland, 1979), p. xxiv.
25. Paul Kaufman, 'A unique record of a people's reading', *Libri*, 14 (1964–5), 227–42; Mark Towsey, *Reading the Scottish Enlightenment: Books and their Readers in Provincial Scotland, 1750–1820* (Leiden and Boston: Brill, 2010), Ch. 4.
26. There is no evidence that any of these families employed specialist librarians in this period, although the librarian was becoming an increasingly well-paid employee at the larger English country houses; Girouard, *English Country House*, p. 140.
27. For Stephen Colclough, books are 'the glue that binds together any community of readers operating within a culture in which books are too expensive to be bought regularly'; *Consuming Texts: Readers and Reading Communities, 1695–1870* (Basingstoke: Palgrave Macmillan, 2007), p. 126.
28. Female use of private libraries in Scotland seems decidedly at odds with private library culture in America, where libraries were considered a 'quintessentially privately male space'; Jessica Kross, 'Mansions, men, women, and the creation of multiple publics in eighteenth-century British North America', *Journal of Social History*, 33 (1999), 393.

29. George Bain, *History of Nairnshire* (Nairn: Telegraph, 1893), pp. 435–8.
30. Mark Towsey, '"An infant son to truth engage": virtue, responsibility and self-improvement in the reading of Elizabeth Rose of Kilravock, 1745–1815', *Journal of the Edinburgh Bibliographical Society*, 2 (2007), 69–92; idem, '"Observe her heedfully": Elizabeth Rose on women writers', *Women's Writing*, 18:1 (2011), 15–33.
31. NLS MS 5118–20, Notebooks of John Erskine of Cambus; *ODNB*.
32. NLS MS 2822, Catalogue of Books of Thomas Crawford of Cartsburn.
33. Cited by Jonathan Rose, *The Intellectual Life of the British Working Class* (New Haven: Yale University Press, 2001), p. 60.
34. Thomas Murray, *Literary History of Galloway: from the Earliest Period to the Present Time* (Edinburgh, 1822), pp. 245–6, 249 (the emphasis is original).
35. *Chapters in the Life of a Dundee Factory Boy: An Autobiography* (Dundee: James Myles 1850), p. 55.
36. James Russell, *Reminiscences of Yarrow* (Selkirk: G. Lewis, 1894), p. 186; *ODNB*.
37. Cited by Arnold Hunt, 'Personal libraries in the age of bibliomania', in *The Cambridge History of Libraries in Britain and Ireland Volume II 1640–1850*, ed. Giles Mandelbrote and Keith Manley (Cambridge: Cambridge University Press, 2006), pp. 438–58 (p. 449).
38. Bryan Hillyard, 'John Kerr, 3rd Duke of Roxburghe (1740–1804)', in *Pre-Nineteenth-Century British Book Collectors and Bibliographers*, ed. William Baker and Kenneth Womack (Detroit: Gale Group, 1999), pp. 198–9.
39. NAS GD136/1195, Books Belonging to William Sinclair Esq. of Lochend, 12 April 1794.
40. *Diary of George Ridpath, Minister of Stitchel 1755–1761*, ed. Sir John Balfour Paul (Edinburgh: Scottish History Society, 1922), pp. 116 and 235.
41. Angus Local Studies Centre, MS 324, Pierson of Balmadies Commonplace Book, 157.
42. NRAS 2614 Bundle 115, Personal Correspondence of William Macpherson, 1818–20; Dick to William Macpherson, 20 July 1820 (the emphasis is original).
43. NAS GD345/800/16, Library records, Monymusk House.
44. Towsey, *Reading the Scottish Enlightenment*, ch. 1; Richard B. Sher, *The Enlightenment and the Book: Scottish Authors and their Publishers in Eighteenth-Century Britain, Ireland and America* (Chicago: University of Chicago Press, 2006).
45. *Ridpath, Diary*, pp. 373, 75 and 117.
46. Ibid., pp. 324, 307 and 324; NAS CH2/555/29, Commonplace Book of Dr David Cruden, minister of Nigg.
47. See Towsey, *Reading the Scottish Enlightenment*, pp. 53–5.
48. Jacqueline Pearson, *Women's Reading in Britain 1750–1835: A Dangerous Recreation* (Cambridge: Cambridge University Press, 1999); Kate Flint, *The Woman Reader, 1837–1914* (Oxford: Oxford University Press, 1995).
49. Fergus, *Provincial Readers*, pp. 41–74.
50. Pam Perkins, '"Too classical for a female pen"? Late eighteenth-century women reading and writing classical history', *Clio*, 33 (2004), 241–64

(p. 264); Jane Rendall, 'Writing history for British Women: Elizabeth Hamilton and the *Memoirs of Agrippina*', in *Wollstonecraft's Daughters*, ed. Clarissa Campbell-Orr (Manchester: Manchester University Press, 1996).

51. NAS GD125 Box 135, undated; cf. Michele Cohen, '"To think, to compare, to combine, to methodise": girls' education in Enlightenment Britain', and Jean Bloch, 'Discourses of female education in the writings of eighteenth-century French women', both in *Women, Gender and Enlightenment*, ed. Barbara Taylor and Sarah Knott (Basingstoke: Palgrave Macmillan, 2007), pp. 224–42 and 243–58.

52. NAS GD125 Box 35, undated.

2
Caroline and Paul: Biblical Commentaries as Evidence of Reading in Victorian Britain

Michael Ledger-Lomas

In Charlotte Brontë's *Shirley* (1849), a novel much concerned with radically opposed readings of shared texts, the vicar's niece Caroline Helstone falls into an argument with the overseer, Joe Scott, about the meaning of Saint Paul's epistles.[1] Joe justifies his bluntly dismissive view of women and their abilities with a hardnosed but orthodox reading of the first epistle to Timothy. 'Let the woman learn in silence with all subjection', it runs. 'But I suffer not a woman to teach, nor to usurp authority over the man, but to be in silence. For Adam was first formed, then Eve. And Adam was not deceived, but the woman being deceived was in the transgression. Notwithstanding she shall be saved in childbearing, if they continue in faith and charity and holiness with sobriety.'[2] Woman succumbed first to temptation and is thus reduced to a subordinate position by the fall of mankind. Caroline and her friend Shirley need to unpick Joe's view of Paul to challenge his views effectively. Whereas Shirley openly ridicules the creation myth of Genesis and Paul's inferences from it, Caroline adopts a softer but more ingenious line. Paul has probably been 'wrongly translated, perhaps misapprehended altogether'. Far from commanding women to be silent and humble at all times, what he really meant was that they should speak out whenever they felt like making an objection.[3]

This short exchange exposes a tension at the heart of nineteenth-century Protestantism. British Protestants constantly reiterated that reading the Bible was both a right and a duty: such was the Bible's authority that proof texts like that from the epistle to Timothy played a consequential part in justifying institutions and in settling the boundaries of race and gender.[4] Yet it was one thing to cite these texts, another to agree on their meaning. Joe was overly sanguine in claiming that the epistle 'is very plain, Miss; he that runs may read'. The inherent difficulty of settling the meaning of opaque texts was exacerbated by the hermeneutic freedom of Protestantism. This chapter therefore investigates structures that guided nineteenth-century readers of the Bible in the exercise of their private judgement and that adjudicated debates like the one between Caroline and Joe. We know a great deal about the entrepreneurial zest with which British and American Bible societies distributed millions on millions of Bibles throughout the nineteenth century.[5] We are less well informed about what governed the reading of those Bibles: the books that guided the reception of the Book.[6] Although there are fine-grained studies of the creative reading of the Scriptures by Brontë and other writers, they often multiply possible interpretations rather than sketching the contours between which most of them fell.[7] There is, though, much evidence about how authority figures tried to determine responses to the Bible, in the form of published commentaries on it. Published as comprehensive exegesis of every word of the Bible, as individual volumes on its particular books or as marginal notes in family Bibles, commentaries preserve in aspic the interpretations that lay readers ought to follow. Neither narrowly homiletic nor purely scholarly, they combine dutiful attempts to recover the original meaning of scriptural terms with blunt recommendations for their application. As one commentator wrote of his decision to mix his 'critical' and 'practical' remarks, there was no point 'retaining all the salt on your plate until the rest of the food is eaten'.[8]

After sketching this market and its importance, this chapter explains what commentaries tell us about efforts to shape Victorian reading and Victorian religion. It concentrates on what commentaries said about a quiver of verses from the epistles of Saint Paul: Caroline and Joe's proof text from the first epistle to Timothy and related verses from the first epistle to the Corinthians and from the epistle to the Ephesians. These texts constituted an obstacle and a resource for evangelical feminists seeking religious and scriptural justification for their activity in the churches and the public square.[9] Their campaign was partly a form of scriptural commentary: it involved extensive use of commentaries and in turn provoked ripostes from the writers of commentaries. This chapter therefore proposes commentaries as evidence of how the most important single text in Victorian Britain was read but also sketches the ways in which commentaries themselves were read.

* * *

The evangelical revival put a new premium on the need not just to read scripture devoutly but to read it correctly and thoroughly. The Bible rewarded intensive attention in an age of extensive reading because it contained a doctrinal system of sin, atonement and justification by faith without which there could be no salvation. 'Would a condemned criminal think the message of his pardon dull?' Thus Edward Bickersteth (1786–1850) scolded those who yawned over their Bibles.[10] For evangelicals, the reading of the Bible was not an accessory to religion but the practice of religion itself, and fraught with ethical consequences. Bickersteth's guide to the art of reading scripture contained prayers to be said before and after every reading. If believers succeeded in internalizing the right message from Paul's writings, they would become 'living epistles, *known and read of all men*'.[11] Evangelical advocacy made Bible reading not just a private but a domestic activity. Bickersteth's son Edward Henry hoped that fathers buying his 1864 commentary would go through the whole of the New Testament during a year of daily prayer, that 'golden girdle of home life'.[12] Paterfamilias needed at least to dip into such works, because he was tasked with securing 'domestic happiness' by placing the Bible at the centre of his family – not just reading it daily but leading his dependents away from fanciful constructions of its meaning.[13] Most of the commentaries this chapter surveys therefore involve men assisting men in hammering the Bible's message into an endorsement of their authority. This source bias invites two provisos. Firstly, there were female writers on scripture who found the commentary genre peculiarly suitable for circumventing the bar on women doing theology, and a chapter that concentrated on them might yield somewhat different results.[14] Secondly, while commentators could counsel readers they could not dictate how their works were used. For every exemplary reader such as Mrs Thornley Smith, a Methodist minister's wife, class-leader – and devout fan of Charlotte Brontë – who diligently copied out nine volumes of notes from commentaries under her husband's approving eye, there was a Harriet Martineau, whose rummaging of 'all commentaries . . . that I could lay my hands on' led her into noto-rious heterodoxy.[15]

Although demand for commentaries flourished in an evangeli-cal climate, there was nothing new about the support they offered to devotional reading. A striking feature of the nineteenth-century market was the enduring appeal of old and familiar commentaries. The appetite for Christian classics even kept up a market for Calvin's commentaries, which were issued by the Calvin Translation Society. Until late in the century, Victorians read and extolled the gigantic commentaries of Matthew Henry (1662–1714) and Philip Doddridge (1702–51) and commentaries produced just before their own day by Thomas Scott (1747–1821) and Adam Clarke (1767–1832).[16] Sometimes excerpts from these works were wedged into the margins of fam-ily Bibles but they were often republished in their own right, the bewigged heads of their authors staring gravely out from their front-ispiece portraits. Editors savoured their notes not so much for their ageing scholarship as for their homely wisdom. John Eadie cherished in Henry's commentary the 'maxims so happily phrased as to merit the currency of proverbs' and its 'deep and exquisite pathos – its racy humour – its pungent and powerful appeals – its homely and unaf-fected imagery – its quaint and striking allusions – its pervading prac-tical applications – its terse and sententious epigrams – its wondrous insight into the working of human nature and passion'.[17]

Not only did older commentaries survive, but the act of producing a commentary encouraged the accretion of past readings. Commentators gloried in being derivative, listing in their prefaces the predecessors that had guided them as a way of establishing their own credit with the reader. Before giving their interpretation of a text, they commonly offered a rummage bag of previous readings, ranging back perhaps to Origen or John Chrysostom. To look at a page from a commentary or annotated Victorian Bible, in which a few lines of Scripture bob on an ocean of scholarly prose, is to see at a glance how private judgement could be trammelled by the history of interpretation. Commentators drew readers into the bewildering game of citing and testing the con-jectures of their contemporaries and predecessors. Readers could easily get lost in the venerable but creaking house of exegesis – like Elizabeth Barrett, who in June 1831 exploded against Chrysostom's commen-tary on Ephesians: 'such a monotony & emptiness!'[18] Commentators thus recognized the risk of losing sight of scripture. Bickersteth senior warned readers 'to be not a slave to' commentaries, even while he recommended some. They should always begin devotional reading by mulling over a text before joining the fray about its meaning.[19] Some editors of Bibles sloughed off the columns of distracting references to Scott and Henry, Locke and Chrysostom, in favour of wide margins and very rudimentary notes. Yet commentary was a resource as well as a distraction. It was by harvesting the past's interpretations that female readers for instance often found the means to challenge the bleak construction that male writers of the present put on Paul's assessment of their rights and abilities.

* * *

The majority of early and mid-nineteenth century commentaries would have backed Joe against Caroline. Paul had put a 'positive, explicit, and universal ban' on women speaking in church and on speaking up for themselves at all, reflecting the divinely ordained subjection of women to men. 'What a sweet course has the Lord marked out for females', trilled Bickersteth's *Family Exposition* on the epistle to Timothy. Men were to enjoy headship over women, while women were to be 'cherished and protected'. Paul could even be read as suggesting that women had all the more reason to keep silent when they knew that men were in the wrong. Bickersteth and other evangelical commentators, not least his son Edward Henry, encouraged readers to follow the epistle to Timothy in grounding Paul's injunction of women's silence in both home and church squarely in the creation story of Genesis. Not only did this establish women's subjection as an intrinsic part of God's design, but it helped defend that creation story as literal fact. Paul's apostolic inspiration and the infallibility of the Old Testament must stand or fall together.[20]

Neither evangelical nor high church commentators could countenance the idea of a Paul in contradiction with himself: his pronouncements added up to a harmonious, authoritative statement of how Christians should live their lives. Christopher Wordsworth's commentary on the New Testament maintained that the epistles 'written by his instrumentality were *given by inspiration of God*'. Paul was the 'great apostolic Architect' and his epistles were not 'mere disjointed essays . . . thrown out extemporaneously on the spur of the moment' but were 'designed by the Holy Spirit of God to bear a reciprocal relation to one another'.[21] Yet commentators had to demonstrate this and not just assert it, by steering readers from passage to matching passage and pre-empting objections that Paul's commandments could not always be reconciled. One of the passages in Paul that remains crucial to this day in discussions of Christianity's teaching on women was also one of the most difficult for Victorian commentators. Verses in the eleventh chapter of the first epistle to the Corinthians not only apparently contradict the epistle to Timothy's absolute injunction of female silence, but also seem to be at variance with Paul's teaching later in the same epistle. Before launching into a complex discussion of the need for women to wear head coverings, Paul wrote that 'every woman that prayeth or prophesieth with her head uncovered dishonoureth her head: for that is even all one as if she were shaven' (1 Cor. 11:5). This verse, which seemed to envisage, perhaps even endorse, women praying and prophesying, seemed to contradict not only the epistle to Timothy but Paul's own words later in the epistle. In the fourteenth chapter he wrote: 'Let your women keep silence in the churches: for it is not permitted unto them to speak; but they are commanded to be under obedience as also saith the law. And if they will learn any thing, let them ask their husbands at home: for it is a shame for women to speak in the church' (1 Cor. 14:34, 35).

Conservative evangelicals such as Bickersteth appealed to earlier authorities such as Calvin and Doddridge in an attempt to massage these contradictions into a consistent demand for women to pipe down in church. 'It was Paul's manner to attend to one thing at a time', wrote the American Charles Hodge, a moderate Calvinist. In the eleventh chapter of Corinthians, he had concentrated on dealing with immediate and flagrant breaches of female modesty. Later on, he could turn to enforcing the fundamental principle that women ought to remain altogether silent in church.[22] This brusquely authoritarian welding together of chapters eleven and fourteen recurred throughout the century and was particularly evident in commentaries written in a Calvinist tradition.[23] Other commentators favoured convoluted solutions of the contradiction. The very widely read American commentator Albert Barnes (1798–1870) argued that the violations of the law of female silence described in Corinthians chapter eleven took place only due to charismatic gifts that had long disappeared and so formed no precedent for the normal practice of the church.[24] Another tactic was to maintain that public breaches of decorum had never taken place at all. The female prophesying mentioned here and elsewhere in the New Testament (Acts 21:9) had probably taken place in private assemblies strictly reserved to women.[25]

These commentators might have reduced Paul's words to an ideology of separate spheres, but those who wished to challenge these interpretations could draw on the concessions made to women's agency by earlier and more authoritative commentators. For John Locke in the early eighteenth century and the Wesleyan Adam Clarke (1762–1832), Corinthians eleven plainly had permitted gifted women to prophesy because it laid down prescriptions for how they should dress when doing so. Clarke's interpretation was especially generous. He argued that when Paul spoke of women prophesying, he referred not only to isolated ecstatic utterances but to everything that now went for teaching and prophesying. For Clarke, the injunction of Corinthians fourteen that women should 'keep silence in the churches' did not negate these earlier words but just modified them. Paul was not demanding absolute silence from women in the church but was just repeating the ban that prevented them from asking questions, quibbling – 'and what we call *dictating*' – in the synagogues that were a model for the first Christian assemblies.[26]

These were not idle distinctions. Clarke belonged to a Methodist movement, many of whose members thought that female preaching was integral to the apostolic Christianity that they sought to revive.[27] The prestige of Clarke's commentary on the Bible has been implicated in the collapse of Methodism's hermeneutical creativity, elevating as it seemed to do male erudition over female inspiration as a qualification for expounding scripture.[28] Yet Clarke's judgements on the epistles were gratefully kept current by women who wanted to preach in the present.[29] Female preachers in early Methodism and among Quakers had constructed many different scriptural justifications for their inspired speech, justifications that were revived following the 1859 preaching tour of the American revivalist Phoebe Palmer (1807–74). Clarke was important to Palmer and the English women who followed in her wake because they wished to make a case for female preaching that did not dispute biblical inerrancy.[30] Palmer did not challenge the idea that the Bible enjoined female submission, but only made the more limited case that it was compatible with the dispensation that made female preaching possible. Catherine Booth, the founder of the Salvation Army, was more forceful in setting out the public as well as the religious role of women, freely quoting Clarke as she did so. Yet even her Salvation Army enforced the injunctions of the epistle to Timothy against wearing gaudy feminine apparel. Almost the only instance in which they would contradict the letter of the New Testament was in using unfermented wine in teetotal communion ceremonies.[31]

* * *

The debate on female preaching was not the only one to be fought out within the medium of devout commentary. The commentaries also illustrate an even thornier debate about how Paul's broader doctrine on the status of women could be explained and therefore justified in a way that made sense to nineteenth-century people. Feminists often accepted the idea that Paul's epistles were internally consistent, while criticizing prejudiced men for 'darken[ing] the text by the multitude of words'.[32] Commentators would have agreed with Caroline Helstone that in reading these epistles it was important to remember that they were written for a 'particular congregation of Christians under particular circumstances' and that they needed to be carefully translated into modern terms. Yet the difficulties of doing so became more and more apparent as commentators reflected on the strangeness of the intellectual background revealed in Paul's epistles. The most puzzling passage of all for commentators was undoubtedly the eleventh chapter of the first epistle to the Corinthians, which put forward a highly involved argument about why women's heads ought to be covered. According to Paul, a man does not have to cover his head because 'he is the image and glory of God'. The case is different for women, because

> the woman is the glory of the man. For the man is not of the woman: but the woman of the man. Neither was the man created for the woman; but the woman for the man. For this cause ought the woman to have power on her head because of the angels. . . . Judge in yourselves: is it comely that a woman pray unto God uncovered? Doth not even nature itself teach you, that, if a man have long hair, it is a shame unto him? But if a woman have long hair, it is a glory to her: for her hair is given her for a covering.

For commentators, this and other passages in Paul's epistles raised numerous questions of detail and principle. What was the 'power' woman was
to wear on her head and why should the 'angels' be involved? In broader
terms, what should readers in the Victorian age regard as the true basis
for Paul's injunction of female modesty: the will of God, the whims of
the angels, or the facts of nature implicit in his discussion of women's
hair?

Commentators understood that Paul's commandment could not
just be read as a naïve command to Victorian women to dress soberly,
although they could not forbear from pointing out that 'the attire
of some among them seems to expose them to the reproof of the
Apostle'.[33] Given that scholars had concluded that Greek women in
places like Corinth had actually worn veils, Paul's words had both to
be understood literally as a demand that Christian converts should
keep them on and as something no longer directly relevant to modern
society, where veils had long ago been cast off. The unanimity of the
commentators here was striking: readers were not meant to forget the
distinction between the first century and the nineteenth. Many argued
that Paul made a simpler and larger point: Christians must conform
to the social conventions of their own day, whatever these might be.
John Hamilton Thom (1808–94), a Unitarian minister who published
his exegetical lectures to his genteel Liverpool congregation, dwelt
approvingly on Paul's sense of decorum. What he had tried to indicate in passages such as Corinthians eleven was that 'felt boundary'
of legitimate social conduct, which was not arrived at through reason,
'but which, nevertheless, the refined and educated sentiments, the
moral *antennae* of the mind, determine with a perfect accuracy'. Paul
had told Christian women that they must be mindful of the scruples
of their peers, a lesson in reticence that still held true.[34] The suggestion
that readers must concentrate on the general principles that informed
the specific sanctions in Paul's writings was especially characteristic
of liberal commentators. It was meant to ensure that they could not
be used to justify social injustices. Thus commentators who wrote
on Pauline texts that apparently condoned slavery stressed that their
counsel to converts to bear with their lack of freedom for the present
did not excuse the institution. Paul could not have imagined the chat-
tel slavery of the American South and would not have endorsed it.[35]

It was difficult to impose limits on this argument. For those like
John Stuart Mill (1806–73) or Frances Power Cobbe (1822–1904) who

challenged the subjection of women, it was easy to suggest that it was not just the head coverings of first-century Corinth that belonged to the past, but the requirement that women abnegate themselves before men. If we no longer needed to heed Paul's tolerance of slavery, an antiquated social institution now hateful to our progressive sensibilities, why worry either about what he had said about the place of women? Mill said the Bible should not be taken 'for a Koran, prohibiting all improvement'.[36] This was the point upon which the Anglo-Catholic Henry Parry Liddon (1829–90) joined battle with him in his posthumously published commentary on the epistle to Timothy. Slavery, Liddon argued, was a 'morbid outgrowth on human society'. By contrast, the subjection of women 'finds its reason in the constitution of human nature, which Christianity can sanctify, but not abrogate'.[37] Liddon's recourse to nature was a well-tried one. In explaining Corinthians eleven, commentators had dwelt with greatest approval on Paul's argument that the differences between men and women were grounded in 'nature' itself, with women's long hair symbolizing the fact that they were the shy and retiring sex. If Paul's Christianity had ultimately transformed society, then it never meant to challenge the facts of life. This was the argument put forward by Arthur Penrhyn Stanley (1815–81) and the Brighton clergyman Frederick William Robertson (1816–53), in commentaries on Corinthians which had a wide and sustained readership among liberal Anglicans. Christianity, wrote Robertson, had made 'man more manly, and woman more womanly'.[38]

These commentaries suggest a shift to a position where Paul's conclusions were to be accepted by readers only insofar as they were endorsed by the scientific and historical study of human nature. Bickersteth's faith, like that of most early nineteenth-century evangelicals, had also been a religion of nature but it was one in which the Bible had had the last and inspired word on the conclusions of natural theology.[39] By contrast, Stanley thought that it did not really matter which text Paul had picked from Genesis to enforce his argument. All that really counted was his correct intuition that nature had marked out men and women for different roles. In expository lectures on Corinthians delivered several decades later, the slum priest Hensley Henson (1863–1907) agreed. Paul's arguments for veils now bore a 'somewhat fantastic appearance' but he had been right to warn women off intruding 'into spheres where, for fundamental reasons of physique and function, they had no place'.[40] The irony was that the more commentators proposed 'nature' rather than inspiration as a touchstone for Paul's words, the more settled their defence of female subordination became. Marcus Dods (1834–1909), a Scottish Free Churchman and relatively liberal critic, complacently explained in his commentary on Corinthians that the 'more graceful form and movement of woman' and her 'mental peculiarities' – a reliance on intuition and an incapacity for abstract thought – proved the justice of Paul's remarks.[41] In his 1898 commentary on the epistle to the Ephesians, the modernist high churchman Charles Gore (1853–1902) cited Havelock Ellis and the biologist George Romanes to claim that those who took issue with Paul were also running against the 'brick wall of fact and science'.[42]

The brick wall was a more imposing defence of male authority than the letter of the epistle, but it was important not to make it look too forbidding. It was difficult to argue that human nature and what this implied for women's social role was fixed or self-evident. Mill's use of the 'extraordinary susceptibility of human nature to external influences' to argue that women's apparent unfitness for political responsibilities might just be the result of centuries of male oppression displeased many clerical authors.[43] Yet by the later nineteenth century many of them nonetheless wanted to claim that Christianity had made women's nature progressive rather than wholly fixed. Centuries of Christian instruction had put the women of today on a higher level than the Corinthians or Ephesian converts who had needed stern lectures from Paul. The rigour of the epistles was a temporary expedient, which was meant to caution converted Greek women not to get carried away in exploiting their heaven-sent liberation from a society that resembled modern India or Turkey in the severity of its patriarchal mores.[44] These later commentators were keen to emphasize that the subjection extolled by Paul's epistles – particularly in the epistle to the Ephesians, which described the husband as being 'the head of the wife' (5:23) – was no charter for male misrule. Commentaries on Ephesians by Gore, the Birmingham Congregationalist Robert William Dale (1829–95) and the Wesleyan scholar George Findlay (1849–1919) all stressed that far from perpetuating an alleged pagan and Jewish contempt for woman as an inferior being, Paul had given her a new dignity and security. The subjection Paul extolled was not servility – as both emancipators and conservatives keen to 'keep women in their place' imagined – but the mutual obedience of men and women to each other and God within marriages 'transfigured' by grace.[45] They welcomed laws designed to protect women against physical abuse by their husbands as a fulfilment of the Pauline ideal and warned incautious advocates of women's rights that the spirit of Christianity would always remain 'their main protection' against the brute force of men.[46]

The mass of Victorian commentaries thus remained pretty far from Caroline Helstone in their reading of Paul's epistles. Henson warned in commentating on Corinthians that while the evolution of marriage into 'equal comradeship' was a welcome development 'thoroughly accordant with the gospel', women who aspired to be the rivals of men by despising marriage and motherhood had embarked on a 'thoroughly anti-Christian' course. The Revd T. Teignmouth Shore's commentary for schools declared brusquely that Paul would not have listened to appeals for 'imaginary rights'.[47] Shore had the suffrage in mind and it is striking that the debate about votes for women took its participants into the same kind of hermeneutical puzzles that had concerned the wearing of veils. Once more those on either side of the question used and composed commentaries. Much the most striking of those was *The Woman's Bible* (1896). Edited by the American Elizabeth Cady Stanton (1815–1902), it was a series of polemical notes on the scriptural passages that had been used to maintain the barriers against female access to power. It aimed to scupper the arguments of 'Paul worshipping male Protestants' by subjecting the texts urged against female political speech and action to fiercely political scrutiny. Paul's command for women to cover themselves is therefore dismissed as a recycled rabbinical superstition; Paul's endorsement of the idea that woman is the origin of sin assailed as introducing a 'poisonous stream' into Christian history.[48] Polemical *The Woman's Bible* might be, but it could draw on a wealth of recent scholarly work that had begun to permeate even the clerical establishment, convincing them that Paul was dominated by the thought patterns of the rabbinical and pagan world to a much greater degree than they had hitherto thought. Many of his arguments involved reasoning 'that could hardly be intelligible except to a Jew'.[49]

This study of the role of biblical commentaries indicates that Victorian readers were not left to their own devices in interpreting

authoritative texts. Yet in the case of the New Testament, the very structures designed to tell readers how to obey Paul's words also recorded
and facilitated doubts about just how and why they were authoritative,
or whether they were so at all. The commentaries therefore show that
what often looks like a quiet process of secularization in nineteenth-
century social attitudes could occur within the culture of devotional
reading itself; and that it was nourished by, even as it broke away from,
the hegemony of the Christian and biblical past.

Notes and references

1. Heather Glen, *Charlotte Brontë: The Imagination in History* (Oxford: Oxford
   University Press, 2002), ch. 6.
2. See 1 Timothy 2:11–15, cited from the King James Bible (also known as the
   Authorized Version), first published in 1611.
3. 'Currer Bell' [Charlotte Brontë], *Shirley: A Tale*, 3 vols (London: Smith,
   Elder, 1849), II, pp. 176–8.
4. See Colin Kidd, *The Forging of Races: Race and Scripture in the Protestant
   Atlantic World* (Cambridge: Cambridge University Press, 2007), ch. 1.
5. Leslie Howsam, *Cheap Bibles: Nineteenth-Century Publishing and the British
   and Foreign Bible Society* (Cambridge: Cambridge University Press, 1991);
   David Paul Nord, *Faith in Reading: Religious Publishing and the Birth of Mass
   Media* (Oxford: Oxford University Press, 1994).
6. For biblical reception and commentaries in the preceding period, see Ian
   Green, *Print and Protestantism in Early Modern England* (Oxford: Clarendon
   Press, 2000), ch. 3; Thomas Preston, 'Biblical criticism, literature, and the
   eighteenth-century reader', in *Books and their Readers in Eighteenth-century England*, ed. Isabel Rivers (Leicester: Leicester University Press, 1982),
   pp. 97–126; Scott Mandelbrote, 'The English Bible and its readers in the
   eighteenth century', in *Books and their Readers in Eighteenth-century England:
   New Essays*, ed. Isabel Rivers (London: Continuum, 2001), pp. 35–78.
7. Marianne Thormählen, *The Brontës and Religion* (Cambridge: Cambridge
   University Press, 1999).
8. Edward Henry Bickersteth, in Bickersteth and Robert Jamieson, *The Holy
   Bible: With a Devotional and Practical Commentary*, 2 vols (London: James
   Virtue & Co., 1861–65), II, 'Preface'.
9. Deborah Valenze, *Prophetic Sons and Daughters: Female Preaching and Popular
   Religion in Industrial England* (Princeton: Princeton University Press, 1985);
   Women Preachers and Prophets Through Two Millennia of Christianity, ed.
   Pamela Walker and Beverly Mayne Kienzle (London: University of California
   Press, 1998); Nancy Hardesty, *Your Daughters Shall Prophesy: Revivalism and
   Feminism in the Age of Finney* (New York: Carlson Publishing, 1991); Pamela
   J. Walker, *Pulling the Devil's Kingdom Down: The Salvation Army in Victorian
   Britain* (London: University of California Press, 2001).

10. Edward Bickersteth, *A Scripture Help: Designed to Assist in Reading the Bible, Profitably* (1817; London: Seeleys, 1852), p. 25.
11. Ibid., p. 37.
12. Bickersteth and Jamieson, *The Holy Bible*, II, iii.
13. H. A. Boardman, *The Bible in the Family: Or, Hints on Domestic Happiness* (London: T. Nelson, 1858), pp. 307–8.
14. See e.g. Robert Kachur, 'Envisioning equality, asserting authority: women's devotional writings on the Apocalypse, 1845–1900', in *Women's Theology in Nineteenth-Century Britain: Transfiguring the Faith of Their Fathers*, ed. Julie Melnyk (London: Garland, 1998), pp. 3–36, and *Let Her Speak for Herself: Nineteenth-century Women Writing on the Women of Genesis*, ed. Marion Ann Tayolr and Heather E. Weir (Waco: Baylor University Press, 1996).
15. Thornley Smith, *A Christian Mother: Memoirs of Mrs Thornley Smith* (London: Hodder and Stoughton, 1885), p. 37; Harriet Martineau, *Autobiography, with Memorials by Maria Weston Chapman* (London: Smith, Elder, 1877), p. 103.
16. On these works see Preston, 'Biblical criticism' and Scott Mandelbrote, 'The Henrys and dissenting readings of the Bible, 1650–1750', in *Dissent and the Bible in Britain, c.1650–1950*, ed. Scott Mandelbrote and Michael Ledger-Lomas (Oxford: Oxford University Press, forthcoming 2012).
17. *The Illustrated National Family Bible: With the Commentaries of Scott and Henry*, ed. John Eadie (London: Leicester & Co., 1863), p. v. Scott, by contrast, 'does not sparkle, but he is always judicious'.
18. *The Barretts at Hope End: The Early Diaries of Elizabeth Barrett Browning*, ed. Elizabeth Berridge (London: John Murray, 1974), pp. 63–4.
19. Bickersteth, *Scripture Help*, p. 54; see similarly idem, *The Christian Student: Designed to Assist Christians in General in Acquiring Religious Knowledge* (London: Seeley & Burnside, 1829), p. 59.
20. Edward Bickersteth, *Family Expositions: On the Epistles of Saint John and Saint Jude and those of Saint Paul to Timothy* (London: Seeleys, 1853); Bickersteth and Jamieson, *The Holy Bible*, II, 336. Sean Gill, *Women and the Church of England from the Eighteenth Century to the Present* (London: SPCK, 1994), p. 17 notes the importance of 1 Tim 2:11–15 in shaping Anglican attitudes.
21. Christopher Wordsworth, *The New Testament of Our Lord and Saviour Jesus Christ*, 2 vols (London: Rivingtons, 1861), I, pp. vi–ii. The words in italic are a quotation from Paul's second epistle to Timothy, 3:16.
22. Charles Hodge, *An Exposition of the First Epistle of Saint Paul to the Corinthians* (London: James Nisbet & Co., 1857), p. 209.
23. Gustav Billroth, *A Commentary on the Epistles of Paul to the Corinthians*, ed. and trans. by W. Lindsay Alexander, 2 vols (Edinburgh: T. & T. Clark, 1837–38), I, p. 273; R. Jamieson, A. R. Fausset, and David Brown, *The Portable Commentary: A Commentary, Critical and Explanatory, on the Old and New Testaments,* 2 vols (Glasgow: William Collins, 1863), II, p. 298.
24. Albert Barnes, *Notes, Explanatory and Practical on the First Epistle of Saint Paul to the Corinthians* (New York: Harper & Brothers, 1837), p. 220.

Barnes was said to have sold over a million copies of his collected *Notes on the New Testament*.

25. Thomas Keyworth, *A Daily Expositor of the New Testament*, 2 vols (London: Richard Baynes, 1825–28), II, p. 99; Joseph Agar Beet, *A Commentary on St Paul's Epistle to the Corinthians* (London: Hodder & Stoughton, 1882); T. Teignmouth Shore, *The First Epistle to the Corinthians: With Commentary by T. Teignmouth Shore* (London: Cassell's, Petter and Galpin, 1879), p. 98.

26. Adam Clarke, *The New Testament of our Lord and Saviour Jesus Christ . . . With a Commentary and Critical Notes, Designed as a Help to a Better Understanding of the Sacred Writings*, 3 vols (London: J. Butterworth and Son, 1817), II, note to 1 Cor 11:5, note to 1 Cor 14:34.

27. See Valenze *Prophetic Sons, passim*, and Gill, *Women and the Church*, pp. 60–4.

28. Phyllis Mack, *Heart Religion in the British Enlightenment: Gender and Emotion in Early Methodism* (Cambridge: Cambridge University Press, 2008), pp. 269–86.

29. See e.g. *The Female Preacher: Or, The Lost Ministry* (1864), p. 6.

30. Hardesty, *Your Daughters Shall Prophesy*, ch. 4.

31. Walker, *Pulling the Devil's Kingdom Down*, ch. 2.

32. Sarah Grimké, *Letters on the Equality of the Sexes and Other Essays*, ed. Elizabeth Bartlett (Yale: Yale University Press, 1988), p. 93.

33. Wordsworth, *New Testament*, p. 119.

34. John Hamilton Thom, *St. Paul's Epistles to the Corinthians: An Attempt to Convey their Spirit and Significance* (London: J. Chapman, 1851), p. 145.

35. Albert Barnes, *An Enquiry into the Scriptural Views of Slavery* (Philadelphia: Perkins and Purves, 1855), ch. 5; Goldwin Smith, *Does the Bible Sanction American Slavery?* (London: Parker, 1863), pp. 112–15.

36. John Stuart Mill, *On Liberty: With, The Subjection of Women; and, Chapters on Socialism*, ed. Stefan Collini (Cambridge: Cambridge University Press, 1989), p. 163.

37. Henry Parry Liddon, *Explanatory Analysis of Saint Paul's Epistle to Timothy* (London: Paternoster Row, 1897), p. 18.

38. Frederick William Robertson, *Expository Lectures on St. Paul's Epistles to the Corinthians* (London: Smith, Elder, 1859), p. 193.

39. Boyd Hilton, *A Mad, Bad and Dangerous People? England, 1786–1846* (Oxford: Oxford University Press, 2006), p. 333.

40. Hensley Henson, *Apostolic Christianity: Notes and Inferences Mainly Based on St Paul's Epistles to the Corinthians* (London: Methuen & Co., 1898), pp. 261–2. See Alfred Rowland, *The First Letter of Paul the Apostle to Timothy, a Popular Commentary, with a Series of 40 Sermonettes* (London: James Nisbet, 1887) for a similar argument. The invocation of Adam and Eve may be an odd way to make an argument, but it is really just a 'vivid illustration' of the different capacities of men and women.

41. Marcus Dods, *The First Epistle to the Corinthians* (London: Hodder & Stoughton, 1889), pp. 254–5.

42. Charles Gore, *St. Paul's Epistle to the Ephesians: A Practical Exposition* (London: John Murray, 1898), p. 224. Gore's book remained in print until the late 1930s.
43. Mill, *On Liberty*, p. 139. On responses to Mill, see e.g. essays collected in *Subjection of Women: Contemporary Responses to John Stuart Mill*, ed. Andrew Pyle (Bristol: Thoemmes, 1995).
44. Rowland, *First Letter of Paul*, pp. 113–14.
45. Gore, *St. Paul's Epistle*, p. 219; Robert William Dale, *The Epistle to the Ephesians: Its Doctrine and Ethics* (London: Hodder & Stoughton, 1882), p. 356.
46. George Findlay, *The Epistle to the Ephesians* (London: Hodder & Stoughton, 1892), p. 359.
47. Henson, *Apostolic Christianity*, p. 265; T. Teignmouth Shore, *The First Epistle to the Corinthians* (London: Cassell, 1879), p. 105.
48. Elizabeth Cady Stanton et al., *The Woman's Bible: The Original Feminist Attack on the Bible*, ed. Dale Spender (Edinburgh: Polygon, 1985), pp. 15–21, 30–5, 162–5.
49. Edward Lyttleton, 'Woman's suffrage and the teaching of Saint Paul', *Contemporary Review*, 69 (1896), 680–91 (p. 685).

3
Reading the 'Religion of Socialism': Olive Schreiner, the Labour Church and the Construction of Left-wing Reading Communities in the 1890s

Clare Gill

> Does it ever strike you, it often does me, how within
> the sixteen miles that make London, lie all the mate-
> rials for heaven on earth, if only something could
> come suddenly and touch our hearts one night;
> there would be nobody sad and lonely: every aching
> head with a hand on it; every miserable old maid let
> out of her drawingroom and her old life-blood flow-
> ing; every wailing little child hushed in somebody's
> arms and making them warm: nobody hungry and
> nobody untaught; the prisons emptied and the back
> slums cleaned, everybody looking with loving eyes
> at the world around them. That would be heaven,
> and it only wants a little change of heart. (Olive
> Schreiner to Havelock Ellis, 1884)[1]

In his discussion of nineteenth-century socialist novels, H. Gustav Klaus advances the notion of socialist literature as a marginalized and dissident force, whose very 'otherness' serves as a possible threat to the prevailing hegemony of the literary mainstream.[2] With Klaus's definition of socialist literature momentarily guiding analysis here, there is no doubt that it would be difficult to make a case for the late-nineteenth-century South African writer, Olive Schreiner, as a socialist writer in this specific conception of the term. Klaus's model for socialist literature perpetuates a dichotomy between popular literature and the ostensibly more marginal subset of socialist fiction, a relationship that is clearly destabilized and problematized in Schreiner's case. Nominated as the 'modern woman *par excellence*' by newspaper editor extraordinaire, W. T. Stead, Schreiner became the darling of London's literati after the publication of her first novel *The Story of an African Farm* in 1883, and enjoyed high sales throughout her career, including fifteen editions of *African Farm* published during her lifetime.[3] Schreiner was, of course, not the only bestselling writer of her day who appealed to mass reading audiences and socialist readers alike, nor was she unique in publishing popular and high-selling texts that espoused distinctly socialistic sentiments. Rather, what set her apart from most of her literary contemporaries was the sheer extent to which her texts were both embraced by the various factions of the wider socialist movement, and promoted as ideologically bolstering their political doctrines, in spite of her evident immersion in the 'dominant literary culture' of her day.[4] Popular writers may well have lined the bookshelves of a host of late-nineteenth-century readers who also defined themselves as socialist, but their works were not necessarily included in the recommended reading lists circulated by the Independent Labour Party, or counted as required reading in socialist correspondence classes as was the case with Olive Schreiner's texts.[5]

This study will go some way to resituating Schreiner's work within the political and cultural contexts of the *fin-de-siècle* 'religion of socialism', the term reappropriated by Stephen Yeo as a signifier for the upsurge in organized left-wing activity that was cultural as well as political in outlook.[6] Through an exploration of her reputation and reception within late-nineteenth- and early-twentieth-century socialist reading circles, I will suggest that, in spite of her evident international acclaim and celebrity-like status in Britain, Olive Schreiner was also very much a writer of the margins. As a freethinking South African woman with feminist, socialist and anti-imperialist convictions, she quite uniquely appealed to a diversity of reading communities that cut across class and gender lines, as well as political and national boundaries. 'I have got scores, almost hundreds of letters from all classes of people', Schreiner told Karl Pearson, 'from an Earl's son to a dressmaker in Bond Street, and from a coalheaver to a poet'.[7] The present research is part of a larger work-in-progress that seeks to situate Schreiner and her fictional and non-fictional texts within concrete publishing and socio-historical contexts, through an exploration of the diverse ways in which her texts were both marketed for and received by a diversity of contemporary reading communities. This chapter focuses upon the promotion of Schreiner's texts amongst one particular *fin-de-siècle* reading community – socialist readers affiliated with the Labour Church movement, and more specifically, those readers, both real and imagined, clustered around John Trevor's periodical, the *Labour Prophet*.

Through an analysis of the letters pages and correspondence class reports published in the *Labour Prophet* throughout the 1890s, this chapter seeks to contextualize the marketing of Schreiner's texts to members of this distinctive socialist reading community and their reception of these texts, disclosing an intriguing and previously unexplored connection between Schreiner, socialist reading materials and Labour Church educational schemes. I will demonstrate how, through the channels of dedicated socialist publications like the *Labour Prophet*, and through the publication of reading lists and the establishment of correspondence classes and left-wing lending libraries, strident efforts were made on the part of labour leaders to construct an active community of socialist readers, encouraged to consume fictional and non-fictional texts imbued with a clear social dimension. As a corollary, this chapter will also offer a timely reappraisal of Schreiner's received reputation as a so-called 'New Woman' writer, a classification that has undoubtedly aided the rediscovery of her work and heralded important discussions of her feminism since Virago's reprint of *Woman and Labour* (1911) in the 1970s.[8] Yet this critical preoccupation with Schreiner's feminism has also had the misfortunate effect of downplaying the ideological importance of left-wing concerns in her work, divorcing texts such as *The Story of an African Farm* (1883) and *Dreams* (1890) from the historical, political and cultural context of a time that Schreiner herself memorably described as the 'brilliant sunrise' of socialist politics.[9]

* * *

Writing in middle age to her brother, William Philip Schreiner in 1912, Olive expresses a misty-eyed nostalgia for the socialist optimism that characterized her formative years living in Britain:

> Just as no one who didn't live through the horror and oppression of Martial Law in this country can dream what it was; so, no one

who did not live through it can ever know the joy, and hope, and passion of enthusiasm with which we worked in those years in the eighties. I was talking about it with Keir Hardie and tears came into both our eyes when we spoke of it.[10]

From the writer's infrequent dalliances throughout the 1880s and 1890s with socialist-inspired, intellectual organizations such as the Progressive Association and the Fellowship of the New Life, to her wide-eyed awe at the Dock Strike of 1889 and close friendships with leading socialists such as Eleanor Marx, Karl Pearson and Havelock Ellis, Schreiner's early years in England were defined – at least in part – by the prevalence of the labour question and an acute intellectual concern for the theoretical tenets of socialism.[11] On the whole, Schreiner eschewed frontline activism in favour of a more theoretical, introspective approach to left-wing concerns, and conceived of her role in the ushering in of this bright new socialist dawn in a strictly aesthetic context. As Ruth Livesey has suggested, Schreiner's ability to situate herself at the vanguard of the contemporary labour movement can be explained by the 'peculiarly idealist and aesthetic nature' of late-nineteenth-century British socialism, in which context, artistic contributions were accorded as much value as political organization or agitation.[12]

Existing evidence for socialists reading Schreiner's texts comes from the whole gamut of left-wing reading communities in Britain at this time. From *Clarion* figurehead, Robert Blatchford (who recommended *Dreams* as essential reading in his bestselling discourse on socialism, *Merrie England*), to labour activists like George Meek ('George Eliot, Mrs Humphrey Ward, and Olive Schreiner are the only three authoresses I could ever read with much pleasure'), Schreiner's appeal appears to have traversed the fissures and factions that scarred the wider late-nineteenth-century socialist and labour movements.[13] Edward Carpenter, Sheffield socialist, poet and philosopher, considered Schreiner's debut novel sufficiently significant to purchase a second copy to send to his good friend, Kate Salt in 1889. Salt, who had tried in vain to procure *African Farm* at the London Library, was so 'delighted' with the gift of Schreiner's celebrated novel that she expressed doubt to Carpenter in her ability to part with the text after reading: 'it is dreadful to think of you getting me a new copy, especially as I know I shan't be good Socialist enough to follow your suggestion and pass it on to someone else'.[14] For many of the novel's first wave of British readers at the

fin de siècle, African Farm seemed to embody the questioning spirit of
the age, and articulated what Henry Norman described in his review of
the novel as all the solutions to 'the simple questions of human nature
and human action'. This sense of Schreiner's novel as an aesthetic
mouthpiece was later compounded by a 'Lancashire working woman'
who, having reread *African Farm* 'over and over', expressed her experience of the novel as effecting a kind of social ventriloquism: 'I think
there is hundreds of women what feels like that but can't speak it, but
she could speak what we feel.' Edward Aveling, partner of Eleanor Marx,
also commended Schreiner's 'bold-out speaking', and championed the
writer in the radical secular periodical *Progress* for giving timely artistic
expression to pertinent social questions.[15]

Schreiner's arrival in England in 1881 significantly coincided with
the popular revival of socialism in Britain: both the formation of the
Marxist-inspired Democratic Federation (later the Social Democratic
Federation) and the genesis of the development of the mass labour
movement in Britain are rooted in this pivotal year.[16] The birth of her
literary career occurred in tandem with the formation of various left-
wing organizations including the Socialist League, the Fabian Society
and the Independent Labour Party. These seminal years in the history of
British socialism also saw trade unions flourish exponentially, the first
Labour candidates elected to Parliament, and crucially, for the dissemination of contemporary socialist ideas and for the purposes of efficient
political organization, the development of a dedicated socialist and
labour press. Socialism was advancing on all fronts at an extraordinar-
ily rapid pace. In as much as the history of the late-nineteenth-century
socialist movement is characterized by mass organization, widespread
support and political progress, it is also just as clearly marked by internal disagreements, defections and divisions: socialism had no coherent
ideology nor any one representative political organization, then or
since. The newspapers and periodicals published by the new and often
short-lived socialist organizations functioned – with varying degrees of
success – as important propaganda tools for the widespread dissemination of left-wing polemic. By far the most popular and influential of
the socialist periodicals was Robert Blatchford's *Clarion*, which reached
peak sales of around 90,000, and is now credited with being Britain's
first mass-circulation left-wing periodical.[17] Cannily employing some
of the publishing tactics marshalled in with the advent of the 'New
Journalism' of the 1890s, Blatchford's paper remained, in spite of

comparatively impressive circulation figures, a commercially unsuccessful publishing venture. As Deborah Mutch has suggested, the 'desire to promote their politics often overwhelmed the socialists' lack of business practices and trade knowledge', continually leading to the rapid appearance and disappearance of a plethora of socialist periodicals that often garnered small, devoted readerships but which ultimately ran at a loss.[18]

John Trevor's *Labour Prophet* was one such publication. First appearing in January 1892, the *Labour Prophet* was issued monthly until September 1898, at considerable economic cost and burden to its editor.[19] Circulation figures amounted to a mere 5,000 per month, yet the paper managed to survive for six years in a saturated, competitive marketplace, owing, at least in part, to the *Labour Prophet*'s vociferously dedicated readership and patrons who donated money to the paper's Central Fund. The sense of community that permeates the *Labour Prophet* is ever palpable, not least because of the interactivity that was encouraged between editorial staff and the paper's readership, via the establishment of correspondence classes, lending libraries and letters pages. As this study will demonstrate, the inclusion of literature within this periodical – in this instance, the fiction of Olive Schreiner – helped to encourage a sense of kinship among readers, as well as serving a distinctive political function within the remit of John Trevor's particular strand of ethical socialism.

* * *

Like many other socialist editors at this time, John Trevor was acutely aware of the power of literature to both educate and inspire, and also of the ability of individual texts to foster a sense of identification and interconnectedness between readers. Railing against the dominant iconography of the figure of the solitary reader, contemporary left-wing organizations promoted an image of reading as a communal activity, as a pursuit that rallied comrades together in socialist solidarity. This notion of a community of readers fused by common experiences and shared goals was also expressed by Olive Schreiner, who claimed to have written *African Farm* expressly for an audience of working-class readers in order that they might feel less alienated as a consequence of the material reality of their lives. As Schreiner noted in a letter to Edward Carpenter in 1892, the modes of production in which a text is created can have a direct bearing upon the audience it will ultimately reach:

> They are bringing out a cheap 2/- edition of Story of an African Farm. I'm glad because the only people I really care to read it are people struggling with material want and the narrowness and iron pressure of their surroundings who won't be so likely to get a more expensive book. The only thing that ever induced me to write it was the feeling that some soul struggling with its material surrounding as I was might read it and feel less alone.[20]

The twin features of Schreiner's letter here – firstly, the importance of working people gaining access to her texts, and secondly, the sense of an ideological community established through the act of reading – are principles that could also be extended to the *Labour Prophet*, the monthly penny paper that served as the official organ of the Labour Church movement. Under John Trevor, a former Unitarian minister and founding father of the Labour Church, the *Labour Prophet* claimed modest circulation figures, comprised of a dedicated and loyal community of regular readers.[21] The network of Labour Church devotees centred around Trevor's publication were actively encouraged to self-educate and to gain access to a prescribed list of fictional and non-fictional texts via a host of innovative modes of distribution, including, for example, liberal access to free lending libraries for Labour Church members. As Sidney E. Dark expressed in a piece for the *Labour Prophet* in 1893, 'the road towards democratic progress' could only be paved via the widespread acquirement of knowledge amongst the working classes:

> Education is a subject that has especial interest for Socialists. The importance of the subject cannot be exaggerated . . . The want of education among the workers is a hindrance. All but a few extra intelligent men and women are unable to think clearly and concisely for themselves, and are thus driven into the hands of leaders who, however able, can never do for the people what the people should do for themselves.[22]

Indeed, so important were the twin doctrines of self-education and personal development to Labour Church philosophy that

John Trevor built them into the movement's founding principles – an oft-published set of five clauses that together formed the Labour Church and *Labour Prophet* manifesto. Clause five states 'That the development of Personal Character and the improvement of Social Conditions are both essential to man's emancipation from moral and social bondage.'[23]

Conducive to the Labour Church's commitment to the intellectual development of its loyal members, the *Prophet* frequently printed a host of original works by some of the period's most eminent social-ists, including pieces by Robert Blatchford, Isabella Ford, Edward Carpenter and William Morris. Readers of the paper were also encouraged to procure suitable literature in the regular book review columns, literary articles and advertisements that together served to expose its readers to a wealth of recommended texts. As important as these constituents were in emphasizing the educative value of litera-ture, it was through the channels of the periodical's correspondence class that the *Labour Prophet* most actively demonstrated its editor's assiduously held conviction that the consumption of suitable read-ing materials could provide an individual with the analytical tools necessary for personal, intellectual and political progression.

The launch of the paper's correspondence class was announced by its editor in the June 1894 number of the *Prophet*. The classes were fundamentally an educational facility, established to guide subscribers through a regimented programme of home study, concomitant with the integral Labour Church doctrine of 'Personal Development'. Yet as John Trevor revealed in the same article, the correspondence classes also functioned to establish formal contact between the *Labour Prophet* and its readership:

> My idea is that each book should be sent out as required with a set of questions accompanying it, and that the reader should send answers to these questions when he returns the book. Upon these answers correspondence would arise, and a suitable book could be suggested for further study.[24]

The prescribed reading lists for the classes included standard non-fictional socialist tracts, such as *England's Ideal* by Edward Carpenter and Robert Blatchford's bestselling treatise, *Merrie England*, but J. W. Longsdon, architect of the reading lists, also extended their remit to include selected works of fiction. Longsdon, who was also one of the examiners of the correspondence class, outlined his case for the importance of an engaged approach to fiction in an 1894 article entitled 'Novel-Reading', in which he claimed that, 'the best moral teaching of the age is to be found in novels'.[25] In both Longsdon's article and in the correspondence class reading lists, Olive Schreiner's *The Story of an African Farm* is singled out for particular praise, endorsed as a worthy, educational read to a two-tiered audience of correspondence class students and readers of the *Labour Prophet* more generally.

Steeped in the transcendentalism of Ralph Waldo Emerson (from whom Schreiner's boy-protagonist, Waldo, acquired his name), and a belief in the 'unity underlying all nature' that emanated from Herbert Spencer, Schreiner and her debut novel appealed philosophically to Labour Church practitioners, who for the most part, as Caroline Sumpter has suggested, 'eschewed Christian Socialism in favour of a democratic theology heavily influenced by Romantic and pantheistic ideologies'.[26] On a monthly basis over the course of two years, readers were encouraged to procure and enter into a dialogue with Schreiner's novel, yet were simultaneously provided with an interpretative framework to guide analysis in the form of a short blurb, reprinted in each number as part of the correspondence class's reading list:

> This story is filled with the same theme – the cruelty and deadness of life without affection and brotherly feeling. Deals in particular with the injustice done to women. The book shows how cruel life often is, but we are also shown why this is so, and how beautiful and noble it may become.[27]

In addition to appealing for their students and general readership to engage with Schreiner's novel, the *Labour Prophet* also implicitly encourages an emulation of the textual interpretation outlined within the parameters of their succinct introduction to the book. So too, the correspondence questions posed to students as part of their course of home study attempted to coach readers in the ways in which the prescribed texts should be both read and understood. One correspondent student's letter to the *Labour Prophet* indicates that this was welcomed: 'The class is a splendid idea. The questions sent touch all the chief points of the book, and help one to thoroughly understand it.'[28] As Margaret Beetham has argued, maintaining a given periodical's regular readership involves offering readers a 'recognizable position' from which to read via the systematic cultivation of a consistent or 'implied' reader within and throughout successive numbers of the publication.[29] In marketing texts such as *African Farm* to the periodical's readers in this way, the *Labour Prophet*'s correspondence classes clearly sought to forge an active community of similarly thinking readers, ideologically bound by common reading materials and shared goals. The dominant position from which to read, constructed within the interactive educational site of the correspondence class column could ultimately be resisted in real terms by Labour Church readers, but nevertheless remains useful in providing a window onto the perceived underlying propaganda function that texts such as *African Farm* could serve. For John Trevor, texts like Schreiner's ultimately functioned for his readers as potential sites of conversion – politically, spiritually and intellectually.

The emphasis placed upon structured, serious reading and the dissemination of appropriate literature across the wider socialist movement at this time, emanated from an earnest belief in the transformative power of print – both as preparation and inspiration for socialist activism for existing enthusiasts of the cause, and also as a recruiting device. Socialist leaders and editors of left-wing periodicals such as Robert Blatchford, Keir Hardie and the current focus, John Trevor, clearly understood that the consumption of appropriately didactic texts could serve as an important propaganda tool in the widespread dissemination of left-wing polemic. To this end, the *Labour Prophet* continually sought to expose its readership to a stream of suitable reading materials and frequently attempted to expand the parameters of its correspondence class community by actively seeking to recruit new members. The formation of local reading groups for the purpose of guided, communal reading was encouraged by the Labour Church in the hope that the construction of formal reading communities would encourage deeper learning via the collective sharing of reading experiences. Reading circles and group discussion performed an important educative function, the social dimension of which encouraged members to dedicate themselves more fully to serious, independent home reading, whilst also inspiring a strong sense of collegiality amongst group members. In November 1896 on the two-year anniversary of the correspondence class's founding, Mary G. Burnett, the class secretary, claimed to

sympathize with those whose working lives and 'material surround-
ings', to borrow Olive Schreiner's phrase, encroached upon their course
of study.[30] Regardless, Burnett cites the example of one periodical reader's evident dedication to the development of her intellectual life as an
encouragement for other readers to emulate her diligence:

> To show what can be done even under great difficulties, I know a
> girl who has in six months read during her dinner hour :– *Sesame
> and Lilies*; *Past and Present*; *Hero and Hero-worship*; *Origin of Species*;
> Olive Schreiner's *Dreams*; and *Biology* (for Preliminary Medical
> Examination). She has read these books thoroughly, and can give
> an intelligent account of every one of them. What one can do,
> another can.[31]

As part of the *Labour Prophet*'s dedication to the expansion of class
sizes, Trevor developed a number of innovative methods of book distribution to help lure new members, whilst simultaneously ensuring
that low-income readers could gain access to prescribed reading
materials. Firstly, free lending libraries were established for students
of the correspondence classes. As Burnett noted in the November
1896 class column in the *Prophet*, the free libraries targeted 'the students who have already gone through most of the books to which
there are set questions', and also, those members of the class, who,
owing to the constraints of labour, 'may not be able to study in
this way'.[32] Secondly, deals were established with publishers so that
correspondence texts could be ordered and purchased at a reduced
rate for class members. When finished with books, students, if they
so wished, could then post them directly to Trevor, who would
advertise them for sale in the *Labour Prophet* on their behalf, so that
other readers could procure second-hand books at a discounted cost,
maximizing the distribution potential of a given text. And finally, for
those who were not within reach of a free library or could not afford
to buy texts either new or second-hand, a postal-based loan service of
correspondence class reading materials was offered, with recipients
simply required to cover the costs of postage both ways. Through
the implementation of such innovative methods of circulation, the
Labour Prophet effectively fostered a community of readers by the
means of an entire 'communication circuit', to use Robert Darnton's

term, which both made use of and bypassed mainstream modes of book distribution and circulation.[33]

* * *

But all of this is not to say that the *Labour Prophet*'s readers were mere passive recipients of the periodical's editorial line. Conversely, internally held evidence within the publication indicates that a portion of its readership were proactive agents in the modification and expansion of the remit of its left-wing educational schemes. By way of a conclusion, I would like to turn briefly to the *Labour Prophet*'s readers and their active role in the promotion of Schreiner's works within the textual boundaries of the periodical. Printed reader's responses are revealing in terms of the sustained popularity of Schreiner's texts throughout the 1890s within correspondence circles. In the April 1896 number of the *Prophet* for example, one correspondence student replied to an offer of a loan of Schreiner's collection of allegories, *Dreams,* from the secretary's personal library, stating that: 'It is good of you to offer to lend me "Dreams", but I already have it among my treasures. The lost one in "Dreams" is a personal favourite of mine.'[34] By both privately consuming and publicly recommending texts that were not strictly prescribed reading materials, this student clearly moved beyond the scope of the course of study outlined in the periodical's reading lists. This particular reader's letter serves both as an endorsement of the extra-curricular *Dreams,* and as an inducement for her fellow students and general readers of the *Labour Prophet* also to procure and read Schreiner's book. Subsequent readers, perhaps coincidentally, proceeded to write to the letters page, urging for *Dreams* be added to the catalogue of the Labour Church lending library and also to the correspondence class study scheme. The eventual addition of *Dreams* to the library in May 1896 is an indicator of the dialogic nature of the periodical form: the *Labour Prophet* was a truly interactive site where readers, along with editors and writers, could participate in the formation of Schreiner's reputation and the establishment of wider reading patterns within their own reading community.

The promotion of Schreiner's texts as suitable reading materials for those readers clustered around the *Labour Prophet* throughout the 1890s emanated from its editor's steadfast belief in both the didactic and propagandistic function of literature. Through the establishment of correspondence classes and a canny network of innovative distribution methods which permitted low-income readers to gain access to texts, John Trevor actively sought to forge an active reading community bound by common reading materials and shared convictions. The evidence of reading Schreiner's texts in left-wing reading communities like the one outlined here also reveals the limits of the feminist repackaging of Schreiner as the first New Woman novelist. The recovery of evidence for the prevalence of Schreiner's works within socialist reading circles at this time provides alternative entry points into her texts today, and ultimately outlines the important role minor periodicals such as the *Labour Prophet* can play in the recovery of forgotten reading communities, reading formations and reading experiences.

Notes and references

1. *The Letters of Olive Schreiner*, ed. Richard Rive (Oxford: Oxford University Press, 1998), pp. 40–1.
2. H. Gustav Klaus, *The Socialist Novel in Britain: Towards the Recovery of a Tradition* (New York: St. Martin's Press – now Palgrave Macmillan, 1982).
3. W. T. Stead, 'The novel of the modern woman', *Review of Reviews*, 10 (1894), 64–74. For further information on the friendship between Olive Schreiner and W. T. Stead, and the publishing history of *The Story of an African Farm*, see Ruth First and Ann Scott's seminal biography of Schreiner, *Olive Schreiner: A Biography* (London: Andre Deutsch, 1980).
4. Klaus, *Socialist Novel*, p. 4.
5. *The Story of an African Farm* was included in the list of the '100 Best Novels in the World' as published in 1899 by *The Daily Telegraph*. This list also included works by a number of popular nineteenth-century novelists including Charles Dickens, Ouida, Mary Elizabeth Braddon, Wilkie Collins, George Lawrence, and Mrs Henry Wood. By contrast, Schreiner's texts were also championed throughout the 1890s by a number of avowedly socialist publications, including, for example, the *Clarion*, the *Labour Leader*, and, the focus of the present study, the *Labour Prophet*. Two of Schreiner's works, namely *African Farm* and *Dreams* were also included in *The Labour Bookshelf*, a circular issued by the publishing department of the ILP comprising reading lists of socialist literature. See, *The Labour Bookshelf*, 3 (1925), p. 3.
6. This term was frequently used in socialist circles throughout the 1890s, but I first encountered it courtesy of Caroline Sumpter's essay: 'Making socialists, or murdering to dissect? Natural history and child socialization in the *Labour Prophet* and *Labour Leader*', in *Culture and Science in*

the Nineteenth-Century Media, ed. Louise Henson and others (Aldershot: Ashgate, 2004), pp. 29–40. See also, Stephen Yeo, 'A NEW LIFE: the religion of Socialism in Britain, 1883–1896', *History Workshop*, 4 (1977), 5–56; and Mark Bevir, 'The Labour Church movement, 1891–1902', *Journal of British Studies*, 38 (1999), 217–45.

7. Rive, *Letters of Olive Schreiner*, p. 109.
8. There are many critical assessments of Schreiner's feminism, but among the best are: Carolyn Burdett, *Olive Schreiner and the Progress of Feminism: Evolution, Gender, Empire* (Basingstoke: Palgrave – now Palgrave Macmillan, 2001); Laura Chrisman, 'Allegory, feminist thought and the *Dreams* of Olive Schreiner', *Prose Studies: History, Theory, Criticism*, 13 (1990), 126–50; Ann Heilmann, *New Woman Strategies: Sarah Grand, Olive Schreiner, Mona Caird* (Manchester and New York: Manchester University Press, 2004); Sally Ledger, *The New Woman: Fiction and Feminism at the fin de siècle* (Manchester: Manchester University Press, 1997); Liz Stanley *Imperialism, Labour and the New Woman: Olive Schreiner's Social Theory* (Durham: Sociology Press, 2002).
9. *The Letters of Olive Schreiner*, ed. S. C. Cronwright-Schreiner (London: Unwin, 1924), p. 278. Critics who have previously situated Schreiner's work within an appropriate socialist framework include: Joyce Avrech Berkman, *The Healing Imagination of Olive Schreiner: Beyond South African Colonialism* (Oxford: Plantin Publishers, 1989); Ruth Livesey, *Socialism, Sex, and the Culture of Aestheticism in Britain, 1880–1914* (Oxford: Oxford University Press, 2007); and Liz Stanley, *Imperialism, Labour and the New Woman: Olive Schreiner's Social Theory* (Durham: Sociology Press, 2002).
10. Rive, *The Letters of Olive Schreiner*, p. 278.
11. Eleanor Marx, Schreiner's 'mental champagne' as she described her friend to Havelock Ellis, was an important figure in the shaping and development of Schreiner's socialism (quoted in Stanley, *Imperialism*, p. 24). As Liz Stanley has suggested, their friendship 'enabled Schreiner to place her developing ideas within a socialist frame concerned with divisions of labour in society' (p. 25). For a full account of the life of Eleanor Marx, including some highly relevant and useful materials relating to Olive Schreiner, Yvonne Kapp's two-volume biography remains unsurpassable: *Eleanor Marx: Family Life 1855–1883* (London: Virago, 1972); *Eleanor Marx: The Crowded Years 1884–1898* (London: Virago, 1976).
12. Livesey, *Socialism*, pp. 3–4. In addition to providing a significant and in-depth account of the aesthetic nature of late nineteenth century socialism, Ruth Livesey's excellent research discusses Schreiner's work both within the context of the contemporary socialist movement and crucially, with relation to other left-wing writers, thus going some way to reinstating the author to her rightful place within the canon of socialist literature.
13. Robert Blatchford, *Merrie England* (London: Clarion Newspaper Company, 1895), p. 205; George Meek, *Bath Chair-man* (London: Constable, 1910), p. 141. The popularity of Blatchford's text and its mobilizing effects upon the socialist movement in the 1890s were extraordinary. Published by Blatchford under his *Clarion* pseudonym, Nunquam, *Merrie England* makes

extensive use of literary reference and allusion throughout, and closes with a list of some sixteen pamphlets and eighteen books that reaches its culmination in *Dreams*. Blatchford's public advocacy of *Dreams* formally politicized Schreiner's aesthetic in the name of *Clarion* socialism, whilst simultaneously promoting her allegories to the hundreds of thousands of *Merrie England* readers throughout the 1890s and beyond. For more on the use of didactic literature in *Merrie England*, see Deborah Mutch, 'The *Merrie England* Triptych: Robert Blatchford, Edward and the didactic use of *Clarion* fiction', *Victorian Periodicals Review*, 38 (2005), 83–103.

14. Sheffield City Council, Libraries Archives and Information: Sheffield Archives, Carpenter/Mss/355/1, pp. 1–2. Kate Salt to Edward Carpenter (5 February 1889), unpublished letter. I would like to thank Mr Jon Wynne-Tyson for kindly granting me permission to quote from this source.
15. Henry Norman, 'Theories and practice of modern fiction', *The Fortnightly Review*, 34 (December 1883), p. 882. Mrs John Brown, *Olive Schreiner, Memories of a Friendship* (Cape Town: n.p., 1923), p. 5.
16. Whilst the final two to three decades of the nineteenth century were an undeniably crucial period in the history of socialism in Britain and Ireland, in accounting for this fact, some historians have downplayed the significance of the post-Chartist decades (from the late 1840s to approximately 1870) for the socialist movement. For a cogent account of why these years must not be dismissed from any comprehensive history of the British socialist movement, see Jon Lawrence, 'Popular Radicalism and the Socialist revival in Britain', *The Journal of British Studies*, 31 (1992), 163–86.
17. Deborah Mutch, *English Socialist Periodicals, 1880–1900: A Reference Source* (Aldershot: Ashgate, 2005), p. xxii.
18. For more on the advent and particulars of the New Journalism, see *Papers for the Millions: the New Journalism in Britain, 1850s to 1914*, ed. Joel H. Wiener (London: Greenwood, 1988); Mutch, *English Socialist Periodicals*, p. xxii.
19. Bevir, 'Labour Church movement', p. 235. For a deeper explication of the economic difficulties experienced at the *Labour Prophet*, see Caroline Sumpter, 'The politics of the fairy tale in the Labour press', in her *The Victorian Press and the Fairy Tale* (Basingstoke: Palgrave Macmillan, 2008), pp. 88–130.
20. Rive, *Letters of Olive Schreiner*, p. 210.
21. According to Mark Bevir, the Labour Church movement and John Trevor are indelibly intertwined. Trevor resigned from his post as a Unitarian minister to found the first Labour Church in Manchester 1891 and conceived of the *Labour Prophet* as a mouthpiece for the Church (p. 217). For Bevir, Trevor's founding of the Labour Church resulted from 'the failure of existing churches to support labour', rendering it 'necessary for workers to form a new movement to embody the religious aspect of their emancipation' (Bevir, 'Labour Church movement', p. 218).
22. Sidney E. Dark, 'Socialists and education', *Labour Prophet*, 2 (January 1893), p. 6.

23. 'The Labour Church is based upon the following principles', *Labour Prophet*, 2 (April 1893), p. 28.
24. 'Our proposed library', *Labour Prophet*, 3 (June 1894), p. 72.
25. J. W. Longsdon, 'Novel-reading', *Labour Prophet*, 39 (March 1895), pp. 36–7.
26. Caroline Sumpter, 'Making Socialists, or murdering to dissect', p. 30.
27. See, for example, 'Our correspondence class', *Labour Prophet*, 4 (January 1895), 15–16.
28. 'Extracts from students' letters', *Labour Prophet*, 5 (April 1896), p. 54.
29. See Margaret Beetham, 'Towards a theory of the periodical as a publishing genre', in *Investigating Victorian Journalism*, ed. Laurel Brake, Aled Jones and Lionel Madden (New York: St. Martin's Press – now Palgrave Macmillan, 1990), pp. 19–32.
30. For more on Labour Church reading classes, see 'Our correspondence class', *Labour Prophet*, 3 (October 1894), p. 139; Mary G. Burnett, 'Our correspondence class: secretary's report', *Labour Prophet*, 5 (November 1893), p. 183.
31. Burnett, 'Correspondence class', p. 183.
32. Ibid.
33. See Robert Darnton's seminal work, *The Kiss of Lamourette: Studies in Cultural History* (London: Faber & Faber, 1990).
34. 'Extracts from students' letters', *Labour Prophet*, 5 (April 1896), p. 55. The student is referring to Schreiner's allegory, 'The lost joy', in *Dreams* (London: Thomas Fisher Unwin, 1890).

Part 2
Reading and Gratification

4
Learning to Read Trash: Late-Victorian Schools and the Penny Dreadful

Anna Vaninskaya

The pernicious effects of reading penny dreadfuls had always been a favourite topic of Victorian cultural commentators, and by the last few decades of the century – although the genre itself was being rapidly transformed by developments in cheap publishing – it grew to be a constant and familiar refrain. In the quarterlies and reviews penny dreadfuls were condemned (and occasionally defended), blamed for every occurrence of juvenile crime, and subjected to disapproving sociological and literary analyses. The emphasis by the 1880s had, along with the publishers' target market, shifted squarely to lower-class boys. The act of reading penny literature was equated with unwholesome eating habits, with the consumption of 'poison' – as damaging to the mental constitution as a poor diet was to the physical.[1] And the epidemic was one of national proportions.

But whence came this huge audience of millions? The answer, so late in the century, was likely to be: from the Board schools. Elementary education was still at the experimental stage, observers complained, 'and one of the first lessons from the experiment is that when we have taught small boys and girls to read, their natural inclination will often be to read what is not good for them'.[2] Any discussion of reading brought in its wake the issue of popular schooling, and articles with titles like 'Elementary Education and the Decay of Literature' began to pepper the pages of the reviews.[3] The errand-boy had learned to read in the classroom, but its barren literary fare had left his appetite for fiction unsatisfied, and his imagination was starved by the fact-cramming exigencies of the three Rs system. The link between juvenile reading practices and the shortfalls of compulsory primary education was rediscovered again and again. Campaigners for elementary curriculum reform were quick to seize upon the connection: the memorization-based system, they argued, may have extended literacy, but it prevented the formation of good reading habits. Board school graduates, if they read at all, inevitably turned to penny fiction. They had access to free libraries, but they preferred 'garbage' to 'wholesome or delicate food', and this 'addiction to low and vitiating forms of reading' was fed by a rising supply.[4] More than one author remarked that a generation before, penny dreadfuls had been neither as numerous nor as directly targeted at boys.

To what extent this picture was a cultural construct – as opposed to an accurate reflection of the reality of the lower-class reading experience – is difficult to determine. Some of the observations have in fact been confirmed by modern scholarship – both on the changing economics of popular publishing and on the nature of Victorian state education. But it is equally easy to disprove other assumptions by pointing to autodidacts' accounts of finding inspiration in the Board school reading books, or of using penny dreadfuls as a ladder to higher forms of literature. As even conservative commentators admitted, 'If to acquire a taste for reading is a good thing by itself, it may be accounted something even that [children] should read "penny dreadfuls". The large number of readers of sensational fiction who do not become criminals may yet rise on stepping-stones of their dead selves to Stevenson or Thackeray.'[5] The autodidacts, if the selections in Jonathan Rose's *The Intellectual Life of the British Working Classes* are anything to go by, heartily agreed.[6] Penny dreadfuls, wrote London hat-maker Frederick Willis, 'encouraged and developed a love of reading that led [a boy] onwards and upwards on the fascinating path of literature. It was the beloved "bloods" that first stimulated my love of reading, and from them I set out on the road to Shaw and Wells, Thackeray and Dickens, Fielding, Shakespeare and Chaucer.' 'Miners' MP Robert Smillie surreptitiously gorged on *Dick Turpin* and *Three-Fingered Jack* as a boy, they too "led to better things": by fourteen he had seen *Richard III*, read some of the Sonnets, discovered Burns, Scott and Dickens.' The ironworker's son Alfred Cox 'attributed his "budding love of literature . . . to an enthusiastic reading of Penny Dreadfuls"'; George Acorn, an East Londoner, read 'all sorts and conditions of books, from "Penny Bloods" to George Eliot'; and Howard Spring, a gardener's son, traced a direct line from the

Magnet to Scott and Dumas.[7] For one miner autodidact 'adventure stories . . . led to more substantial material, including Dickens, Scott, Eliot, and the Brontës', while the future poet W. H. Davies, growing up in Newport in 1885, 'began with the common penny novel of the worst type, but acquired a taste for better work in a shorter time than boys usually do'.[8]

The commentators also did not take into account the possibility that some working-class children may have entered school already knowing how to read, having devoured classic literature at home with their parents or siblings: sometimes in tandem with the less elevated fare of the streets, sometimes exclusively. The shortcomings of the elementary school curriculum had little to do with their reading development, and such students were usually capable of finding literary inspiration even in the poor teaching materials condemned by middle-class observers. *Their* imaginations were certainly not starved by the system: the selection in Nelson's *Royal Readers*, as Flora Thompson famously recalled, 'was an education in itself for those who took to it kindly'.[9] Thompson was able to extract enough Scott, Byron and Tennyson to keep her happy from the same reading book that her classmates found tedious and dry. She was not unusual. As Davies' biographer describes, although 'his first attraction was to the penny-dreadfuls of his day, which he read in secret',

> The school-books he read [also] contained poems that stirred him deeply. One of the school texts he used contained long passages from *The Lady of the Lake*, with a prose commentary attached. And there was a favourite schoolboy poem starting with the resounding line: 'A Soldier of the Legion lay dying in Algiers', with a refrain that the boys loved to chant at play. There were extracts from Shakespeare, the usual lyrics, and a few heavily didactic poems intended to inculcate morality in the boyish heart.[10]

Jonathan Rose provides many more examples of working-class child readers who not only indulged equally and simultaneously in both the 'classics' and the 'trash', but also drew from their Board or church society school curriculum a deep appreciation of literature for its own sake. 'Jones . . . attended a Board school, where he found "salvation" in an old cupboard of books presented by the local MP. They were mainly volumes of voyages and natural history, "which took a

Rhymney boy away into the realms of wonder"'; 'H. M. Tomlinson, a successful author and dockworker's son, credited his East End Board school with encouraging free expression in composition classes and giving him a solid literary footing in the Bible, Shakespeare and Scott.' One headmaster 'read aloud from *Macbeth*, *The Pickwick Papers*, and *The Water Babies*', and another acquainted his students with '*Robinson Crusoe, Gulliver's Travels*, and *Tales From Shakespeare*'. '"Thinking back, I am amazed at the amount of English literature we absorbed in those four years", recalled Ethel Clark.'[11] Many of these children were born shortly after the end of the Victorian period, but Rose adduces as much evidence from those who went to school before 1900: Edgar Wallace, the future best-selling writer, enjoyed most of all precisely that routine memorization and recitation of poetry and scenes from Shakespeare's plays that critics of the system condemned as mindless and incapable of imparting any proper understanding of literature. Testimonies like his were not exceptional. 'Mark Grossek (b. 1888), son of a Jewish immigrant tailor, concluded that his Board school in dismal Southwark was in many respects superior to the genteel grammar schools he later attended on scholarship', for instead of Latin grammar 'he was treated to Byron [and] Shakespeare'.[12] It was probably only a minority of students who believed that Board schools successfully 'introduced the best in English literature, then set their pupils free at adolescence to read on their own', but it was a minority the contemporary critics resolutely ignored.[13]

These children may have been precocious (their subsequent careers are certainly far from representative), but their reading experiences often betrayed remarkable similarities despite widely differing circumstances. Flora Thompson's case, for instance, may be compared with that of another well-known autobiographer, Robert Roberts.[14] On the surface they had little in common: Thompson attended a small rural Oxfordshire school in the 1880s, Roberts a large urban one in the Salford industrial slum of the 1910s. Thompson's peers left by the age of eleven or twelve at the very latest to take up agricultural labour (she and a friend were the only pupils to reach Standard V), and no special subjects like history or geography were on offer. By Roberts' time, some students stayed on until thirteen or fourteen (up to Standard VII – the highest available), and benefited from history lessons, art and music. Though they were not put in for examinations by the headmaster, there was nothing to prevent them from trying for technical or commercial colleges instead of going straight to work. Yet both schools were poor National (Church of England) primaries, staffed for the most part by unqualified teachers, and offering, according to the HMI Inspectors who visited them, an execrable education concentrating mainly on the three Rs and Scripture. Both made it their chief business to inculcate patriotism and class subordination, and both produced semi-literate readers of illustrated comic papers as well as future writers who amused themselves in their spare time outside school by reading or writing poetry. Unlike Thompson, Roberts also enjoyed boys' penny papers and adult penny periodicals churned out by the presses of Harmsworth and Pearson, but this did not prevent him from patronizing the public library.

Of course, for every child like Thompson or Roberts, there were several others who gained even less from their training in the three Rs than the most pessimistic school inspector feared. Memoirs, as well as more systematic recent research, confirm that a by no means negligible number of pupils remained illiterate upon leaving school, or lost their reading and writing skills through lack of use. The percentage of those who even reached the higher standards where genuine ability to read was tested was tiny: in 1882, 'a mere 1.9 percent proved their capacity to "read a passage from one of Shakespeare's historical plays, or from some other standard author, or from a history of England" as demanded by Standard VI'.[15] If the more gifted children had little to fear from penny dreadfuls because they were already educated enough to appreciate 'healthy literature', those who were let down by the system were even less likely to be tempted by something they barely had the skills to consume.

But whatever the actual reader experience may have been, the cultural construct it gave rise to deserves to be considered on its own terms. The observations that follow are based on a close reading of over fifteen articles spanning the period from 1870, the year of Forster's landmark Education Act, to 1901, the end of the Victorian era and the year before the passage of the equally monumental 1902 Act, which abolished the Board schools, established the Local Education Authorities and put the provision of secondary education for the working classes on the national agenda. There were, of course, more than fifteen articles, but the extent of repetition over the thirty year span, both with regard to complaints and to proposed remedies, and the fact that some articles published decades apart actually came from the same pen (Francis Hitchman, Thomas Wright), make even a random selection at least partially representative.[16] The publication venues ranged from *Macmillan's Magazine* to the *Quarterly Review*, although the biggest proportion of such articles was to be found in the *Nineteenth Century* and the *Contemporary Review*. The spread of authors was even more impressive: from Helen Bosanquet, leader of the Charity Organization Society and author of the Poor Law Majority Report (1909), to popular middle-brow novelists like H. Rider Haggard and James Payn; from Thomas Wright, a working-class School Board visitor and social commentator, to Hugh Chisholm, Conservative editor of the famous eleventh edition of the *Encyclopaedia Britannica*, and Alexander Strahan, Liberal publisher of the *Contemporary Review*.[17] James Greenwood, brother of the editor of the *Cornhill* and the *Pall Mall Gazette*, and one of the first of the late-Victorian social explorers, who dressed as a tramp and slept in workhouses in order to gather material for his journalism thirty-five years before Jack London and sixty-five years before Orwell, also pitched into the debate about the 'Penny Awfuls'. What all these people had in common was a concern with the link between lower-class schooling and reading experience, and the belief, as one article in the *Nineteenth Century* phrased it, that 'the instruction imparted through the Board school has not superinduced any large amount of reading, except in a shape contemptible and worthless'.[18] It was not sufficient to teach children *how* to read, Greenwood wrote: the newly set-up London School Board should also have been empowered 'to root up and for ever banish from the paths of its pupils those dangerous weeds of literature that crop up in such rank luxuriance on every side to tempt them'.[19] Teaching reading was not difficult; guiding pupils away from the tempting and dazzling dreadfuls that beset on every side to more 'wholesome and profitable' matter was the more necessary task.

Despite the diversity of their backgrounds, most of these critics were in some way involved with popular education, popular literature, or the cultural life of the working and lower-middle classes. Chisholm described the purpose of the *Encyclopaedia Britannica* as 'democratizing the means of self-education';[20] Haggard wanted to know where the audiences for his romances came from – romances which were routinely accused of plumbing the depths of penny-dreadful awfulness, and which sold in the millions when reprinted in one-penny formats. One of the answers he proposed was the new Board schools that 'pour[ed] out their thousands every year'.[21] Thomas Wright, one of the most perceptive commentators on the issue of penny reading, was the most suited by his background to the task. He was a member of the self-educated, local Mechanics' Institute-attending respectable working class, a prolific observer of its ways of life, as well as of the culture of the poorer casual labourers his school visiting brought him into contact with. Helen Bosanquet, through her work for the COS, also had a direct acquaintance with the penny dreadful-consuming public, though her paternalistic perspective had none of the participant–observer authenticity of Wright's. Strahan, the publisher, was known for his zeal in providing 'good but inexpensive literature "for the people"', which might go some way towards explaining the recurrence of enlightened publishing self-interest as a proposed panacea for the horrors of cheap print.[22] In 1870, in his own *Contemporary Review*, Strahan asked whether it was 'worthwhile to agitate for compulsory education, if, when people have learnt to read, they will content themselves with such poor innutritious stuff?'[23] The solution lay firmly in the hands of private enterprise, and Strahan took comfort in the fact that tastes would improve if a better kind of cheap literature were made available by businessmen like himself.

The belief that publishers rather than educational institutions held the key gave comfort to many other commentators over the next thirty years. Although remedies like the provision of good literature in the classroom received the obligatory nod, this school of thinking pinned its hopes primarily on the market. In 1880 Francis Hitchman, having given an extensive survey of penny journals, boys' story papers and penny dreadfuls, acknowledged that matters might mend with the further diffusion of education. But since such education routinely excluded 'culture', it was better to rely on enterprising publishers to supply good literature, and to expunge the 'tract element' associated with poorly selling philanthropic attempts to wean the working class off their poisonous addiction. Businessmen knew best.[24] After ruling out censorship as a solution, and admitting that the introduction of religious teaching in the Board schools to fill up the moral void was politically out of the question, Hitchman turned to the 'healthy and natural light' of capitalist enterprise: 'Publishers are beginning to awaken to the fact that the spread of education and the increased facilities of communication have created a vast new public to which it is worth while to appeal.' 'The extent of the sale of the trash . . . proves the existence of a public . . . from whom a large profit may be drawn.' If books, illustrations and systems of distribution were selected judiciously, and good literature published in 'penny number form', return on speculation would be at least as good as that 'yielded by the shabby, vulgar, and vicious prints' of Drury Lane.[25]

The device of starting reviews of penny fiction with perorations on the state of elementary education and ending with appeals to progressively minded publishers to step into the breach was a favoured one. G. B. Johns, in an *Edinburgh Review* article of 1887, began with a description of the vast audience of shop-girls, errand-boys, and street arabs: the millions of Board school pupils and graduates whose demand for fiction and excitement was met with an overabundant supply of penny dreadfuls. The solution was to 'Flood the market with good, wholesome literature, instead of the poisonous stuff to which the hapless purchasers are now condemned', to make it 'as easy and profitable' to potential publishers to supply the pure as it was to supply the tainted. Although the reprint series could already boast horrible abridgements of Dickens and Thackeray, Johns proposed an entirely new penny library of healthy fiction. 'Romances' and 'Lives', 'tales of history, love-making, adventure, crime, and fairyland', wonder and mystery, could be written not by the anonymous purveyors of trash, but by writers such as Wilkie Collins, Elizabeth Braddon, Mrs Oliphant, G. A. Henty and Walter Besant. Even the old Gothic romances of Walpole and Radcliffe could be resuscitated and repackaged for a modern readership. Though to reach their target working-class audience these authors would have to dispense with preaching and simply amuse, Johns saw no reason why they could not sell as well as the rubbish currently dominating the market.[26]

A few years later, Hugh Chisholm echoed Johns in calling upon publishers to make good fiction available as cheaply as the bad. Like Hitchman, he realized that it was unworkable to censor the dreadfuls by state legislation: they did not fall under the acts dealing with blasphemous, obscene or seditious literature, and suppression did not in any case deal with the root of the problem. But if 'the schoolboy [could] get the *Prisoner of Zenda* for a penny he [would] not be obliged to buy the only thing which that modest sum will now procure in the market, some choice morsel like *Sweeney Todd*'. The reduced prices could be made up for in greater circulation, and as copyrights ran out, good readable fiction from the previous fifty years would fill the shelves:

> With Penny Populars like Dickens, Thackeray, Scott, the two Kingsleys, Marryat, Whyte, Melville, Lytton, G. P. R. James, Wilkie Collins, Grant . . . and all the rest of them, including Stevenson, Rider Haggard, and Sir Walter Besant himself, the well-directed young glutton for fiction in the next century will have the very best chance of neglecting the rubbish-heap of badly-written and clumsy sensationalism to which the protection of better literature by the Copyright Act has resulted in confining the larger number of the poor in our own day.[27]

'Cheap wholesome literature for the poor' had in fact been suggested as an alternative to the penny dreadful since at least the 1860s, and both religious societies like the Society for the Promotion of Christian Knowledge and mass-market publishers like Harmsworth, with his halfpenny juvenile periodicals intended to 'counteract the pernicious influences of the Penny Dreadfuls', attempted to provide it. The new publishing tycoons, however, were significantly more successful than the Religious Tract Society and its ilk in achieving 'domination of popular publishing in Britain', and by the turn of the twentieth century the market was monopolized 'by a handful of large firms'.[28] The Amalgamated Press is the most famous, but the anti-dreadful counter-attack was many-pronged: W. B. Horner & Son, for example, specialized in proper and wholesome 'Penny Stories for the People', with hundreds of thousands of copies of hundreds of titles printed.[29] Chisholm had of course been disingenuous in making his argument: as David Vincent points out, 'This reduction of "choice" to a stark contrast between the elevating and the corrupting was both misleading and perceptive.'[30] For a penny one could already get a reprinted classic or an improving monthly as readily as a dreadful – and the children knew it. Joseph Stamper, an iron-moulder-novelist, had to 'ponder whether to buy Thomas à Kempis or *Deadwood Dick*',[31] and in his autobiography he gave an overview of the wholesome literature on offer to the youthful working-class consumer:

> Maybe to neutralise the Penny Dreadful, Cassells brought out the Penny Classics. These had a bluish-green cover and were world

famous novels in abridged form, but sixty or seventy pages. And
W. T. Stead brought out the Penny Poets. The covers of these were
pimply surface-paper, a bright orange colour, and they contained
selections from Longfellow, Tennyson, Keats, and many others.
I first read *Hiawatha* and *Evangeline* in the Penny Poets and thought
them marvellous; so marvellous that I began to write 'poetry'
myself. Stead also brought out another penny book; this had a pink
cover and contained selections from the ancient classics: stories
from Homer, the writings of Pliny the younger, Aesop's *Fables*.[32]

In the very year that Chisholm penned his plea, 1895, W. T. Stead
started his famous *Library of Penny Poets, Novels, and Prose Classics*,
and he was by no means the first in the field.

But if publishers were the answer, the schools were the problem.
In an 1890 review of penny fiction, ranging from old favourites like
Spring-Heeled Jack, *Sweeney Todd*, and *Turnpike Dick*, to papers like
the *London Journal*, the *Family Herald* and the *Boys of London and
New York*, Francis Hitchman took up the subject again. The opening of his article made the roots of the evil absolutely clear: '"We
must educate our masters", said Lord Sherbrooke (then Mr Lowe),
in the course of the debates on the Reform Bill of 1867. The remark
fell upon fertile soil, and Mr Forster's Education Bill of 1870 sprang
directly out of it.' Hitchman continued with a highly partisan
account of the Victorian debates over state education, coming at last
to the main question:

> We have been 'educating our masters' in the three Rs for nearly
> twenty years, and some of us are beginning to ask, to what use
> they have put that painful training in the rudiments which has
> cost the country so much solid money. The natural inquiry is,
> what do they read? Not indeed that they read much. The modern
> system of education, with the pressure of impending examina-
> tions for ever weighing upon teachers and children, is admirably
> adapted to prevent the youth of the period from troubling itself
> greatly about literature in any form.

But after he has left school at thirteen, 'the working lad finds that
the enterprising publishers of Shoe Lane and the purlieus thereof
have provided him with a certain store of amusement . . . the lads

employed in City offices and warehouses, who in many cases have a great deal of leisure', are occupied in reading, but reading 'which is not precisely of the kind for which Cobbett and Franklin hoarded their pence. No small proportion of it comes under the category of "Penny Dreadfuls".'

> This foul and filthy trash circulates by thousands and tens of thousands week by week amongst lads who are at the most impressionable period of their lives, and whom the modern system of purely secular education has left without ballast or guidance, it is not surprising that the authorities have to lament the prevalence of juvenile crime, and that the Lord Mayor and Alderman should constantly have to adjudicate in cases for which these books are directly responsible.[33]

Even commentators like Thomas Wright, who did not endorse the view that penny reading led to juvenile crime, agreed that 'the cram system, at its present high-pressure pitch', contributed to a hatred for real books and increased susceptibility to the widely advertised penny dreadful or serial. Compared with the age before the Education Acts, the number of subjects had increased, the workload was heavy enough to 'bewilder' the brain, and schoolboys no longer had the time or the stamina to pursue outside reading.[34] As a school visitor, Wright may have been echoing contemporary concerns about 'overpressure': a scare of the mid-1880s which attributed child death and insanity to overwork in the Board schools. But the cramming system was being condemned from all sides: the conservative Chisholm expressed the prevailing view when he claimed that its only purpose was to 'gain prestige for the school (and the headmaster) at the examinations'.[35]

Most observers by the end of the century agreed that the extension of popular education did not in itself equal the extension of culture, and that without reinforcement it would produce people capable only of reading newspaper police reports. But for education professionals like Wright, schools were not just part of the problem, they could also be part of the solution. He welcomed the fact that authors like Dickens, Bulwer-Lytton, Gaskell, Reade, Trollope, Ainsworth and Braddon had already written for the twopenny or onepenny public, but this was not enough.[36] What was needed was collaboration

between publishers and schools. 'Popular education and cheap literature are tunnelling ignorance from either end':

> Happily inspired publishers have issued in school book-form
> 'Robinson Crusoe', Southey's 'Life of Nelson', and one or two other
> works of a like interesting character. The leading school-boards
> have been wise enough to place these volumes on their Requisition
> Lists . . . as they are found by experience to give schoolchildren a
> much greater interest in their work than the older forms of 'read-
> ing book'.[37]

These older general readers – the only kind of textbook millions
of children had access to for most of the Victorian period[38] – were
'patchwork' concoctions, not 'incentives to higher forms of reading
[but] the task-work reading of the school'.[39] So if on the streets tales
of crime and violence were to be challenged by easily accessible high
quality romances from big-name novelists, in the schoolroom scrappy
reading books had to be replaced by whole literature classics. Wright
was predicting a trend: towards the end of the century educational
publishers did begin to issue abridged or edited texts of nineteenth-
century novels for school use. They were not often read continuously
or for their own sake: 'The interest of the narrative', Wright pointed
out, was 'necessarily . . . impaired by being read not only in piecemeal,
but, so to speak, in sandwich fashion – between, say, slices of grammar and arithmetic'. But even when employed for boring dictation
lessons, the impression they made, Wright claimed, was great enough
to 'create a taste for reading', and to inspire some students to pursue
it outside the classroom. Such books could also be used to make other
subjects, like geography or history, more interesting: 'a cut-and-dried
geographical lesson-book' was less effective, Wright argued, than an
'illustration of the voyages of Robinson Crusoe'.[40] The argument eventually bore fruit: Rose refers to one early twentieth-century teacher
'who disregarded the timetable that prescribed one hour each for history, geography, and English. Long before the word "interdisciplinar-
ity" had been invented, he taught them all together as one subject.'[41]
There were probably many others like him.

　School libraries of the kind established by the London School Board
were another way forward. According to Wright, 'they constitute[d]
a recognition of the importance of general reading as an instrument

of an improved elementary education'. They had to contain books of interest to students, not 'goody' morality tales which would fail to attract the readers of penny dreadfuls as surely as the unsuccessful journals of pure literature. But 'if a well-selected library formed part of the apparatus of every public elementary school, we might confidently expect to see the reign of the penny dreadfuls come to a speedy close'.[42] Progress on the school library front was certainly being made: in 1880 twelve per cent of 'inspected schools in England and Wales had their own libraries', and the figure rose to forty per cent by 1900, though there is no evidence to suggest that their existence had any effect on combating the popularity of penny reading.[43] Hugh Chisholm also supported the move to start Board school libraries: 'The best way to counteract the penny dreadful is to provide an equally attractive substitute, and the teachers might do a great deal by seeing that the young folk should have access to a good supply of healthy fiction.' 'If the Education Department would get Parliament to make a grant for extending these "juvenile" libraries, it would be money well spent.'

But Chisholm also went further, proposing a solution that the working-class Wright would never have contemplated. Unlike upper-class boys who were educated either at Public boarding Schools or at home, Chisholm pointed out, Board school pupils were raised in an environment without discipline. Teachers had no authority outside school and were afraid to enforce discipline within it; parents had no time or desire to control their children at home. Something had to be done

> to equalize the chances of the neglected Board school children with their more fortunate brothers at the Public schools . . . the State must recognize that its responsibilities are not finished when it compels children to come and be taught. If we only teach them how to read stuff which poisons their minds we are doing them a wrong, and it is our duty to prevent that to the best of our power.

The answer was to make Board schools into imitation Public Schools, with houses, team games, 'a regular system of moral and religious training', and the rest of the paraphernalia, including the 'intervention of Dr Stick, of whose valuable ministrations our modern sentimentalists fight so uncommonly shy'. Greater involvement by the teachers in the moulding of the 'new generation of the lower class', on the lines of Public School masters, was a prerequisite. 'When one thinks of what the teachers might make of the Board schools, it is not difficult to imagine a healthier state of things among the children, which would of itself go far to counteract the morbid influences of sensational fiction.'[44]

In other words, if you wanted lower-class boys to stop reading penny dreadfuls you had to transplant them to an upper-class environment. This kind of solution could never be tested in practice, but it would, ironically enough, be tested many times in the imagination of the lower-class boys in question, and teachers would have nothing to do with it. For if a Public School ethos did eventually permeate the boys' lives, it was through the school stories found in the Amalgamated Press penny and halfpenny papers, in particular Frank Richards' stories in the *Gem* and the *Magnet*. These taught Frederick Willis 'to be "very loyal" to the headmaster and teachers at his old Board school: "We were great readers of school stories, from which we learnt that boys of the higher class boarding schools were courageous, honourable, and chivalrous, and steeped in the traditions of the school and loyalty to the country. We tried to mould our lives according to this formula . . . the constant effort did us a lot of good."'[45] Robert Roberts shared the experience: 'Through the Old School we learned to admire guts, integrity, tradition.' So did numerous other boys whose testimonies Rose adduces,[46] and whose involvement stretched beyond imitation of the characters' lingo and body language to the absorption of a 'moral code': 'Over the years these simple tales conditioned the thought of a whole generation of boys. The public school ethos, distorted into myth and sold among us weekly in penny numbers, for good or ill, set ideals and standards.'[47] The worlds of the Board school and the Public School were light years apart, but unfamiliar realities could still be emulated if they were presented in the familiar format of the boys' paper. This type of identification may not have resulted in a 'common schoolboy culture that . . . transcended class', as Rose opines, but it certainly proved that the reading habits condemned by critics could produce the most unexpected results.[48] Working-class pupils were not cured of their addiction to penny fiction by the salutary influence of a Public School environment: on the contrary, it was only through penny fiction that they gained access to it.

Notes and references

1. For a general examination of the vocabulary of poisonous consumption, see Patrick Brantlinger, *The Reading Lesson: The Threat of Mass Literacy in Nineteenth-Century British Fiction* (Bloomington: Indiana University Press, 1998). For penny dreadfuls see John Springhall, '"Pernicious reading"? "The penny dreadful" as scapegoat for late-Victorian juvenile crime', *Victorian Periodicals Review*, 27 (1994), 326–49 and idem, '"Disseminating impure literature": the "penny dreadful" publishing business since 1860', *Economic History Review*, 47 (1994), 567–84; Patrick Dunae, 'Penny dreadfuls: late nineteenth-century boys' literature and crime', *Victorian Studies*, 22 (1979), 133–50; Elizabeth James and Helen R. Smith, *Penny Dreadfuls and Boys' Adventures: The Barry Ono Collection of Victorian Popular Literature in the British Library* (London: The British Library, 1998); and Judith Rowbotham and Kim Stevenson, *Behaving Badly: Social Panic and Moral Outrage – Victorian and Modern Parallels* (Aldershot: Ashgate, 2003), pp. 163–8.
2. Hugh Chisholm, 'How to counteract the "penny dreadful"', *Fortnightly Review*, 58 (Nov. 1895), 765–75 (p. 771).
3. Joseph Ackland, 'Elementary education and the decay of literature', *Nineteenth Century*, 35 (Mar. 1894), 412–23.
4. Thomas Wright, 'On a possible popular culture', *Contemporary Review*, 40 (Jul./Dec. 1881), 25–44 (p. 27).
5. Chisholm, 'How to counteract', p. 771.
6. Jonathan Rose, *The Intellectual Life of the British Working Classes* (New Haven: Yale University Press, 2001).
7. Ibid., pp. 368–70.
8. David Vincent, *Literacy and Popular Culture: England 1750–1914* (Cambridge: Cambridge University Press, 1989), p. 223; W. H. Davies, *The Autobiography of a Super-Tramp* (London: A. C. Fifield, 1908), p. 10.
9. Flora Thompson, *Lark Rise to Candleford* (Harmondsworth: Penguin Books, 1973), p. 181.
10. Richard James Stonesifer, *W. H. Davies: A Critical Biography* (London: Cape, 1963), p. 21.
11. Rose, *Intellectual Life*, pp. 33, 157–8.
12. Ibid., p. 159.
13. Ibid., p. 162. For just one example of the type of literature such working-class intellectuals went on to read see Rose, pp. 191–2.
14. Robert Roberts, *The Classic Slum: Salford Life in the First Quarter of the Century* (1971; Harmondsworth: Penguin Books, 1973), and idem, *A Ragged Schooling: Growing Up in the Classic Slum* (1976; London: Fontana, 1978).
15. Vincent, *Literacy and Popular Culture*, p. 90.
16. For many more examples see *Popular Print Media, 1820–1900*, ed. Andrew King and John Plunkett, 3 vols (Abingdon: Routledge, 2004).
17. Helen Bosanquet, 'Cheap literature', *Contemporary Review*, 79 (Jan./June 1901), 671–81; James Payn, 'Penny fiction', *Nineteenth Century*, 9 (Jan. 1881), 145–54.

18. Edward Salmon, 'What the working classes read', *Nineteenth Century*, 20 (Jul. 1886), 108–17 (p. 117).
19. James Greenwood, 'Penny awfuls', *St. Paul's Magazine*, 12 (Feb. 1873), 161–8 (p. 161).
20. Nigel Hamilton, 'Chisholm, Hugh (1866–1924)', *Oxford Dictionary of National Biography*, Oxford University Press, 2004, http://www.oxforddnb.com/view/article/32404 [accessed 10 Jan. 2010] (para. 3 of 9).
21. H. Rider Haggard, 'About fiction', *Contemporary Review*, 51 (Jan./June 1887), 172–80 (p. 174).
22. Patricia Srebrnik, 'Strahan, Alexander Stuart (1833–1918)', *Oxford Dictionary of National Biography*, Oxford University Press, 2004, http://www.oxforddnb.com/view/article/40987 [accessed 10 Jan. 2010] (para. 3 of 5).
23. Alexander Strahan, 'Our very cheap literature', *Contemporary Review*, 14 (Apr./Jul. 1870), 439–60 (pp. 458–9).
24. Francis Hitchman, 'The penny press', *Macmillan's Magazine*, 43 (Nov. 1880/Apr. 1881), 385–98 (pp. 385–9).
25. Francis Hitchman, 'Penny fiction', *Quarterly Review*, 171 (Jul. 1890), 150–71 (pp. 170–1).
26. G. B. Johns, 'The literature of the streets', *Edinburgh Review*, 165 (Jan. 1887), 40–65 (pp. 62–3).
27. Chisholm, 'How to counteract', p. 774.
28. Joseph McAleer, *Popular Reading and Publishing in Britain, 1914–1950* (Oxford: Clarendon Press, 1992), p. 23.
29. Victor Neuburg, *Popular Literature: A History and Guide* (London: The Woburn Press, 1977), p. 228.
30. Vincent, *Literacy and Popular Culture*, pp. 222–3.
31. Qtd. in Rose, *Intellectual Life*, p. 371.
32. Joseph Stamper, *So Long Ago* (London: Hutchinson, 1960), p. 162, http://www.open.ac.uk/Arts/reading/record_details.php?id=11365 [accessed: 10 Jan. 2010].
33. Hitchman, 'Penny Fiction', pp. 150–1, 154.
34. Wright, 'On a possible popular culture', pp. 32, 34.
35. Chisholm, 'How to counteract', p. 772.
36. Thomas Wright, 'Concerning the unknown public', *Nineteenth Century*, 13 (Feb. 1883), 279–96 (p. 296).
37. Wright, 'On a possible popular culture', p. 40.
38. See Christopher Stray and Gillian Sutherland, 'Mass markets: education', in *The Cambridge History of the Book in Britain*, ed. David McKitterick, 6 vols (Cambridge: Cambridge University Press, 2009), VI: *1830–1914*, pp. 359–81.
39. Wright, 'On a possible popular culture', p. 41.
40. Ibid., pp. 40, 41.
41. Rose, *Intellectual Life*, p. 159.
42. Wright, 'On a possible popular culture', pp. 41–2.
43. Rose, *Intellectual Life*, p. 149.

44. Chisholm, 'How to counteract', pp. 771–3.
45. Rose, *Intellectual Life,* p. 323. School Boards were abolished by the 1902 Education Act, so the *Gem* and *Magnet*'s Edwardian readers could not have attended 'Board schools', but in practice the elementary educational establishments in question would have been the same.
46. See Rose, *Intellectual Life,* pp. 322–31.
47. Roberts, *Classic Slum*, pp. 160–1.
48. Rose, *Intellectual Life,* pp. 328–9.

5
'Something light to take my mind off the war': Reading on the Home Front during the Second World War

Katie Halsey

In February 1916, the *New York Times* published an interview with the publisher George H. Doran, entitled 'The war is making England a nation of readers', which was an account of what Doran had seen while visiting Britain that year. According to Doran, during the First World War 'millions of readers are being made. The cheap editions of the novels are selling as they never sold before . . . People are reading who have never read before, and those who read before are reading more extensively – and more intensively.'[1] In *The People's War 1939–45* (1969), Angus Calder identifies a similar reading 'addiction' during the Second World War, noting that 'With reading for pleasure, as with religion, the war made the addicts keener.' He suggests, however, that there was a shift in the *kind* of reading engaged in during the later conflict. Calder claims that the war 'reduc[ed] the calls for "good light reads" among housewives of all classes, now much overworked', and that 'there was a clear trend towards more serious reading', thus implying that most readers read not primarily for 'pleasure' but for other purposes during the Second World War.[2]

The material considered in this chapter suggests that Calder's assertions need some qualification, as well as some explanation. Firstly, his assumption that 'good light reads' (by which he means predominantly popular fiction) were the preserve of housewives is inaccurate. A large number of both men and working women surveyed by the Mass Observation project expressed a preference for 'light reading'.[3] It is clear also that 'light reading' does not always mean fiction to these Mass Observation participants, being used to denote a variety of genres, including sports, biography and the popular press, as well as fiction. Calder's claim that there was a 'clear trend' towards 'more serious reading' is also debatable, not least because he does not satisfactorily define what he means by 'serious reading', although it is implicit that this category primarily means reading for information, and includes works on politics, philosophy, economics, the sciences, agriculture and general reference works. In contrast to Calder's view, the evidence considered in this chapter demonstrates not only a hunger for books of all kinds, including 'serious' reading, but also a thirst for 'light' or 'escapist' reading – books that 'take my mind off the war', as a number of readers described them.[4] Drawing on the evidence collected in the Mass Observation archives and the *UK Reading Experience Database 1450–1945*, and a case study of one individual reader, I discuss the attitudes towards reading matter of 'ordinary' British readers on the home front during the Second World War and its immediate aftermath, looking at the period from 1939 to 1950. Before turning to the individual testimonies, however, it is necessary to consider some of the general factors affecting all readers of the period: specifically, the role of censorship, the availability of printed matter, the price of books and other texts, and the time (or lack of it) existing for reading.

As Calder makes clear, during the war years, Britain enjoyed significant political and cultural freedom, at least in comparison with the other warring nations. It was possible to be a pacifist, to read subversive or unpatriotic literature, or even to suggest that Britain might be at fault in entering the war. Press censorship only applied to news; commentary was (in theory) free. However, in practice, 'defeatist' and pacifist attitudes were unpopular, and newspapers tended to work with the government ministries to suppress news that might adversely affect morale. Newspapers (such as the *Daily Worker*) that the government believed to be hindering the war effort could be closed down. British citizens frequently complained that their newspapers did not contain enough real hard news. Books, however, were a different story. Unlike newspapers, radio and films, which were subject to both security censorship (designed to keep important tactical information from the enemy) and policy censorship (which was intended to prevent the spread of ideas that would improve enemy morale or decrease British morale), books were only limited by security censorship. This meant that many of those who held 'unpatriotic' opinions, such as pacifists, and who could not express themselves in newspapers or on the radio, could still publish books. Calder notes that the prominent pacifist Vera Brittain's book *Humiliation with Honour* sold ten thousand copies in five months in 1942–43.[5]

The imposition of limits on paper supplies posed a very serious problem for the publishers of both books and newspapers. Newspaper editors were forced by the shortages of paper and of journalists to reduce the size of newspapers, so despite the avidity with which the British bought and read newspapers, added demand did not create more supply. The Ministry of Supply limited book publishers, first to 60 per cent, then to 37½ per cent of the paper they had used during the last twelve months before the war. In any given year of the war, the majority of all paper was used in official publications. At the height of the war, therefore, book publishers had only 22,000 tons of paper available to them for books. Amy Flanders points out that publishers also faced restrictions in the supply of other necessary materials – binding cloth, boards for book covers, even glue – and suffered (sometimes severe) shortages of personnel.[6] In addition, the blitz destroyed books – twenty million unissued volumes were destroyed in the course of the war. Four hundred libraries were bombed, and their collections went up in flames.[7] Approximately one million books were lost from these libraries, and many, too, would have been lost from bombed bookshops, private homes or institutions such as schools, colleges and universities. New books became shorter, with a minimum number of words per page, and reprints of classic works became rare and rarer. There was huge demand for books in the armed services, but the services depended on donations of books from the public, and as book shortages increased, the demand was harder to meet.

Demand for books, then, consistently outstripped supply. They were, in addition, exempt from purchase tax, while other kinds of entertainment were not. Citizens who could not afford other entertainment such as the cinema could, therefore, sometimes afford books. These tended to be of a fairly poor quality, though there was a thriving black market in books as in everything else. The quality of editions printed during the war years and their aftermath was understandably bad, with gaudy dust-jackets failing to disguise the thin paper and cramped print. Gollancz editions cost between three shillings and sixpence and four shillings and sixpence per book. Given that the average wage was around twenty-three shillings a week, a book of that kind was a reasonably substantial investment for Britons of all classes except the very rich; nonetheless existing historical records show clearly that readers continued to purchase books despite their inferior physical appearance and relative cost.

It might be assumed that there was less time for reading available during the war. In many ways, this is, of course, true – British citizens who had previously been unemployed found themselves with jobs in the armed services, factories, volunteer organizations, or on the land. Retired people came out of retirement to work as air raid and fire wardens, or in the Home Guard. Housewives joined the paid workforce. Ever-increasing restrictions on fuel, food, clothing and luxuries meant that those doing the marketing spent more time in queues, and less time at home. Spare time was used turning sheets sides to middle, digging for victory, collecting scrap iron, or trying to stretch the week's meat ration. Free time, we must assume, was at a premium. However, it is also the case that some of the restrictions (on fuel, for example), and rising costs (on cinema tickets, for instance) simply meant that people spent more time at home. The blackout made it difficult, and sometimes dangerous, to go out, and this also kept people at home in the evenings. Time spent in air raid shelters could be used for reading (although limited light supplies in the shelter meant that often only the person nearest the light could see to read, and so that person read aloud while others listened). A Blackpool insurance manager wrote sardonically in November 1939:

> Had a nice night last night. Tommy Bloody Handley on the wireless again, read every book in the house. Too dark to walk to the library, bus every 45 minutes, next one too late for the pictures. Freedom is in peril they're telling ME![8]

A female draper's assistant in 1944 makes much the same point about enforced reading, saying, 'I do like reading, and I spend most of the evening reading because there's nowhere to go.'[9] Some British citizens found that their work actually gave them more time to read, as in the case of this Civil Defence warden, interviewed in 1943: 'Well, I think Civil Defence is a marvellous racket. It's given me the spare time I've been wanting for years – I've done more solid reading, for instance, than I've done since I was twenty-one.'[10] Nonetheless, the majority of those surveyed by Mass Observation agreed that they 'read less now than before the war, owing to pressure of work',[11] or, more pointedly, that 'the only books I have the opportunity of reading are ration and points books'.[12]

* * *

With the issues of availability, cost, time and censorship in mind, we can now consider the testimony of individual readers in greater detail. When surveying such material, what is immediately obvious is not only the difficulty of making generalizations, but also the extent to which, for many people, the war impinged surprisingly little on their lives. My case study, Hilary Spalding, a manufacturer's daughter from County Durham, born in 1927, is one of these. As a teenager at boarding school during the war years, she felt 'very untouched by the war'.[13] Although her father ran the Air Training Corps in Darlington, and worked for the ARP, and her mother was in the WVS, she herself was 'always very unpolitical' and deliberately avoided the newspapers left in the school common-room.[14] At home in the holidays, she read her parents' copy of the *Observer*, but only the theatre and book reviews.[15] She read other material voraciously, however. Her diary begins in 1943, and includes reading lists of all the books read from 1943 to 1948 (see Figure 5.1).

Many of the books she read were borrowed from the school and public library, and later the library at King's College, Newcastle, but some were given to her as gifts from friends and family members, and she enjoyed buying books herself. A sample from her diary of 1946, the year after the end of the war, shows the kind of time and money that Spalding invested in books. She was relatively well-off, with an allowance of twenty pounds a month, of which two pounds ten shillings a week was spent on full board in her lodgings. The other two pounds ten shillings per week was spent on lunches, stockings, cosmetics, books, train travel and other living expenses. On 24 January, she notes that she 'Bought a complete Spenser (6 shillings only)' with money borrowed from a friend 'as I'd run out'. On 21 March, she bought *Other Men's Flowers* (ed. Archibald Percival Wavell, 1944) for ten shillings and sixpence 'which I really shouldn't have'. On 26 March, she bought C. S. Lewis's *The Problem of Pain* (1940), but did not note its cost. On 11 May, she sold her collection of childhood books for five pounds, and expended some of it on George Borodin's *This*

89

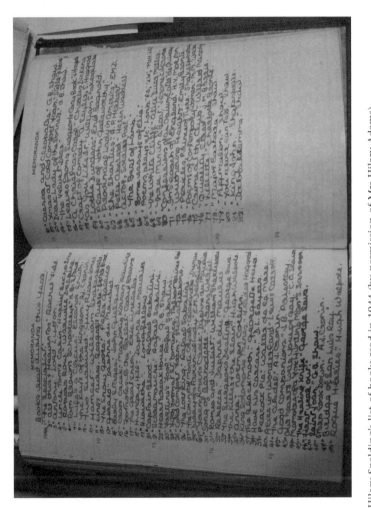

Figure 5.1   Hilary Spalding's list of books read in 1944 (by permission of Mrs Hilary Adams)

Thing Called Ballet (1946). On holiday in Exeter, she spent eighteen shillings on Donald Brook's *The Romance of the English Theatre* (1945), and six shillings on *Hassan*, by James Elroy Flecker (1922). A friend sent her as a gift the just-published *Life of Oscar Wilde* by Hesketh Pearson (1946), and she notes the price as sixteen shillings. She also frequently records borrowing books from the public library, and from her friends, including Kathleen Winsor's notorious *Forever Amber* of 1944.[16] When her mother discovered the copy, she was so horrified that she threw it on the fire.[17]

She recorded her reading carefully, often with comments on it. As I have argued elsewhere, it is always wise to treat diary entries about reading with care,[18] and an example from Spalding's diary illustrates this well. One of the diary entries reads: 'I have started *Ben Hur* and like it very much.' When interviewed in December of 2007, Spalding revealed that this was a 'pious lie' – her father had given her *Ben Hur* (by Lew Wallace) in a slip case. She never got beyond the first few pages, and, when she gave the book to a charity shop half a century later, it was still in the slip case.[19] It is important to remember that diary entries about reading are not necessarily either transparently truthful or, indeed, comprehensive.

These caveats notwithstanding, the diary gives a fascinating insight into the popular reading of the war years, and helpfully reminds us of the extent to which light fiction was still a staple of the reading public at this time. Spalding's reading lists include such bestsellers as Margaret Mitchell's *Gone With the Wind*, Winsor's *Forever Amber*, Howard Spring's *Fame is the Spur*, works by Dorothy L. Sayers, John Buchan, Arthur Ransome, Daphne du Maurier, Rudyard Kipling, Alexandre Dumas, Helen Waddell, Georgette Heyer, and a host of now-forgotten authors, as well as the classics, including Shakespeare, the Brontës, Jane Austen, the Elizabethan playwrights, Walter Scott, Edmund Spenser, Tobias Smollett, Anton Chekhov (of Chekhov's *Three Sisters*, she wrote, 'a simply terrible play in which everyone is quite crazy. We laughed a lot at it!'),[20] Thomas Gray, George Bernard Shaw, John Steinbeck, Harriet Beecher Stowe, William Hazlitt, Thomas de Quincey and Charles Dickens. Unsurprisingly, given that she was first at school, and then at university reading English Literature during the years under consideration, her diary also records the reading of set books at school. Interestingly, however, she told me when I interviewed her that the English Literature course at King's College, Newcastle in the 'forties, which began with Anglo Saxon and ended with George Bernard Shaw, had no set books. Students devised a course of reading for themselves. Reading choices for those years therefore reflect an implicit rather than explicit reading list – and thus an implicit rather than explicit canon – as well as the restrictions on printed matter discussed above.

When I interviewed her, I asked Spalding whether she had ever read the Public Information Leaflets, distributed by the Ministry of Education, or other propaganda materials disseminated by the government. She said she could not remember anything of that kind at all. I also asked whether she, or the school, had ever collected books to send to soldiers at the front, but the answer was again in the negative. She did, however, remember staff at the school receiving books from the Boots Postal Library with great enjoyment, and clearly remembered the difficulty of getting hold of books, both new books and reprints of the classics. She and her friends shared their books around, with a waiting list for the favourites. Showing me a Gollancz edition of Dorothy Sayers' *The Nine Tailors*, from 1946, she remembered the poor quality of the books available during and immediately after the war:

> Look at this. It's tiny print, it's horrible paper, and look, it's going brown at the edges. You couldn't get hold of decent books – this *was* a decent book – it was the best that was on offer. These are Gollancz publications and they had bright yellow covers and they were really a staple . . . they were very very poor quality and this went on for about 2 or 3 years after the war.[21]

Her diary bears out her memories of the difficulty of getting books. In the 1947 diary, for example, she writes on 7 February, 'I got a copy of *Rebecca* at last! I've wanted one for ages, but it's only just been reprinted' (as a Gollancz edition).[22] Readers were often, in fact, grateful for the Gollancz editions – as Spalding points out, they were 'the best . . . on offer', and frequently, indeed, the only editions on offer. Winifred Moore, a Quaker teacher and Labour councillor, was one of those who were thankful for Gollancz. She wrote to her son Gerald in January 1941, of her pleasure in a 'wonderful' Gollancz book:

> Stanley sent me a wonderful book of Gollancz: *The Musical Companion* edited by Bacharach . . . This book is jolly for me. It's just

a straightforward manual of music, and fills in all the gaps of one's knowledge that get in the way when trying to listen intelligently.[23]

* * *

Much of the material in the Mass Observation archives also comments on the scarcity of reading matter. In 1942, an anonymous reader surveyed by Mass Observation observed: 'There's nothing worth reading these days – nothing – in fact I'm turning more and more to the old books.'[24] On the other hand, also in 1942, another of Mass Observation's readers found no difficulty in getting hold even of books that had been censored:

> [I read] Oh, anything political – I'm mad about politics – you know, India today and all that sort of thing and all those red books that aren't allowed, I get all those . . . one of the best books I've read is 'What Next Germany' or some such title – I can't remember. It was wonderfully interesting.[25]

Constance Reaveley, a lecturer in political philosophy, who worked as a machinist in a factory during the war, used her experience there to reflect on the importance of literature to the general public in wartime:

> It seemed to me that the girls I knew at the works needed a better literature to feed their minds. Fiction, like poetry, should be an interpretation and criticism of life; the stories they were reading were nothing but wish-fulfilment fantasy, and they got sick of them. I thought I would write to the head of a women's college, and suggest that a girl who wanted to write, and would work in a factory for a few months, could produce stories for factory girls about factory girls which would give them a lot more interest than anything there is on the market for them at present.[26]

One reader did claim to like the sort of fiction recommended as ideal for factory girls by Constance Reaveley:

> I read what I call semi-serious novels. That is, it's got to have a love story woven through it, but at the same time well written,

unlike the trashy love stories of Ethel M. Dell or Ruby M. Ayres' kin . . . I liked books by Phillip Gibbs: 'The Nettle Danger' [*sic*], 'The Sons and Others', 'The Amazing Summer', and now his newest 'Through the Dark Night', which brings war events almost up to date. It isn't anything new, but at the same time, I enjoyed reading them.[27]

The majority of those surveyed by the Mass Observation project, however, did not want fiction that was 'an interpretation and criticism of life'. Many wanted precisely *not* to engage with their real lives, and some explicitly recognized that their taste for 'light books and escapist stuff'[28] was related to a desire to forget the world of war for a brief moment. A naval officer, for example, read James Joyce's *Dubliners* repeatedly in order to transport himself into 'another world':

Whenever I feel fed up I read one of these sketches and find myself in another world – Dublin, 20 years ago. Dublin saloon bars, street children, catholic priests, and inconspicuous clerks – all ordinary people but real. The stories are slightly tinged with melancholy. That soothes me.[29]

Similarly, a female Mass Observation participant told her interviewer in 1942, 'I like books by Ruby M. Ayres and Anne Duffield. The young lady [the librarian] usually chooses the books for me – she knows what I want. Something light to take my mind off the war – a straight romantic tale.'[30] Another participant agreed that what she wanted was 'books of the romantic and family kind', adding 'just now I've got at home the "Home Divided" by Pearl Buck – it's the simple love-story kind of book, but it holds your interest'.[31] Despite what was often assumed (and, indeed, is still sometimes suggested) by the press, female readers did not necessarily opt for romance when they were looking for escapist fiction – another female respondent preferred 'any author, so long as it's a genuine western story'. She 'always read purely western, because they're more or less full of action, and I can get into it in the first chapter. No war books for me, I can read all that boasting and piffle in the papers.'[32]

The dislike of 'war books' articulated by this reader surfaces repeatedly in the Mass Observation surveys and diaries. 'I won't read war books', said one Mass Observation participant.[33] Another read 'thrillers and mysteries and oriental tales. Anything mystery which has nothing whatever to do with the war.' This reader also enjoyed P. G. Wodehouse, whose books acted 'as a kind of tonic'.[34] A different female respondent also wanted 'books of the humorous kind', naming Ian Hay's *Night on Wheels* and *The Diary of a Provincial Lady* by E. M. Delafield, and this reader too was 'not keen to read books dealing with the current situation'. She continued: 'War's grim enough, I prefer to choose books without war interest.'[35] A male participant described the way he chose books for his wife:

> Most of the books I choose from the free library are for the wife. I cast my eye over the books vaguely searching for likely looking binding. If one catches my eye, such as a new looking book, I glance at the title and author. If that looks promising, I take the book out and scan the synopsis, if there is one, and then scan the first page, before flicking over the pages and reading snatches of the dialogue. If there seems to be plenty of action, I choose the book. I avoid books about the present or last war.[36]

Again, we see that 'war books' are shunned, while books with 'plenty of action' to distract the mind are valued.

Escapism was not the only motivation for indulging in 'light' rather than 'serious' reading. Many readers found that they were unable to concentrate on political, philosophical or scientific works, because of anxiety, poor light during the blackout, or lack of time: 'I read more. But cannot concentrate on the type of literature I like, preferring now a light novel or auto-biography to escape the present day.'[37] Another of those surveyed agreed that he read more, and also read 'fewer political works and more fiction'.[38] A female participant made much the same point: 'Yes, I read more as have more time – but have gone onto novels and escapist literature – cannot read such books as "The Mortal Storm" and books like "Fallen Bastions" now. I also try to keep up with political reading but find it rather difficult.'[39] That is not to say, of course, that no one read 'serious' literature. Many did read political or philosophical books, as well as fiction that engaged with the issues of the day. One participant recorded reading 'about the same amount of non-fiction, but far more biographies and autobiographies'.[40] Other participants identified a new sense of purpose in their reading, sharpened by lack of time:

> Since the war began I have read less because my working hours have been lengthened and ARP duties and various social activities leave me less leisure. My reading however is much more purposeful (as I have no time to waste). I read little fiction now, but much [*sic*] political and social books. This is, I think a natural development, but much hastened by the war and the conditions which caused it.[41]

Similarly, an Engineer in the Royal Marines reflected on the purpose of his reading in 1942:

> I read less now than before the war, owing to pressure of work – of a mental nature – and consequently prefer to spend most of my leisure in exercise. Thus what I read now is more carefully chosen, and read over several times. I squeeze more of the innards from my reading. I copy out passages here and there and make my own anthology.[42]

Like this engineer, many readers chose their reading carefully, and tried to use it purposefully to understand the background to the war, or to make sense of the political climate, as in the case of this participant:

> Lately, I've been reading books about China and Russia. I figure it out this way: I read the newspapers and meet different kinds of people, and they all have to say something different. It makes me want to read and know more myself. I don't think the ordinary person knows much about the people in other countries except what we hear now. If we can get some idea of the way they live and work, [it will] go a long way towards understanding them.[43]

In this case, the reader perused newspapers for political news, but found them insufficient for his purposes, and so turned to books to give him a better understanding of the lives of others involved in the war. As Adrian Bingham also shows in Chapter 8 of this volume, many British subjects lost faith in the newspapers over the course of the war, complaining that patriotic bias made them unreliable, that they did not separate out news and comment, and that they did not have enough hard 'facts' about the progress of the war. One Mass Observation reader wrote in 1940: '[I] cling desperately to "The New Statesman & Nation" in the hopes of gleaning a few facts which newspapers and radio studiously avoid'.[44] In 1943, another participant summed up a common view, preferring the *Monitor* to 'any English papers' on the grounds that 'it doesn't mix its news and views up together, like Beaverbrook's dirty rags do'.[45] Readers clearly felt that the hand of the censor fell heavily on British newspapers, and so supplemented their reading of newspapers with other sources:

> I am forming my opinions mainly from what I read in books on economics, politics, history, etc. I read the daily papers, but I do not take a lot of notice of what I read in them from the point of view of their opinions on the war, and what shall be done after it. I get far more satisfaction from reading articles or books by authors such as C. E. M. Joad, H. G. Wells and Huxley.[46]

* * *

From the evidence discussed throughout this chapter, it is clear that the reading of both fiction and non-fiction texts co-existed during the years of the Second World War, as they had during the First World War. Readers engaged both with 'serious' works of literature, and with 'light reading', putting their reading to a variety of uses, and many readers did not concentrate exclusively on either type of reading, turning to fiction when they wished, but continuing to read political, philosophical and scientific works on other occasions. First-hand testimonies in the *UK Reading Experience Database* and *Mass Observation Online* show the diversity of reading experience during the war and its aftermath. A brief statistical analysis of the 395 different Mass Observation readers collected in the *UK Reading Experience Database* clearly demonstrates, in contrast to Calder's view that fiction-reading decreased in the war years, that readers predominantly read newspapers and fiction during the war years, with other genres hardly making a showing (see Table 5.1).

'Fiction' here is of course a very broad category, including both canonical works and non-canonical fiction in a variety of sub-genres.

Table 5.1   War-time reading by genre (Mass Observation data as recorded in the *UK Reading Experience Database*)

Genre	Number of entries
Newspaper	143
Fiction	127
Politics	29
Magazines	17
Public Information	16
Philosophy	5
Advert	5
History	4
Spiritualism	4
Biography	4
Medicine	4
Professional	2
Letters	2
Poetry	2
Religious	2
Literary Criticism	1
Diaries	1
Travel	1
Drama	1

Both men and women read and enjoyed mysteries, detective stories, gothic novels, romances, comic novels, historical novels, school stories and science fiction, as well as the works of Austen, Dickens, Thackeray, Voltaire, Tolstoy, Orwell, Aldous Huxley, Evelyn Waugh, H. G. Wells, James Joyce and D. H. Lawrence among many others.[47] Some readers (such as Spalding) clearly read both 'highbrow' canonical texts as well as lowbrow and middlebrow popular fiction, while others tended to stick to what they knew best. Despite the clear bias shown for the reading of fiction and newspapers, however, the records also show that readers of this period were additionally reading a large variety of other kinds of material – including Churchill's and Hitler's speeches, Proust's *À la recherche du temps perdu*, Freud's lectures, Shakespeare's plays, Darwin's *Origin of Species*, poetry by A. E. Housman and Louis MacNeice, public information leaflets, magazines, even tombstone inscriptions.[48] As every historian of reading knows, readers are as various as they are numerous. Of the readers represented in the *UK Reading Experience Database*, some read more, some less than they had before the war. Some bought books, some borrowed them. Some read escapist fiction, others read political philosophy. Some read *Mein Kampf*, some read *Gone with the Wind*. Some believed what they read in the papers, others looked elsewhere for their hard facts. It is absolutely clear from a survey of the available material that fiction did not give way to more 'serious' reading in the war years. Readers continued to demand, and to enjoy, 'light reading'. What unites these very different pieces of evidence is the way that, taken as a whole, they express the vivid *need* that ordinary British subjects felt for books and other printed matter during the war years, and the real deprivation they felt when it was not possible to obtain the books they wanted to read.

Notes and references

The author wishes to thank Hilary Adams (née Spalding) for permission to quote from her manuscript diary and interview transcript, and Shirley Gould-Smith for permission to quote from unpublished family letters.

1. 'The war is making England a nation of readers', *New York Times*, 27 February 1916.
2. Angus Calder, *The People's War, 1939–45* (1969; London: Pimlico, 1992), p. 512.
3. See, for example, Mass Observation, File Report 1332, July 1942, 'Books and the public', p. 70c; File Report 126, May 1940, 'Report on the press', p. 11, and File Report 62, March 1940, 'Literary questionnaire by H. P. Elderton and G. L. Wallace,' p. 5, all in *Mass Observation Online*, http://www.massobservation. amdigital.co.uk [accessed 1 December 2009]. All material from the Mass Observation Archives online will hereafter be referenced as MOAO, name of file report, diary or survey, and page number (if relevant) only.
4. MOAO, 'Books and the public' (1942), p. 70c.
5. Calder, *People's War*, p. 511.
6. Amy Flanders, '"Our ambassadors": British books, American competition and the great book export drive, 1940–1960', *English Historical Review*, 125 (2010), 875–911 (p. 877).
7. For a fascinating history of the destruction of books, see Lucien X. Polastron, *Books on Fire: The Tumultuous Story of the World's Great Libraries* (London: Thames and Hudson, 2007), esp. pp. 169–266.
8. MOAO, File Report 15A, December 1939, Wartime Directive No. 4.
9. MOAO, File 2018, February 1944, 'Books and the public', p. 18.
10. MOAO, Advertising Service Guild, 'The journey home: Advertising Service Guild's Report on the problems of demobilisation conducted by Mass-Observation' (London, 1944), p. 70.

11. MOAO, 'Books and the public' (1942), p. 5.

12. MOAO, 'Books and the public' (1942), p. 6.

13. *UK Reading Experience Database* Archive, interview with Hilary Adams (née Spalding), 16 December 2007.

14. Ibid.

15. Hilary Spalding, private correspondence, 19 December 2009.

16. Hilary Spalding, MS Diary 1947, private collection.

17. Hilary Spalding, private correspondence, 19 December 2009.

18. See, for example, Katie Halsey, 'Reading the evidence of reading', *Popular Narrative Media*, 2 (2008), 123–37, and Rosalind Crone, Katie Halsey and Shafquat Towheed, 'Examining the evidence of reading: three examples from the *Reading Experience Database*', in *Reading in History: New Methodologies from the Anglo-American Tradition*, ed. Bonnie Gunzenheimer (London: Pickering & Chatto, 2010), pp. 29–45 (31–2).

19. Spalding, MS Diary 1945 and interview, 16 December 2007.

20. Spalding, MS Diary 1945.

21. Spalding, interview, 16 December 2007.

22. Spalding, MS Diary 1947.

23. Winifred Agnes Moore [née Booth], MS Letters from Winifred Moore to her family, 1928–41, private collection, recorded in *UK The Reading Experience Database,* http://www.open.ac.uk/Arts/reading/record_details.php?id=14141, accessed: 04 December 2009.

24. MOAO, 'Books and the public' (1942), p. 164.

25. MOAO, 'Books and the public' (1942), p. 163.

26. Constance Reaveley, in Jenny Hartley, *Hearts Undefeated: Women's Writing of the Second World War* (London: Virago, 1999), pp. 148–9.

27. MOAO, 'Books and the public' (1942), p. 162.

28. MOAO, File Report 492, November 1940, 'Directive results', p. 11.

29. MOAO, 'Books and the public' (1942), p. 171.

30. MOAO, 'Books and the public' (1942), p. 70c.

31. MOAO, 'Books and the public' (1942), p. 162.

32. MOAO, 'Books and the public' (1942), p. 70e.

33. MOAO, 'Books and the public', (1942), pp. 162–3.

34. MOAO, 'Books and the public' (1942), p. 162.

35. MOAO, 'Books and the public' (1942), p. 105.

36. MOAO, 'Books and the public' (1942), p. 145.

37. MOAO, 'Directive results', p. 11.

38. MOAO, 'Directive results', p. 11.

39. MOAO, 'Directive results', p. 10.

40. MOAO, 'Books and the public' (1942), p. 5.

41. MOAO, 'Books and the public' (1942), p. 5.

42. MOAO, 'Books and the public' (1942), p. 5.

43. MOAO, 'Books and the public' (1942), p. 163.

44. MOAO, 'Directive results', p. 11.

45. MOAO, File Report 1569, January 1943, 'Feelings about America and the Americans', p. 30.

46. MOAO, File Report 126, May 1940, 'Report on the press', p. 15.

47. For full records of the reading experiences mentioned here, see *UK Reading Experience Database* (http://www.open.ac.uk/Arts/reading/uk), ID numbers: 11962 (on reading Austen); 10042 (Dickens); 11944 (Thackeray); 9988 (Voltaire); 10097 (Tolstoy); 10108 (Orwell); 11969 (Huxley); 11862 (Waugh); 10156 (Wells); 11958 (Joyce) and 11967 (Lawrence).
48. For full records of the reading experiences mentioned here, see *UK Reading Experience Database* (http://www.open.ac.uk/Arts/reading/uk), ID numbers: 10061 (on reading Shakespeare); 10062 (Freud); 10334 (Churchill); 10610 (Hitler); 10018 (Darwin); 11829 (MacNeice); 10068 (tombstone inscriptions).

Part 3
Reading and the Press

6
What Readers Want: Criminal Intelligence and the Fortunes of the Metropolitan Press during the Long Eighteenth Century

Rosalind Crone

From the late seventeenth century onwards, Londoners witnessed the tremendous proliferation of commercial printing generally and of newspapers in particular. In addition, during the eighteenth century, newspapers began to develop a modern layout and to incorporate more variety in their content. Historians have described the shift away from newspapers that strove to emulate the essay sheet towards newspapers that featured large numbers of advertisements and non-political news.[1] Advertisements became increasingly important to newspapers over the course of the century as proprietors recognized the potential profits they offered and as readers began to demand them. For example, the success of one newspaper launched in 1731, the *Daily Advertiser*, led to the rapid emergence of several newspapers which included the term 'Advertiser' in their titles.[2] While newspapers included advertisements for a wide range of goods and services, amongst these 'crime advertisements' became a typical feature.

The rise of crime advertisements in the eighteenth century represented the collision of new print culture with the peculiar English criminal justice system. Before significant reforms in policing and prosecution during the early nineteenth century, responsibility for the recovery of stolen property and the prosecution of the offender(s) fell to the victim of the crime. Victims had to locate their missing goods, apprehend suspects and bear the costs associated with the pursuit of the offender and his or her trial. Newspaper advertisements, with their ability to reach large audiences, could form an important part of this process. Readers were, of course, essential to the success or failure of an advertisement. Victims who chose to advertise their missing property were dependent upon individuals with particular forms of knowledge to read the advertisement buried in the columns of the newspaper, and then to take action.

The first and most substantial studies of the use of print in the recovery of goods and apprehension of suspects by private individuals, prosecution associations and law enforcement agencies focused largely on the provinces.[3] The authors of these studies showed that victims continued to employ a range of methods to combat crime, and that, especially in regions where newspapers were not distributed daily, there was a clear preference for the handbill, which was cheaper and speedier to disseminate. Yet, at the same time, their research proved that over the course of the century printed forms replaced the traditional 'hue and cry' system (verbal and later written dissemination of information between parish constables), and that even if handbills were used more often, advertisements in newspapers did have some 'positive' impact on crime clear-up rates.

This level of success has been measured in two ways. First, by using evidence from the text: crime advertisements in newspapers increased over the course of the eighteenth century. For instance, according to Peter King, their number more than tripled in the *Chelmsford Chronicle* during the last third of the century.[4] Such substantial growth probably would not have occurred unless victims had some confidence in the viability of crime advertisements. Second, success has been demonstrated by using evidence of reading derived from Assize records. For example, in a small, but significant number of trial depositions (interrogations of witnesses by magistrates who made the decision whether or not to commit the accused for trial), historians have been able to establish a direct link between the placement of an advertisement and the resultant prosecution process.[5] Much more interesting, though, are the gaps and silences in the evidence, and the apparent incongruity between the growing number of advertisements and the rate of prosecution based on these. In other words, the loose language used by victims in describing the 'crime' suggests that advertisements may have served to open negotiations with an offender allowing the victim to recover his or her goods while avoiding the inconvenience of prosecution.[6]

If John Styles and Peter King have indirectly proposed that in the provinces advertisements sustained a system of resolution outside of the realm of authority, Robert Shoemaker has argued for the reverse in London. Gathering evidence of the use of crime advertisements found in the *Old Bailey Sessions Papers* (*OBSP*), transcripts of trials for felonies and serious misdemeanours heard at the central criminal court for London and Middlesex, Shoemaker has attempted to demonstrate how Londoners increasingly distanced themselves from the pursuit of offenders as the century progressed and official involvement in the detection of crime increased. Although references to printed notices of crimes grew from 51 during the 1720s to 285 during the 1750s (or, as proportionate to the number of trials, from 1.04 per cent to 6.94 per cent), Shoemaker concludes that advertising in newspapers and on handbills first absolved those on the streets from intervening out of a sense of duty by offering payment to witnesses for information, and second, as an extension, allowed for the growth of more professional agencies for solving crime, for example, thief takers.[7] The evidence would thus seem to suggest that, over the course of the eighteenth century, Londoners welcomed the gradual extension of the power of the state in the area of law enforcement.

However, it could also be argued that in this case, Shoemaker might have relied too heavily on evidence of reading found in the *OBSP*. In other words, in order fully to understand the reading communities – particular groups of individuals who shared similar characteristics or motives for reading (for example, victims, pawnbrokers, thieves who stole property in order to return it to gain a reward) – that emerged around crime advertisements, we need a more balanced approach, one that combines evidence from the text with a large body of evidence of reading. This chapter examines the editorial policies of one newspaper, the *Public Advertiser*, in conjunction with evidence of reading crime advertisements found in the Old Bailey trials. Even though historians have stressed the importance of handbills in crime announcements, and some witnesses at the Old Bailey mention reading them, handbills were not as frequently referred to as the newspapers. In fact, handbills were not mentioned in any of the trials heard during the 1720s and 1750s. Moreover, newspapers published and circulated in London did not have the same problems of dissemination as those in the provinces. There were several daily newspapers that carried large numbers of advertisements and which were available in numerous coffee shops and public houses.

Not only was the *Public Advertiser* a daily newspaper with an expanding readership, but from the mid-century onwards the editors, in association with new 'policing' institutions, actively encouraged the publication of crime advertisements within its pages. The text was shaped with specific communities of readers in mind, namely, victims of property crime and retailers who might encounter the missing goods. However, as this chapter will show, ultimate power rested with the readers, whose reaction to these editorial policies dictated the fortunes of the newspaper, at least in relation to this profitable arm of its business. And in this case, the evidence of reading can only provide a portion of that story. After all, courtroom narratives only tell us about those cases which came to court, an end desired by the editors and the authorities, but not necessarily by the victims of crime who paid for the advertisements and the readers who came forward to help resolve the situation. Much more revealing are the gaps and silences between the text and the readers: when combined with external evidence, these shed a great deal of light on the preferences of the general public in combating crime.

The *London Daily Post and General Advertiser* was launched in 1734, but became known simply as the *General Advertiser* in 1744. In 1753, the newspaper was renamed the *Public Advertiser*, and in 1794 its name was changed again to the *Oracle and Public Advertiser*. As it was known as the *Public Advertiser* for the greater part of its existence, this is how I will continue to refer to it. Throughout the century, the *Public Advertiser* comprised four pages of print, three of which were devoted exclusively to advertisements. The price of the newspaper remained fairly constant over the century, rising from two pence half-penny to three pence half-penny by the 1790s. For most of its life (until 1793) the newspaper was controlled by Henry Woodfall and his son, Henry Sampson Woodfall. The *Public Advertiser* was a successful newspaper as demonstrated by both its long life and its circulation rates. Contemporary accounts claim that the newspaper sold between 3,000 and 4,000 copies each day in 1779.[8] The actual readership of the newspaper would have been much larger than this though it is difficult to provide an estimate. Disagreement persists among historians on how to calculate accurate numbers of readers. While some insist that, on average, one newspaper would have been read by five different people, others suggest that this figure should be as high as twenty, given the significant accessibility of newspapers in

London.[9] Following the latter formula, the *Public Advertiser* may have been read by up to 80,000 men and women each day.

The Woodfalls devoted between seventy-five and eighty per cent of the newspaper to advertising. A brief glance at the dense columns quickly reveals that crime advertisements did not dominate the content of the *Public Advertiser*. More prominent were the advertisements for new books and playbills from the London theatres, as well as the notices of significant auctions and sales and lettings of expensive property. The historian R. B. Walker suggests that this correlated with a high social class of readership.[10] The first two columns of Table 6.1 provide an illustration of the rather small number of crime advertisements that appeared in the newspaper each month in comparison with the total number of advertisements. However, as the third column demonstrates, even if the total number of crime advertisements was small, their presence in the *Public Advertiser* was both consistent and increasingly frequent. Until the mid 1750s, there was always almost one crime advertisement in each daily issue, and after that date the place of crime advertising in the newspaper grew at a significant rate until the 1780s.

Table 6.1 also demonstrates the spread of crime advertisements across four different categories. Variety as well as patterns in crime advertising was important, and each category used here refers to the different character and purpose of the type of advertisement placed by victims or the authorities. The first category of advertisement was usually inserted by the authorities and contained a description of an offender, sometimes an escaped felon, to be apprehended by the public for a reward, or of a suspect already in custody whom it was hoped would be identified by a victim. For example:

> STOLEN three shifts marked M.M. and numbered, one shift marked E.D., a quantity of table linen marked M.M., one apron marked E.D. and Two Black Hen Turkies. . . . The Person suspected is a short well-set Man, with a Black Beard, grey Eyes, Pepper and Salt coloured Burtout Coat, blackish wig, and looks country-fied . . . give notice to John Fielding, Esq; and you shall receive One Guinea Reward.[11]

The second category includes notices, placed privately by individuals or through the authorities, calling attention to property recently stolen.

Table 6.1 Crime advertising in the *Public Advertiser*, 1744–98

Date	Total ads	Crime ads	Frequency (crime ads)*	Cat 1	Cat 2	Cat 3	Cat 4
Apr 1744	1404	17	0.62	10	1	5	1
Sep 1746	858	29	1.11	23	1	4	1
Jan 1750	1593	20	0.74	0	7	13	0
Nov 1752	1092	6	0.23	0	1	5	0
Jul 1755	1161	49	1.81	3	24	19	3
Dec 1759	1161	72	2.66	8	31	27	6
Mar 1763	1971	105	3.88	22	41	37	5
Nov 1768	1215	60	2.22	7	36	14	3
Feb 1772	2184	87	3.3	12	42	30	3
Oct 1778	1215	80	2.9	16	50	10	4
Apr 1782	1161	29	1.07	1	19	7	2
Sep 1784	598	19	0.73	3	13	0	3
Jan 1787	540	22	0.81	3	10	4	5
May 1791	405	9	0.33	4	2	3	0
Nov 1795	832	1	0.038	0	0	0	1
Jun 1798	650	1	0.038	0	0	1	0

*Average number of crime advertisements published in each daily issue of the *Public Advertiser*.

These advertisements contained a very comprehensive description of the property as well as a short account of the circumstances of the theft and very often an offer of a reward for the return of the goods:

> STOLEN out of a House in Ormond-street, Yesterday Evening A Silver Cruet Stand, With a Handle, containing two large Cruets with tops, and a Silver Pepper-box, the Pepper-box and Stand have double arms engraved on them; on one side three birds with a Chevron; on the other Bars embattled. And also Stole at the same time, a parcel of Silver Tea-spoons, and two small Silver Salt Shovels, and some other things not known. Whoever will bring them to Brown's Coffee-house in Great Ormond-street, shall have Two Guineas Reward and no Questions asked; if pawn'd or sold, the Money return'd with thanks.[12]

Category three refers to property advertised as 'lost', for example, items left in carriages, or 'dropt' out of someone's pocket. Sometimes these advertisements strongly hinted that the property was probably stolen and a reward was always offered for its return:

> To all Pawnbrokers, etc., LOST, on Saturday last, between the Bank and St Paul's, a neat, flat, Pinchbeck WATCH almost new, Number 1428, with an enamell'd Dial-Plate; the Maker's name on the Plate, Tautrin, London. Bring it to the Bar of the Chapter Coffee-house and you shall have two Guineas Reward. If offer'd to be sold or pawn'd, stop it, and you shall have the same Reward.[13]

Advertisements in the final category appeared with the least frequency. These were notices about property that had been found, sometimes by individuals walking through the city streets, potentially by gangs of thieves who sought to return property they had stolen for a reward, but mostly by pawnbrokers who had 'stopt' the suspicious items at their shops:

> STOPT from a poor Girl, at Mr Harvard's, Pawnbroker, in Great Maddox-street, Hanover-square, a Gold Seal with a full Coat of Arms. Any Person proving it their Property and paying the Expense of this Advertisement may have it again; and if not owned in a few Days it will be returned to the Person who brought it.[14]

Thus far, the *Public Advertiser* looks much like other London news-papers of the eighteenth century, particularly those dominated by advertising, as most featured crime advertisements as an additional profit-making enterprise. However, early in the life of the *Public Advertiser*, Henry Woodfall made some crucial editorial decisions that he intended to have a dramatic impact on the readership of these notices. In November 1752, a large notice appeared on the front page of the newspaper, not only announcing the change of name in the New Year, but, more importantly, declaring the establishment of a close relationship with Henry Fielding and the law enforcement authorities located at Bow Street.[15]

Henry Fielding and his half-brother John Fielding were key reform-ers of the criminal justice system in the eighteenth century. In 1749, as Court Justice, Henry Fielding established the famous office at Bow Street from which he directed a force of thief takers known as the 'Bow Street Runners', and often regarded as London's first profes-sional police force. John Fielding was similarly ambitious and in 1751 became Justice of the Peace for Westminster. Both brothers, but especially John Fielding, were enthusiastic about the use of print for gathering criminal intelligence and solving crime. In early 1752, Henry Fielding launched the *Covent-Garden Journal*, an entertaining periodical which, among other things, he used to promote his mag-isterial activities.[16] But the endeavour was short lived, and by the end of the year he had decided to use an established newspaper to fight crime in the city. There is no mystery in his choice of the *Public Advertiser* as he was, after all, a shareholder. When Henry became ill during 1753, John Fielding, who at first acted as locum and then officially replaced Henry as JP for Middlesex and Court Justice on his death, consolidated and extended the work begun by his brother.[17] In sum, Henry Woodfall and the Fieldings entered into a special agreement: articles lost or stolen reported at the Fieldings' offices in Bow Street would be 'exclusively' advertised in the *Public Advertiser*.

Moreover, as part of this arrangement, a deal was struck with the London pawnbrokers. The notice of November 1752 declared that the principal pawnbrokers of the metropolis had agreed to consult the lists of the lost and stolen property in the *Public Advertiser* every day and their names and addresses were inserted for public interest. For the pawnbrokers, this was, potentially, beneficial. They were already all too aware of the need to read crime advertisements in order to avoid receiving stolen goods and the risk of criminal prosecution. This new relationship offered the possibility that now only one newspaper would need to be consulted for such intelligence. Over the next few decades, John Fielding inserted similar, prominent notices in the *Public Advertiser*. These emphasized the benefits of crime advertisements, promoted the arrangement between Bow Street and the newspaper and drew attention to the wide readership of pawnbrokers and other dealers in second-hand goods who had been attracted to read them. An example of these notices is the following one, which appeared every Friday from August through November 1768:

> From the POLICE. The extensive Sale of the PUBLIC ADVERTISER (joined to the Variety of Channels thro' which it passes) has always been the Means of *detecting of many* ROBBERIES, and of *apprehending so many* OFFENDERS, that it may be proper to give THIS PUBLIC NOTICE, That, for the Future, all Information of this Kind, sent to BOW-STREET, will be *constantly inserted* in THIS PAPER: And if SUCH INFORMATIONS are *properly* attended to, by PAWNBROKERS, JEWELLERS, SILVER-SMITHS, STABLE-KEEPERS, BUYERS OF SECOND-HAND CLOATHES, &c. *few Robberies will escape Detection*; especially if ALL PERSONS ROBBED *make use of* THIS PAPER *to advertise their Losses in.* J. FIELDING.[18]

While drawing victims towards this particular publication, John Fielding also used the crime advertisements to reshape methods for fighting crime in London. Whereas during the first half of the century, advertisements for stolen, lost and found property were taken in at coffee shops and public houses, and these locations were often also used for the negotiated return of goods, Fielding began to promote the Bow Street office as the sole location for the receipt and dissemination of criminal intelligence as well as the primary site for the processing of 'found' items. Although the *Public Advertiser* continued to list coffee shops and public houses that would take advertisements for the newspaper, these locations featured less and less in the crime advertisements generally as Bow Street took control. On one level, Fielding believed that by centralizing such activity more crimes would be solved and more offenders caught. But on another level, the magistrate was also determined to bring negotiations under the surveillance of the authorities.

His drive was in some respects justified. Advertisements for stolen property carrying rewards for its return with 'no questions asked', like the one featured above, had encouraged the emergence of a number of individuals and groups who had transformed the practice of returning stolen goods for monetary rewards into a regular income. Thus legislation passed in 1752, which placed restrictions on the types of rewards offered, combined with Fielding's insistence on processing all complaints through the Bow Street office, meant that advertisements for stolen property (category two) became tied to the pursuit of offenders.[19] Rewards were now distributed on the conviction of the thief (or thieves) rather than on the recovery of the missing property. It was a high-risk strategy. In a metropolis which lacked a formal police force, promises of rewards encouraged ordinary people to return stolen goods and, on a more general level, to uphold justice and preserve the public peace. Even though they represented a significant advancement, the Bow Street runners hardly constituted an effective crime-fighting team which could replace existing structures. Rather, they were conceived of as an additional tool to be used. Ordinary people still needed to be encouraged to participate in the criminal justice process. In addition, this policy also relied on the willingness of both victims and witnesses to become involved in the prosecution process, for which they would be forced to bear the costs. Did the Fieldings, especially John Fielding, expect too much? How successful were the attempts of Fielding and Woodfall to determine the production and readership of crime advertisements?

The data contained in Table 6.1 would indicate at least some success. Both the quantity and frequency of crime advertisements increased with the involvement of authorities after 1752. However, a close examination of the content of these advertisements reveals that they were in the main placed by those affluent men and women of the merchant, professional and ruling classes who formed the original, primary readership for the *Public Advertiser*. The stolen property featured was often of considerable value – watches, gold seals, plate and delicate candlestick holders, for example. And when the crime referred to was a theft from a dwelling house, the residence mentioned was often in a fashionable, metropolitan neighbourhood. The cost of placing an advertisement in the newspaper – two shillings, rising to three shillings in 1768 and three shillings and sixpence in 1782 – was prohibitive for all except wealthy people and this, combined with the drive to prosecute those responsible for the theft, restricted the extent to which more ordinary Londoners could take advantage of this method to recover their property. Although legislation in 1752 gave courts the authority to pay expenses in felony cases if the prosecutor was poor, a provision extended to all prosecutors in 1778, payment was dependent upon the successful prosecution of the accused and did not compensate the victim for costs incurred in the pursuit of the offender.[20] Prosecution associations did exist in London precisely for this purpose, their membership largely composed of tradesmen and small businessmen who paid a regular subscription fee into a common fund from which the costs of pursuit and prosecution could be drawn when a member became a victim of crime.[21] But the *Public Advertiser* seemed to have limited appeal for these associations as the very small number of advertisements placed by them after 1774 suggests.

If those wealthy members of London society who did decide to place an advertisement to draw attention to their stolen property were attracted by the promise that metropolitan pawnbrokers consulted the newspaper regularly, their money was probably well spent. Evidence of reading derived from the *OBSP* indicates that pawnbrokers and dealers in second-hand goods did consult the crime advertisements in order to assess the legitimacy of items brought to their shops. For example, in the trial of William Wilson for the theft of two saws in 1759, pawnbroker Robert Alexander gave the following testimony:

[Wilson] brought a saw to pawn. He was alone: I asked him his name; he told me his name was Pollard. . . . I lent him two shillings upon it; the next morning I was reading the *Public Advertiser*, I saw this saw expressed particularly, and mentioned to have been stolen, I went to Mr Fielding's as the advertisement directed.[22]

Significantly, in the *OBSP*, no pawnbrokers seem to have been charged with the receipt of stolen goods and to have used the lack of information contained in newspapers as a defence. It may be that such an assertion proved to be routinely believable at the point of investigation, so that no further action was taken by the victim and the authorities.

This defence was certainly used by ordinary men and women who were accused of various property crimes. For instance, Edmond Lovell, charged with forgery, claimed that he had found the two 'bad' bank notes on 17 or 18 January 1798 in a letter on the ground:

> From that time I went to the public house to see the paper, to see if such notes were advertised; the last time I went into the public house was the Saturday, the day I was taken up.[23]

In December 1789, Esther Radford, wife of a clerk, appeared as a witness in the trial of David Bevan for theft. Radford stated that on the night of 31 October, Bevan brought a parcel to her house containing a pair of pearl earrings set in gold which he claimed he had found at the top of Pond Street. On Bevan's instruction, Radford placed the earrings in her bureau,

> and I desired my servant, when she went out, to get me a newspaper; which was produced to me on the Monday; I read it through, to see if such things were advertised; I saw no such thing.[24]

In consequence, she returned the property to Bevan. But claiming to have consulted the newspaper did not always get the accused out of trouble: while Lovell was acquitted, Bevan was found guilty and sentenced to transportation.

However, what we might infer from this evidence is that the increasing use of crime advertisements, by individuals and, more significantly, by the authorities, might have encouraged rather than discouraged ordinary people from getting involved in solving crime, even if the case in question did not end up in the courtroom. It certainly became much more expedient to check if found goods had been advertised in order to avoid potential prosecution. Despite Fielding's best efforts, as the above testimonies demonstrate, the location of choice in this endeavour remained the public house or the coffee shop. These bustling social spaces not only often contained a number or choice of newspapers for consultation, but also made the process of participation in the criminal justice system much more informal and controllable at the level of the individual. Moreover, reading the newspaper at the pub or coffee shop was often part of eighteenth-century Londoners' daily routines, as the many casual references to it in the *OBSP* highlight.

Witness testimonies also stress the degree of informality that persisted in the negotiation of the return of property, even when it was necessary to involve the authorities. On 8 July 1766, a mug was stolen from a public house in Darkhouse Lane. The landlord, John Smith, advertised it in the newspaper the following day. On the same day, 9 July, Mary Leech, servant at the Whitehorse Inn in Fleet Market found a mug under the bed of the lodger, John Newman. She called her master, landlord Anthony Sawrey, and they both consulted the newspaper where they found the mug advertised. Sawrey contacted Smith and the authorities at the same time and waited until they had both arrived before any action was taken. Although the matter was settled in the courtroom, the return of the mug combined with the character reference Sawrey provided for his lodger ensured John Newman was acquitted of the crime.[25]

In this case, the newspaper of choice for both the victim and the witnesses who found the mug was not the *Public Advertiser*, but a strong rival, the *Daily Advertiser*. In fact, if we take a top-down view of the evidence of reading crime advertisements contained in the *OBSP*, the limits of Fielding and Woodfall's efforts to make the *Public Advertiser* the chief organ of crime news become clear. Table 6.2 shows how many times the *Daily Advertiser*, the *Public Advertiser* and other newspapers containing the word 'advertiser' were mentioned in Old Bailey trials each decade. Where a newspaper was referred to by name, which was relatively infrequent, it was more likely to be the *Daily Advertiser* than the *Public Advertiser*. Although we see a sharp rise in references to the *Public Advertiser*, after Fielding and Woodfall

Table 6.2   References to named newspapers in Old Bailey trials, 1740–1819

	Daily Advertiser	*General/ Public Advertiser*	*Advertiser*
1740s	4	0	10
1750s	19	7	9
1760s	8	3	10
1770s	5	0	2
1780s	12	3	2[a]
1790s	3	1[b]	2[c]
1800s	0	0	1
1810s	2	0	3[c]

[a] One of these is a mention of the *London Courant and General Advertiser*.
[b] Not a crime advertisement.
[c] All references to the *Morning Advertiser*.

entered into their agreement in 1752, these references also rapidly declined during the next decade, the 1760s.

The comparative popularity of the *Daily Advertiser* is confirmed by an in-depth look at the text. As Table 6.3 illustrates, many more crime advertisements were placed in this newspaper than ever appeared in the *Public Advertiser*. As the *Daily Advertiser* appealed to a different primary audience (other categories of advertisements suggesting it was read by shopkeepers and tradesmen), this newspaper certainly helps to redress the balance in our perspective of crime in the metropolis. Victims did come from all levels of society, and the use of crime advertisements for the recovery of property did extend below the more affluent.[26] Also very evident in these advertisements is the significant lack of involvement from the authorities. Although the *Daily Advertiser,* like other London newspapers, had not entered into an arrangement with Bow Street, we might still expect to see the insertion of notices by officials alerting readers to offenders at large, or suspects taken into custody. Almost no advertisements along these lines featured in the *Daily Advertiser.* Category one advertisements featured in Table 6.3 were almost exclusively placed by individuals searching for a suspect on a personal level or by masters chasing runaway apprentices.

But by far most noticeable in the *Daily Advertiser* is the very large number of advertisements for lost property, the quantity increasing after the restriction on rewards for stolen property in 1752. From the description of the circumstances surrounding the loss of the goods, in most cases it was likely that the property advertised as lost was in fact stolen. Declaring property to be lost instead of stolen allowed victims to offer a reward for its return and to avoid the costs and inconvenience of prosecution which could follow the accusation. Because John Fielding monitored the content of the *Public Advertiser* and insisted that even lost and found items be processed at Bow Street, many victims may have chosen to place advertisements in the *Daily Advertiser* instead. In this case, it is the lack of evidence of reading combined with the growth of lost advertisements in the newspaper which confirms the assumption. Reading and acting upon lost advertisements in newspapers was probably more commonplace than reading and acting upon crime advertisements in any other category.

Unexpectedly, however, the fortunes of the *Public Advertiser* and the *Daily Advertiser* took a similar turn with respect to crime advertising

Table 6.3 Crime advertising in the *Daily Advertiser*, 1744–96*

Date	Total ads	Crime ads	Frequency (crime ads)	Cat 1	Cat 2	Cat 3	Cat 4
Apr 1744	2650	267	10.7	47	39	159	22
Feb 1772	5175	388	15.5	19	45	274	50
Mar 1796	3024	179	6.62	4	19	143	13

*Unfortunately, we are at the mercy of surviving issues of the *Daily Advertiser*, especially issues in sequence, which makes data comparison more limited than would have been ideal.

after the 1770s. Both the number and frequency of crime advertisements fell into decline. In the case of the *Public Advertiser*, this decline most likely forms part of the story of the newspaper's relationship with Bow Street. As part of his General Preventative Plan of 1772, which aimed to extend the advertisement of crimes and circulation of intelligence to a national level, John Fielding ultimately dispensed with the services of the *Public Advertiser*, and by 1773 had begun to publish his own newspaper, the *Hue and Cry*, which solely contained criminal intelligence, gathered by the authorities, and distributed nationally.[27] Moreover, under the direction of Henry Sampson Woodfall, the *Public Advertiser* had at times excited political controversy through its publication of parliamentary news and critiques of George III's government. Perhaps the authorities had come to realize that the use of commercial publications to develop specific policies had substantial limits. In the case of the *Public Advertiser*, from Table 6.1 above it is clear that the withdrawal of Bow Street did not encourage victims of crime once again to place advertisements to communicate with potentially knowledgeable readers.

At the same time, however, the concurrent decline in crime advertising in the rival newspapers suggests that victims were beginning to make more use of other methods for restitution after the 1780s. It would be wrong to assume that these were options provided by the extension of authority, or that Londoners on the whole were increasingly willing to hand over responsibility for crime fighting to the new policing forces. Evidence from the nineteenth century has shown that many ordinary men and women used the services of the metropolitan police and the prosecution process if and when it suited them: the rate of private prosecutions remained high, and informal methods of restitution within communities continued to provide satisfaction for many victims.[28] This chapter has sought to contribute to that body of evidence, to demonstrate the extent to which both wealthy and especially ordinary Londoners remained reluctant to hand over responsibility for solving crime to newly established institutions.

As for the implications of this small study for the history of reading, I hope I have shown how using evidence of reading alone has the potential to be as misleading as a purely text-based approach. The two methods need to be closely intertwined. Furthermore, we must never take the survival of evidence of reading for granted, but should question why some sources survived over others, or why some readers left a trace and others did not. The evidence of reading used in this chapter obviously forms just the tip of the iceberg, present in the historical record solely because of peculiar circumstances, for example, the recovery of the stolen property combined with a victim's decision to prosecute. As shown above, for reasons of expense, inconvenience or even potential criminal prosecution, many readers of crime advertisements may have wished to erase any evidence of their reading, something that the victims of crime (or the producers of crime adverts) recognized and then exploited to their own advantage. In this case then, the evidence of reading in the historical record may blind us to more widespread practices.

Notes and references

1. Jeremy Black, *The English Press in the Eighteenth Century* (London: Croom Helm, 1987); idem, *English Press, 1621–1861* (Stroud: Sutton Publishing, 2001); Hannah Barker, *Newspapers, Politics and English Society, 1695–1855* (Harlow: Longman, 2000); idem, *Newspapers, Politics and Public Opinion in Late Eighteenth-Century England* (Oxford: Clarendon, 1998); Michael Harris, *London Newspapers in the Age of Walpole: A Study of the Origins of the Modern English Press* (London: Associated University Presses, 1987). Crime reporting in the eighteenth-century press has recently received attention. See, for example, Esther Snell, 'Discourses of criminality in the eighteenth-century press: the presentation of crime in *The Kentish Post*, 1717–1768', *Continuity and Change*, 22 (2007), 13–47; and Peter King, 'Newspaper reporting and attitudes to crime and justice in late-eighteenth and early-nineteenth century London', *Continuity and Change*, 22 (2007), 73–112.
2. R. B. Walker, 'Advertising in London newspapers, 1650–1750', *Business History*, 15 (1973), 112–30.
3. John Styles, 'Print and policing: crime advertising in eighteenth-century provincial England'; David Philips, 'Good men to associate and bad men to conspire: associations for the prosecution of felons in England, 1760–1860'; and Peter King, 'Prosecution associations and their impact in eighteenth-century Essex'; all in *Policing and Prosecution in Britain, 1750–1850*, ed. Douglas Hay and Francis Snyder (Oxford: Clarendon, 1989); Peter King, *Crime, Justice and Discretion in England, 1740–1820* (Oxford: Oxford University Press, 2000), pp. 57–62.
4. King, *Crime, Justice and Discretion in England*, p. 59.
5. Ibid., pp. 59–62; Styles, 'Print and policing', pp. 76–81.
6. Ibid.
7. Robert Shoemaker, *The London Mob: Violence and Disorder in Eighteenth-century England* (London: Hambledon and London, 2004), pp. 36–8, 49.

8. Walker, 'Advertising in London newspapers', pp. 122–3.
9. Black, *English Press* pp. 104–9; Barker, *Newspapers, Politics and Public Opinion*, pp. 25–31.
10. Walker, 'Advertising in London newspapers', p. 123. See also Hannah Barker, who argues that the fluctuations in the circulation rates of the newspaper correspond directly with the London season; Barker, *Newspapers, Politics and Public Opinion*, p. 25.
11. *Public Advertiser*, 1 December 1759, p. 3.
12. *Public Advertiser*, 17 March 1744, p. 3.
13. *Public Advertiser*, 21 March 1763, p. 4.
14. *Public Advertiser*, 24 December 1759, p. 3.
15. *Public Advertiser*, 15 November 1752, p. 1.
16. Martin C. Battestin, 'Fielding, Henry (1707–1754)', *Oxford Dictionary of National Biography* (Oxford: Oxford University Press, 2004), s.v.
17. Clive Emsley, *Crime and Society in England, 1750–1900*, 2nd edn. (Harlow: Longman, 1996), pp. 220–1; idem, *The English Police: A Political and Social History*, 2nd edn. (Harlow: Longman, 1996), pp. 19–20; Anthony Babington, *A House in Bow Street: Crime and the Magistracy in London, 1740–1881* (London: Macdonald & Co., 1969); Martin Battestin and Ruth R. Battestin, *Henry Fielding: A Life* (London: Routledge, 1989).
18. *Public Advertiser*, 4 November 1768, p. 1.
19. 26 Geo. II, c.36 (1752).
20. Emsley, *Crime and Society in England*, pp. 186–7.
21. See Philips, 'Good men to associate', pp. 113–70, and King, 'Prosecution associations', pp. 171–207.
22. *Old Bailey Proceedings Online* (www.oldbaileyonline.org, accessed 17 December 2009), Feb 1759, trial of William Wilson (t17590228–13).
23. Ibid., Feb 1798, trial of Edmond Lovell (t17980214–3).
24. Ibid., Dec 1789, trial of David Bevan (t17891209–111).
25. Ibid., Sept 1766, trial of John Newman (t17660903–30).
26. See also Peter King, 'Decision-makers and decision-making in the English criminal law, 1750–1800', *Historical Journal*, 27 (1984), 25–58, who emphasizes the strong presence of victims from across the social spectrum, including the 'labourer, servant, gardener and husbandman' social group, in the prosecution process.
27. John Styles, 'Sir John Fielding and the problem of criminal investigation in eighteenth-century England', *Transactions of the Royal Historical Society*, 5th Ser., 33 (1983), 127–49.
28. See, for example, the work of Jennifer Davis: 'Prosecutions and their context: the use of the criminal law in late-nineteenth century London', in Hay, *Policing and Prosecution in Britain*, pp. 397–426; and idem, '"A poor man's system of justice": the London police courts in the second half of the nineteenth century', *Historical Journal*, 27 (1984), 309–35; and Emsley, *Crime and Society*, pp. 187–92.

7
The Reading World of a Provincial Town: Preston, Lancashire 1855–1900

Andrew Hobbs

This chapter attempts to recreate the circumstances of reading in an industrial town in northern England in the second half of the nineteenth century. 'The "where" of reading is more important than one might think, because placing the reader in [their] setting can provide hints about the nature of [their] experience.'[1] Few historians of reading have followed Darnton's suggestion, neglecting place as they have neglected newspapers and periodicals, or non-literary texts such as advertising or train timetables. Instead, the literary roots of the discipline have skewed scholarship towards the historical reading of high-status literary texts.[2] However, if we start from the reader rather than the text, a different picture of nineteenth-century reading emerges, one in which

> the book was not the predominant form of text and, more than likely, was not therefore the thing most commonly or widely read . . . The most common reading experience, by the mid-nineteenth century at latest, would most likely be the advertising poster, all the tickets, handbills and forms generated by an industrial society, and the daily or weekly paper.[3]

This chapter focuses on two reading institutions where newspapers were found, the news room and the newsagent's shop.

In 1855, Preston was recovering from the 1853–4 lock-out, an event used as raw material by Charles Dickens and Elizabeth Gaskell for their novels *Hard Times* and *North and South*. Preston was an ancient market, legal and administrative centre for northern Lancashire, with an economy dominated by cotton spinning and weaving. The population grew from 69,000 in 1851 to 125,000 by 1901.[4] Table 7.1 shows approximate numbers of reading institutions in Preston during the period, recorded in trade directories, library reports, autobiographies, newspaper articles, oral history and photographs. The numbers are almost certainly underestimates.

Table 7.1   Some Preston reading institutions, 1853–1901[5]

	1853	1873	1901
Schools	66	77	86
Booksellers	27	30	28
Newsagents	7	33	75
Libraries, news rooms and reading rooms	9	10	13
Lending & circulating libraries	3	4	2
Publishers	4	6	7
Printers	18	10	32

It should also be noted that the institutions listed in Table 7.1 are all formal reading places, whereas most reading probably took place at home, in public houses, or on the street. It was the norm for even the smallest public house to provide at least one newspaper, while larger commercial hotels advertised the number of titles available.[6] In Preston, reading the paper aloud and discussing its contents had been a formalized event during the excitement of the 1830 by-election, at which the radical Henry Hunt defeated Lord Stanley. Voters

> flocked to the public-house on a Sunday evening . . . to hear the newspaper read. The success of the landlord depended, not on the strength of his beer altogether, but on having a good reader for his paper . . . it was not the general custom to drink during the reading of the paper. Every one was expected to drink during the discussion of any topic, or pay before leaving for the good of the house.[7]

It is likely that pubs were significant reading places, particularly of newspapers, into the twentieth century.

Libraries, news rooms and reading rooms

Public places set aside for reading were common in nineteenth-century Preston, among them news rooms, established for no other purpose than reading and discussing the news.[8] There was no clear distinction between news rooms, reading rooms and libraries.[9] In the Institution for the Diffusion of Knowledge (a mechanics' institute established in 1828), they occupied three respective spaces; in others, the library (a cupboard or a few shelves) may have been in the corner of a news room; while the Harris Free Library, purpose-built in 1893, contained a news room and reading room alongside reference and lending libraries. Smaller news rooms and reading rooms such as those in commercial hotels stocked nothing but newspapers, but most also took quarterly and monthly periodicals. Other news rooms and reading rooms, such as those run by church mutual improvement societies, also included books.

Places set aside for reading needed to be warm, comfortable and well-lit. The Exchange and News room, opened for the use of businessmen in Preston's new town hall in 1867, was furnished with four tables each measuring 9 ft × 3 ft, 9 in.; four loose newspaper stands with reading table; two tables with tops; twenty chairs; one telegraph stand, 6ft, 6in. high; two benches with back rails, 10 ft × 1 ft, 6 in.; two umbrella stands; inkstands; one towel rail and roller; a letter box, blackboard, toilet materials and six spittoons. 'All the furniture [was] to be of best Dantzic Oak – French polished.' The rules of the Exchange and News room stipulated no smoking and no dogs, and requested 'that no person detain a newspaper longer than fifteen minutes after its being asked for; and that no preference be shown by the exchange of papers'.[10] A comment from a member suggests groups of friends or like-minded acquaintances gathered for conversation in different parts of the room:

> Occasionally on a very cold day there was only one fire, the consequence being that all political creeds and set classes of theologians were pitched into one corner . . . when there was no doubt but that they desired being seated with their own fellows.[11]

The news room of the Central Working Men's Club presented a cosy picture in 1864:

> The fire was blazing cheerfully, the paper and pictures upon the walls were as beautiful as any artist could desire, and the general effect was decidedly one of comfort and quiet enjoyment. The

library or reading room, as the adjoining apartments were designated, was furnished in a similar manner, only books took the place of newspapers.[12]

In 1893 the news room and reading room of the Harris Free Library accommodated 276 people, with a separate ladies' reading room (news rooms, like pubs, were overwhelmingly male places).[13] Figure 7.1, from 1895, shows light streaming onto the high, sloping reading desks of the news room in the background; newspaper readers are standing, unlike the book and magazine readers in the reading room.[14] The row of men standing on the left are working class, judging by their caps. The two on the left stand close together, perhaps in whispered conversation. The men facing them are taller, perhaps because they had been better fed. Behind them is a man in a top hat who looks as though he could afford the subscription of a more exclusive news room, and facing him are two men in bowler hats. All classes appear to be using this news room.

As its name suggests, the free library was free to use, but in the 1850s, the cost of using a news room or reading room ranged from £2 12s 6d per year at the Winckley Club to a penny a week at institutions aimed at operatives, such as church mutual improvement societies. However, even the Winckley Club subscription was cheaper than buying a few of the quarterly reviews and general magazines, and suggests that private ownership of reading matter was beyond the means of even many wealthy men.[15] Until the opening of the Free Library and the Co-op's reading rooms, poorer readers' access to reading material was limited, segregating them from middle-class readers.[16]

Private ownership of newspapers and periodicals was available at reduced rates, however, through a recirculation system which challenges ideas of the newspaper as ephemeral. Some newsagents sold day-old papers at half-price, and reading rooms and news rooms reduced their costs by selling back-copies to members.[17] The enduring value of used newspapers is shown by an appeal for reading material from the curate of St Paul's church, for a parish reading room: 'We would promise to send for the papers, keep them clean, and return them at any time that might be wished.'[18]

The Winckley Club took twenty-two papers and periodicals in 1851, rising to fifty-five titles by 1900, with London daily papers the single most popular genre.[19] For the proposed reading room at

Figure 7.1 Reading room with news room at rear, Harris Free Library, Preston, 1895 (courtesy of the Harris Museum & Art Gallery, Preston)

St Paul's school, mentioned above, 'the sort of papers that would be useful are the London and Manchester daily and weekly papers, the local papers, *Household Words*, the *Leisure Hour, Family Economist,* &c., &c.'[20] The middle-class Institution for the Diffusion of Knowledge took fifty-two titles in 1861, with an emphasis on literary and technical publications. Provincial dailies were the most common type of newspaper, and Preston papers were more popular than at the Winckley Club, judging by the multiple copies required. Local newspapers featured in an announcement of the opening of the new Free Library in 1879 among a detailed list of forty-eight titles (books were not mentioned). A year later the Free Library offered eighty-one titles (five quarterlies, thirty-three monthlies, thirty-five weeklies and nine dailies), increasing to 171 by 1900 (nine quarterlies, seventy-three monthlies, sixty-five weeklies and twenty-four dailies). The most popular publications were local newspapers, if we take multiple copies as an index of demand.[21]

A mixed economy of news rooms reigned in Preston at the start of the period, including larger institutions such as the Institution for the Diffusion of Knowledge, the Winckley gentleman's club established in 1846 and the Literary and Philosophical Institute, founded in 1848.[22] Paternalistic mill owners provided workplace libraries, and there was a handful of small trades union and commercial news rooms.[23] Contemporary commentators believed that reading was moving away from the pub and into public libraries, news rooms and workers' clubs as early as the 1850s and 1860s.[24] In Preston, there is not enough evidence to track trends in pub reading, but there was certainly change and expansion in other reading places. One factor was a reduction in newspaper prices after the abolition of Stamp Duty in 1855, which led to a fall in news room subscriptions at the Institution for the Diffusion of Knowledge, and the closure of Cowper's Penny News and Reading Room in Cannon Street.[25]

Church-sponsored reading rooms, aimed at working-class adults, flourished in the 1850s and '60s. In the 1850s, rooms in at least five Church of England parishes opened in connection with mutual improvement societies. The 250 members of St Peter's Young Men's Club paid 1d per week in 1861 for

> a reading room supplied with the leading papers; a library, containing 400 volumes; educational classes, three nights a week;

> a conversation room, where bagatelle, chess, draughts &c. are
> allowed; and an excellent refreshment room . . . The club . . .
> affords to the working man opportunities for spending his time
> rationally and instructively, without resort to the pot-house,
> where his money is wasted, and himself ultimately reduced to
> beggary.[26]

The aim of keeping men away from the pub, to prevent drunken-
ness and poverty (perhaps to control political discussion, too) was
behind many other reading rooms, such as the Temperance Hall in
the 1850s and '60s, the Alexandra coffee tavern, opened in 1878, and
reading and recreation rooms opened for dock workmen in 1886.[27]
The denominational flavour of church reading rooms reflected their
balance among the population, with Anglicans in the lead, followed
by Catholics and then Nonconformists.

Commercial news rooms such as Cowper's (1854–55) and the
Exchange and News Room (1867–78) were most numerous from
the 1850s to the 1870s.[28] Political parties opened reading rooms, to
educate, entertain, or both, from the late 1860s, particularly around
the time of the 1867 Reform Bill, which extended the franchise to
working-class men in urban constituencies such as Preston. The
local branch of the National Reform Union opened a reading room
in March 1867, and in November 1869, within a week of each
other, Preston's General Liberal Committee opened a reading room
in Fishergate and the Central Conservative Club opened in Lord
Street. Trades union rooms multiplied in the 1860s, and all kinds of
clubs and associations offered reading rooms as a benefit for their
members, such as the 11th Lancashire Rifle Volunteers, the Preston
Operative Powerloom Weavers' Association and the Central Working
Men's Club.[29]

The reading ecology of the town changed with the opening of the
council-funded Free Library in 1879, in the former premises of the
loss-making middle-class Exchange News room.[30] The Free Library's
arrival led to another fall in membership of the Institution's news
room, especially among subscribers on the lowest rates, followed by
the room's amalgamation with the reading room two years later. The
Free Library had less impact on news rooms provided by organizations as part of wider membership benefits, notably those of the
Preston Industrial Co-operative Society, the single biggest provider

Table 7.2   Approximate numbers of news rooms, reading rooms and libraries, Preston, 1850–1900

Pre-1850	1850s	1860s	1870s	1880s	1890s
5	27	27	24	16	16

of reading rooms in the town from the 1890s to the early decades of the twentieth century.[31] In 1889 there were six Co-op reading rooms; ten years later there were fourteen Co-op groceries in Preston, and it is possible that each one had a reading room (for Table 7.2, it has been assumed that 50 per cent of the branches did so).[32] There is little evidence here for the thesis that, from the 1880s, newspapers were no longer seen as educational or morally uplifting.[33]

The number of individual institutions and organizations offering reading facilities rose to a peak in the 1850s and '60s and then fell, as can been seen from Table 7.2. However, those that remained were larger – pre-eminently the Free Library, the two Conservative clubs and the Liberal club. Exceptions to this pattern were the Co-op's many small reading rooms. There was a decline in middle-class institutions and free-standing news rooms not connected to a club or organization, but an increase in working-class ones, perhaps reflecting a middle-class shift from reading in public to reading in private. It was no longer necessary to join a news room, thanks to falling cover prices, rising incomes and the growth of free public libraries. But many people still preferred to read newspapers and periodicals in pubs and less formal news rooms, where they could also discuss the news with like-minded people.

Newsagents

Mr John Proffitt ran one of nine Preston businesses described as newsagents around 1860. The advertisement (Figure 7.2) for his shop, on the main north–south route through Preston, tells us a great deal about newsagents at the start of the period. Although most of the text is devoted to newspapers and periodicals, he describes himself as a 'hair dresser' first, 'news agent' second. This was a time when newsagents, or news-vendors, were starting to distinguish themselves from booksellers and grocers, but a shop devoted mainly to papers

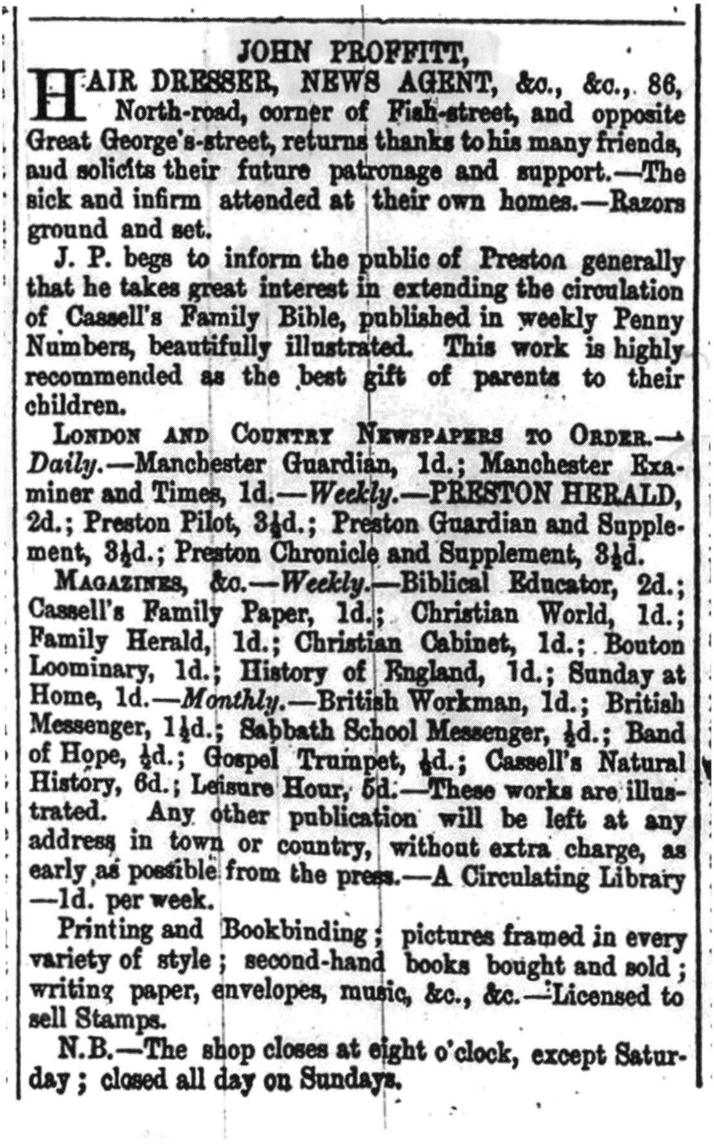

JOHN PROFFITT,

HAIR DRESSER, NEWS AGENT, &c., &c., 86, North-road, corner of Fish-street, and opposite Great George's-street, returns thanks to his many friends, and solicits their future patronage and support.—The sick and infirm attended at their own homes.—Razors ground and set.

J. P. begs to inform the public of Preston generally that he takes great interest in extending the circulation of Cassell's Family Bible, published in weekly Penny Numbers, beautifully illustrated. This work is highly recommended as the best gift of parents to their children.

LONDON AND COUNTRY NEWSPAPERS TO ORDER.— *Daily.*—Manchester Guardian, 1d.; Manchester Examiner and Times, 1d.—*Weekly.*—PRESTON HERALD, 2d.; Preston Pilot, 3½d.; Preston Guardian and Supplement, 3½d.; Preston Chronicle and Supplement, 3½d.

MAGAZINES, &c.—*Weekly.*—Biblical Educator, 2d.; Cassell's Family Paper, 1d.; Christian World, 1d.; Family Herald, 1d.; Christian Cabinet, 1d.; Bouton Loominary, 1d.; History of England, 1d.; Sunday at Home, 1d.—*Monthly.*—British Workman, 1d.; British Messenger, 1½d.; Sabbath School Messenger, ½d.; Band of Hope, ½d.; Gospel Trumpet, ½d.; Cassell's Natural History, 6d.; Leisure Hour, 5d.—These works are illustrated. Any other publication will be left at any address in town or country, without extra charge, as early as possible from the press.—A Circulating Library —1d. per week.

Printing and Bookbinding; pictures framed in every variety of style; second-hand books bought and sold; writing paper, envelopes, music, &c., &c.—Licensed to sell Stamps.

N.B.—The shop closes at eight o'clock, except Saturday; closed all day on Sundays.

Figure 7.2 Advertisement for John Proffitt, *Preston Herald*, 1 September 1860

and magazines was still a rarity. As well as cutting hair and sharpening razors, Proffitt also offered printing, bookbinding, picture-framing, stationery, second-hand books and a circulating library. At this time it was the norm for a purchaser to buy their paper in a grocer's or corner general store, a bookshop, stationer's, or tobacconist's, even fruit-shops, oyster-shops or lollipop-shops, as Wilkie Collins found in his survey of sellers of 'penny-novel Journals'.[34] For Proffitt, however, the periodical press seems to have been an important part of his business. The periodicals advertised are mainly family magazines with a strong Christian or temperance slant, although there is also the *Bouton Loominary*, a Lancashire dialect title published in Bolton. Newsagents' shops could also serve as informal reading rooms, where reading and discussion were combined.[35]

Trade directories and newspapers show how protean was the emerging category of newsagent. The *Preston Herald* published a list of sixty-six Preston agents for the paper in 1870, twenty-four of whom did not appear as newsagents or booksellers in the trade directories of the 1860s and 1870s.[36] Conversely, twenty-two newsagents listed in the 1873 directory did not appear in the *Herald* list, emphasizing the unreliability of trade directories. The twenty-four *Herald* outlets absent from the directories were spread evenly around the town, including five in the slum area south-east of the town centre. These were probably small grocer's shops; other outlets are listed under different classifications in earlier directories, including a confectioner, a retailer of beer, grocers, a chemist and druggist, and a milliner and dressmaker, demonstrating the variety of shops and offices where one might encounter reading matter for sale, and the types of businesses that developed into newsagents (see Figure 7.3). Neither were there any clear demarcations between new or second-hand bookshops, booksellers or newsagents, shops or libraries. WH Smith was not unusual in selling newspapers, new and second-hand books and periodicals, and operating a circulating library (like Smith's, Mudie's circulating library also sold used periodicals).[37]

The population of Preston increased by roughly fifty per cent during the period, and the proportion able to read probably doubled, yet the number of newsagents increased tenfold (see Table 7.3).[38] However, the figures for the 1850s and 1860s are probably bigger underestimates than later figures, for the reasons discussed above. The development of newsagents as a distinct type of shop, away from

Figure 7.3   E. Smith, 'stationer, newsagent, toy dealer', Fylde Street, Preston, c.1908 (by permission of Mr William Smith)

Table 7.3 Preston booksellers and newsagents, with indices of readership, 1853–1901

	1853	1860	1870	1880	1889	1901
Booksellers & stationers	27	31	28**	22	26	28
Newsagents	7	9*	38**	53	66	76
Preston population (10,000s)	6.9		8.5	9.7	10.8	12.5
% men signing marriage register		64.7	72.3	92.4		
% women signing marriage register		30.7	47.4	81.7		

*1861; **1869; population figures from Censuses of 1851, 1861, 1871, 1881, 1891 and 1901.

their origins as a sideline to bookselling and grocery can be seen in the fact that all seven 'news-vendors' identified in 1853 were also classified as booksellers.[39] By 1901, however, only twelve newsagents out of seventy-six were also booksellers. The expansion of news-selling outlets between 1853 and 1873 is striking, particularly their spread into respectable working-class areas. The greatest expansion was in those areas populated by textile worker households whose relatively high disposable incomes drove the growth of music hall, the seaside tourism industry and professional football.[40] Did the reading habits of this culturally dynamic group shape the publishing industry in equally distinctive ways?

While population growth and advances in literacy must be among the reasons for this expansion of the news trade, the explosion of cheap reading matter, including the provincial press, could also be an important factor. In Preston, the biggest leap in literacy was in the 1850s and 1860s, before compulsory education, but during the ten years of greatest print expansion, beginning with the abolition of Newspaper Stamp Duty in 1855. This can be deduced from the steep increase in signatures on marriage registers during the 1870s, double the rate of growth of the previous decade, these signatures of young adults in their mid- to late twenties reflecting their schooling some fifteen years earlier.[41] This sharp rise in literacy overlaps with the time of greatest expansion in the Preston news trade, which quadrupled during the 1860s (if we take the directory figures at face value).

Conclusions

The second half of the nineteenth century was a dynamic period in the history of reading as the explosion of cheap print (including local and regional newspapers) combined with a steep growth in reading ability to change the nature of the newspaper-reading experience. Before the repeal of Newspaper Stamp Duty in 1855, public houses were the most accessible places to find a newspaper, and there were only half a dozen rooms in Preston set aside for the reading of newspapers. Less than ten years later there were more than twenty-five, but their numbers declined sharply after the town's first state-funded reading place, the Free Library, opened, with newspaper-reading central to its purpose. By the end of the century, the halfpenny local evening newspaper had made ownership of a daily paper commonplace, even for working-class readers, reducing the need for public news rooms. However, the news and reading rooms of the public library, political clubs and the Co-op movement survived into the twentieth century.

In Preston, the opening of the public library ended the need for free-standing rooms, unattached to any organization, devoted solely to the reading of newspapers. It brought a certain amount of public reading experiences under state control, however benevolent (as symbolized by the policeman in the Free Library reading room, Figure 7.1), and its rule of silence influenced the style of reading, and began to break the old association between reading and discussing the news.[42] While limited social mixing had always taken place in inns and public houses, the Free Library was Preston's first reading institution to be used by all classes and both sexes.

The decline in middle-class news rooms, and the huge increase in newsagents, suggests a trend away from sharing newspapers in public places, associated with discussion and conversation, to buying them for private consumption.[43] However, this requires qualification: middle-class news rooms declined more than working-class ones and working-class readers continued to read in pubs. Here, discussion could continue alongside reading, as it could in the reading rooms above Co-op shops, in Labour and Conservative clubs, or at home. Reading newspapers aloud in public places probably declined as literacy increased, but oral history evidence suggests that it continued at home into the twentieth century.[44] More research is needed on where and when newspapers were read aloud in this period, and more generally on reading in the public house and the home.

Working-class news rooms were set up by conservative, respectable groups such as the notoriously conservative textile unions and Preston's equally conservative co-operative movement. Similarly, if the creation of church reading rooms and a public library were part of a civilizing project by the local middle classes, reading places and reading material had to be negotiated with readers and their 'gatekeepers', such as the librarian of Preston's Free Library, who allowed a wide range of reading matter, and refused to censor betting news on principle. The growth of newsagents shows that the capitalist publishing market gave working-class people the freedom to create their own reading worlds – a democratization of print. These new purchasers (as opposed to new readers) encouraged newspaper publishers to adapt their publications, in their content, writing style and address, and their price.

The comparative significance of newspapers in the public life of a town is illustrated by the lack of any institutions dedicated to the reading of fiction in volume form, for example. Local and regional newspapers appear consistently in lists of papers taken by all kinds of reading institutions in Preston, from small pubs to the reading rooms of the town's elite. They were more popular in places lower down the social scale. News rooms, like pubs, offered a range of papers, which encouraged 'promiscuous' reading, thus complicating simplistic ideas of inferring readers from single texts. The tradition of discussion alongside reading the newspaper brought oral and print culture together, creating a public sphere.[45] Facilities to read and discuss the news were thought attractive enough to be offered as benefits for members of clubs and societies, and to be used as bait to lure men into churches and political parties, pubs and temperance halls. Newspapers were central to the reading world of a provincial town.

Notes and references

1. Robert Darnton, 'First steps towards a history of reading', in his *The Kiss of Lamourette: Reflections in Cultural History* (London: Faber & Faber, 1990), p. 167.
2. Leah Price, 'Introduction: reading matter', *PMLA*, 121 (2006), 9–16, cited in Stephen Colclough, *Consuming Texts: Readers and Reading Communities, 1695–1870* (Basingstoke: Palgrave Macmillan, 2007), p. viii; Richard D. Altick, *The English Common Reader: A Social History of the Mass Reading Public, 1800–1900* (Chicago: University of Chicago Press, 1963); Jonathan Rose, *The Intellectual Life of the British Working Classes* (London: Yale University Press, 2001).
3. Simon Eliot, 'The Reading Experience Database; or, what are we to do about the history of reading?' http://www.open.ac.uk/Arts/RED/redback.htm [accessed 24 January 2010] (para. 10 of 25).
4. David Hunt, *A History of Preston* (Preston: Carnegie, 1992).
5. Information in tables was compiled from trade directories and from word-searching the digitized *Preston Chronicle,* 19th Century British Library Newspapers, http://find.galegroup.com/bncn [accessed 10 June 2010].
6. Altick, *English Common Reader*, pp. 200–1; Arthur Aspinall, *Politics and the Press, c.1780–1850* (Brighton: Harvester Press, 1973), pp. 9, 29.
7. W. Pilkington, *The Makers of Wesleyan Methodism in Preston, and the Relation of Methodism to the Temperance and Teetotal Movements . . . With a Preface by the Rev. C. Garrett* (Preston: W. Pilkington, 1890), p. 183; see also *Cobbett's Political Register*, 26 September 1807, quoted in Aspinall, *Politics*, p. 11.

8. John B. Hood, 'The origin and development of the newsroom and reading room from 1650 to date, with some consideration of their role in the social history of the period' (unpublished FLA dissertation, Library Association, 1978); Colclough, *Consuming Texts* pp. 88–145; Martin Hewitt, 'Confronting the modern city: the Manchester Free Public Library, 1850–80', *Urban History*, 27 (2000), 62–88; Patrick Joyce, *The Rule of Freedom: Liberalism and the Modern City* (London: Verso, 2003), p. 132; Aspinall, *Politics*, pp. 6–32; Christopher M. Baggs, 'The libraries of the Co-operative movement: a forgotten episode', *Journal of Librarianship and Information Science*, 23 (1991), 87–96.

9. Baggs, 'The libraries', pp. 87–96.

10. Preston, Lancashire Record Office (LRO), Minutes of Exchange & News Room committee, 24 June 1867, CBP 53/4.

11. 'Annual meeting of the subscribers to the Exchange Newsroom', *Preston Chronicle (PC)*, 19 November 1870.

12. 'Travels in search of recreation II, Central Working Men's Club', *PC*, 20 February 1864.

13. John Convey, *The Harris Free Public Library and Museum, Preston 1893–1993* (Preston: Lancashire County Books, 1993).

14. William Bramwell, *Reminiscences of a Public Librarian: A Retrospective View* (Preston: Ambler, 1916). Many libraries only had standing accommodation; see Robert Snape, *Leisure and the Rise of the Public Library* (London: Library Association, 1995).

15. Altick, *English Common Reader*, p. 319.

16. See David Barton and Mary Hamilton, *Local Literacies: Reading and Writing in One Community* (London: Routledge, 1998), p. 17, on 'inequality . . . in the access to literacy resources' in the late twentieth century.

17. For example, 'The Daily Telegraph may be had at half price the morning after publication, at [Lytham] Times office' (advertisement in *Preston Pilot*, 18 November 1885, p. 4).

18. *PC*, 6 September 1856.

19. Winckley Club minute books, LRO DDX 1895.

20. *PC*, 6 September 1856.

21. The centrality of the local press to Preston's reading world is examined in more detail in Andrew Hobbs, 'Reading the local paper: social and cultural functions of the local press in Preston, Lancashire, 1855–1900' (unpublished PhD thesis, University of Central Lancashire, 2010).

22. *PC*, 3 January 1852; 8 June 1867; 28 December 1867; 29 December 1877; 26 January 1878.

23. John Goodair, *Strikes Prevented* (Preston, 1854), cited in Harold Dutton and John King, *'Ten Per Cent and No Surrender': the Preston Strike, 1853–1854* (Cambridge: Cambridge University Press, 1981), p. 85.

24. 'Manchester free libraries', *Chambers' Journal*, 3rd ser., 13 (1860), 341; [Henry Solly,] 'Working men's clubs and institutes', *Fraser's Magazine*, 71 (1865), 391; 'Popular reading-rooms', *Chambers' Journal*, 3rd ser., 20 (1863), 411–12; 'Refreshments and reading-rooms for the working classes', *Leisure Hour*, 1 (1852), 526–7; [George Dodd and Henry Morley,]

'Accommodation for quidnuncs', *Household Words*, 8 (1853–54), 88–91, all cited in Eugenia Palmegiano, 'A conundrum on character: periodical perceptions of press readership in the nineteenth century', paper given at the conference 'Characters of the Press', Roehampton University, London, 4 July 2008.

25. Preston, University of Central Lancashire, Livesey Collection (LC) uncatalogued, Institution for the Diffusion of Knowledge, annual report for 1855, p. 5. However, the 1858 annual report stated that 'The News-room . . . is well sustained by numerous subscribers' (*PC*, 30 June 1855).

26. *PC*, 31 October 1861. See similar descriptions of St Luke's Conservative Association (*Preston Herald* (*PH*), supplement, week ending 17 September 1870, p. 3) and LC M [Pre]), Preston Temperance Society annual report for 1862, p. 7.

27. *Preston Guardian* (*PG*), 4 September 1886, p. 6.

28. LRO CBP 53/4.

29. *PC*, 5 September 1863; 22 December 1861; 1 July 1871.

30. *PG*, 3 August 1878, p. 10; 2 January 1878, p. 6.

31. In 1889 there were six Co-op reading rooms 'well supplied with daily and weekly papers' (*PC*, 6 April 1889, p. 5), but it has not been possible to confirm their addresses.

32. In 1879 the Rochdale Pioneers Co-operative Society had eighteen news rooms, Bury's had twelve, Oldham's seventeen (Baggs, 'The libraries', pp. 90, 92).

33. See Mark Hampton, *Visions of the Press in Britain, 1850–1950* (Urbana: University of Illinois Press, 2004) for a recent exposition of this view.

34. Wilkie Collins, 'The unknown public', *Household Words*, 21 (1858), 217–22. Boys' adventure stories were sold from 'lollipop and toy shops, sweet-stuff vendors, and small chandler's shops' in London (John Springhall, '"Disseminating impure literature": the "penny dreadful" publishing business since 1860', *Economic History Review*, 47 (1994), 567–84 (p. 572)) and Preston grocers sold newspapers (Zoe Lawson, 'Shops, shopkeepers, and the working-class community: Preston, 1860–1890', *Transactions of the Historic Society of Lancashire & Cheshire*, 141 (1991), 309–28 (p. 311)). Such shops were still selling newspapers in Middlesbrough at the start of the twentieth century (Lady Florence Bell, *At the Works: A Study of a Manufacturing Town*, ed. Jim Turner (Middlesbrough: University of Teesside, 1997), p. 144).

35. James Ogden, 'The birth of the "Observer"', *Rochdale Observer*, 17 February 1906; Hartley Aspden, *Fifty Years a Journalist: Reflections and Recollections of an Old Clitheronian* (Clitheroe: Advertiser & Times, 1930), p. 9.

36. *PH*, 3 September 1870, p. 5.

37. Stephen Colclough, '"A larger outlay than any return": the library of W. H. Smith & Son, 1860–1873', *Publishing History*, 54 (2003), 67–93; Guinevere L. Griest, *Mudie's Circulating Library and the Victorian Novel* (Newton Abbot: David and Charles, 1970). See list of 'second hand reviews and magazines' from Mudie's 1890 catalogue, reprinted in Laurel Brake, '"The trepidation of the spheres": the serial and the book in the 19th century', in *Serials and Their Readers, 1620–1914: 14th Annual*

Conference on Book Trade History, ed. Robin Myers and Michael Harris (Winchester/New Castle, DE: St Paul's Bibliographies/Oak Knoll Press, 1993), p. 82.

38. The signing of the marriage register (as opposed to making a mark) is here used as an index of the ability to read. For justification of this method, see David Vincent, *Literacy and Popular Culture: England 1750–1914* (Cambridge: Cambridge University Press, 1989), pp. 17–18.

39. Oakey's 1853 directory of Preston.

40. John K. Walton, *Lancashire: a Social History, 1558–1939* (Manchester: Manchester University Press, 1987), p. 190; Robert Poole, *Popular Leisure and the Music Hall in Nineteenth-Century Bolton* (Lancaster: Centre for North-West Regional Studies, University of Lancaster, 1982); Dave Russell, *Football and the English: A Social History of Association Football in England, 1863–1995* (Preston: Carnegie, 1997); John K. Walton, *The English Seaside Resort* (Leicester: Leicester University Press, 1983).

41. William B. Stephens, *Education, Literacy and Society, 1830–1870: The Geography of Diversity in Provincial England* (Manchester: Manchester University Press, 1987), p. 13.

42. Hewitt, 'Confronting the modern city', pp. 86–7.

43. Aled G. Jones, *Press, Politics and Society: A History of Journalism in Wales* (Cardiff: University of Wales Press, 1993), p. 105.

44. For example, oral history interviewee Mr T2P (b. 1903), Lancaster, Lancaster University, Elizabeth Roberts, 'Social and family life in Preston, 1890–1940': transcripts of recorded interviews, 1981.

45. Jürgen Habermas, *The Structural Transformation of the Public Sphere: An Inquiry into a Category of Bourgeois Society* (Oxford: Polity, 1992).

8

'Putting literature out of reach'? Reading Popular Newspapers in Mid-Twentieth-Century Britain

Adrian Bingham

For ordinary Britons in the twentieth century, reading meant, above all, the consumption of newspapers. Surveys found that whereas almost half of adults said they never read books, only a tenth did not regularly see a daily newspaper.[1] The newspaper was one of most successful products of the twentieth century, and provided, as Chris Baldick puts it, 'the most regular and most formative relationship between the majority of the population and the written word'.[2] And newspapers were particularly successful in Britain. In the middle decades of the twentieth century, the British read more newspapers per capita than any other people in the world – almost twice as many as Americans in the mid-1950s, and nearly three times as many as the French.[3] In no other country have mass market newspapers been as fiercely competitive or achieved quite the same influence and prominence as in Britain. Fleet Street's uniquely successful brand of popular journalism has provided millions of ordinary readers with one of their main windows onto the world, and has shaped the nation's political and social life in countless ways.

In order to achieve such popularity, newspapers had to mould themselves to fit into the rhythms of everyday life. This chapter will explore the ways in which ideas about reading practices shaped the layout and content of newspapers. The first section will outline how the desire to make the reading experience as easy, convenient and interesting as possible strongly influenced the evolution of the popular newspaper in the opening third of the twentieth century, and led to the forging of a template from which there has been little variation in subsequent decades. This desire to achieve ease of reading generated considerable anxieties among critics like Q. D. Leavis, who claimed that the younger generation were becoming addicted to the 'cheaper gratification' offered by newspapers and thereby prevented from obtaining the 'finer cumulative pleasure that literature gave their fathers'.[4] But the fears of such commentators tell us little about the realities of the newspaper reading experience. So the second part of the chapter will examine readership surveys from the period – conducted by Mass Observation and a variety of research and commercial organizations – to offer some suggestions about what ordinary readers thought they were getting from their newspapers. It will argue that newspapers offered broader horizons beyond normal routines, provided an agenda for everyday conversations, and encouraged a sense of engagement in a national community.

The convenience of readers was not a high priority for most Victorian editors and journalists, unless they worked for one of the popular Sunday newspapers, such as *Lloyd's Weekly News* (1842) or the *News of the World* (1843). These weeklies, which offered a cheap and entertaining miscellany of stories about unusual events, sensational court cases and the latest political dramas, circulated widely among the working classes and demonstrated the commercial potential of the mass market.[5] But morning daily newspapers were still very much targeted at the respectable middle classes, and the most striking features of these newspapers were their formality, density and visual austerity. The morning press was dominated by lengthy reports of the happenings of the public sphere – party politics, financial news, international diplomacy, the activities of 'high society' – lightened with a sprinkling of crime and sports stories. Political speeches and public meetings were reported at great length, with little attempt to summarize or analyse their content. Very few illustrations were included, and there was no attempt to guide readers to important stories with eye-catching headlines. After all, the projected reader was an urbane 'man of affairs', able to form his own conclusions from this untreated material.[6] The imagined reader was also expected to have the leisure to work carefully through the paper column by column. In reality, as one observer noted, this meant that the newspaper was 'suitable only for those who could retire to their clubs at four o'clock and spend two or three hours digesting it'.[7] The Victorian morning newspaper was, furthermore, an overwhelmingly masculine product. Women were largely invisible in its columns: they were located instead in the domestic, 'private' sphere, which was considered to be the proper subject of women's magazines rather than of a 'serious' organ of political affairs. In general, editors were too busy pursuing the intricacies of party politics to be concerned with extending the readership of their papers. As the historian Lucy Brown concluded in her survey of the Victorian press, the morning newspapers 'made no attempt . . . to adjust their presentation of the news to people of limited education' and 'did not try to attract readers through a simplification of thought and vocabulary'.[8] Political influence at Westminster, not a large circulation, was the most sought-after prize.

This is the culture that Alfred Harmsworth (later ennobled as Lord Northcliffe) sought to change with the launch of the *Daily Mail* in 1896.[9] The *Mail* was an immediate success, and was soon selling around a million copies a day: it was the first genuinely mass market daily.[10] Northcliffe thought deeply about the actual reading experience of readers, and tried to shape his newspapers around it. This was by no means an easy task, because there was so little reliable information about reading – even circulation figures were untrustworthy until the establishment of the Audit Bureau of Circulations in 1931. In November 1920 – twenty-four years after launching the *Daily Mail* – Northcliffe was presented with the findings of a house-to-house survey conducted in several provincial towns by the *Mail* circulation team, and declared that it was the first time that he had been able to discover with any accuracy 'the foundation of our sale and the kinds of people who read the Paper'.[11] Much of Northcliffe's success was due to his perceptiveness in assessing the information available to him about popular tastes. Throughout his career he remained eager to discover the views of his readers. He paid close attention to the letters pages, he obsessively watched people reading newspapers in public places (trains, parks, streets), and he organized mini-surveys of his own. In May 1920, for example, he informed the *Daily Mail* office that he had 'nearly fifty women of all classes' looking at the women's pages; nine days later he announced that he had taken 'twenty-five opinions on our new serial story'.[12] He also encouraged his journalists to involve themselves in the ongoing task of testing the popularity of certain features, declaring in January 1921, for example, that 'It would help me greatly if the staff would get their womenfolk to read and criticise the Serials'.[13]

Northcliffe sought to redefine traditional notions of news and newspaper content. Rather than thinking of his reader as an elite man relaxing at his club, he visualized an aspirational lower-middle-class family sitting around the breakfast table. He tried to provide respectable but entertaining content that would appeal to this notional family, with particular sections targeted at different members so that they would pass the newspaper round and lengthen the lifespan of the newspaper. He demoted the masculine public sphere from its position of overwhelming dominance in the news pages: no longer would dry parliamentary speeches be recorded in full, and political events would now be reported not for the educated elites, but for the average reader. Instead, there were to be human interest stories about crimes and unusual events, and more about personalities in the public eye. Northcliffe repeatedly told his staff that 'people are so much more interesting than things' and called for stories which would feed the curiosity of readers about their fellow citizens.[14] Northcliffe demanded prose that was simple and direct enough to be understood by anyone who might be tempted to buy the paper. He was well aware that many potential readers had received only a very limited education, and continually reminded his journalists not to adopt a style that such people would find difficult to interpret. His right-hand man, Kennedy Jones, told his staff to:

> Make the news clear. Avoid technical terms or explain them. State who the persons are whose names are mentioned. . . . Don't forget that you are writing for the meanest intelligence.[15]

Northcliffe also recognized the need for frequent repetition and heavy emphasis for his papers to make an impression on the public. He reminded his journalists that just because they were familiar with the complexities of public life, they should not assume that their readers were too. 'The Paper is constantly referring to "contingent guarantees" and the "Osborne judgement"', he complained to the *Mail*'s news editor in 1910. 'Nobody knows what these phrases mean, and they will not know until you have explained them twenty or thirty times. The parochial Fleet Street view of the world explains the inability of the public to understand what the average newspaper is talking about.'[16] Northcliffe tried to rid his staff of the assumptions that people scrupulously read the whole paper, that they were always concentrating fully, and that they would be able to remember what had been written in previous editions. He was fond of observing that 'Most people have never heard of Pears' Soap', at a time when the soap seemed to have an almost ubiquitous presence on advertising hoardings.[17]

One of the main ways in which Northcliffe sought to make the newspaper more attractive to the family was to include feature pages with material directed at women. The first issue boasted that this was nothing less than a 'Daily Magazine, an Entirely New Idea in Morning Journalism', which would provide every week 'matter equivalent to a sixpenny monthly'.[18] The *Mail* justified its focus on female readers by arguing that:

> Movements in a woman's world – that is to say, changes in dress, toilet matters, cookery, and home matters generally – are as much entitled to receive attention as nine out of ten of the matters which are treated of in the ordinary daily paper. Therefore, two columns are set aside exclusively for ladies.[19]

In the *Mail*, the editorial matter became explicitly gendered. 'The man who has not time for this class of reading', the editor remarked of the women's columns, 'can leave it severely alone and lose nothing; he gets his Money Market and all the latest news on the other pages.'[20] Northcliffe was, therefore, inviting men and women to take different routes through the newspaper. The first issue also contained the opening instalment of a fiction serial, aimed mainly at women. Northcliffe hoped it would encourage wives to remind husbands to bring their paper back home, again extending its lifespan.[21] Northcliffe's research found that the fiction serial was the most important feature for many women: 'I know how surprised Fleet Street was when it discovered that the majority of women readers started their perusal with the serial.'[22] Children's features were also included, and were designed to familiarize the very youngest readers with the paper in the hope that they might buy it themselves when they were older.[23]

Northcliffe is often described as the man who ushered in the industrialization of the press by basing the *Mail*'s finances on revenue from branded advertising.[24] Ironically, though, Northcliffe initially believed that many readers were irritated by the amount of space taken up by advertising in their newspapers and predicted that his publication would be able to reduce this burden. The first issue boasted that:

> The *Daily Mail* gives exactly the same news, but fewer adver-
> tisement sheets . . . the 'note' of the *Daily Mail* is not so much
> economy of price as conciseness and compactness. It is essentially
> the busy man's paper [and readers will save time by avoiding] the
> usual puzzling maze of advertisements.[25]

But when the *Mail* quickly achieved record circulations, it was evident that this policy was letting major revenue-raising opportunities
slip by, and it was soon reversed. The *Mail*'s advertising department
rapidly expanded the space allocated to display advertising, in the
process transforming the appearance of the paper. Northcliffe justified the reversal by admitting that he had come to recognize the
importance of advertising for the reading experience of many people,
especially women. When the *Mail* had to reduce its size during the
First World War, for example, he urged his care in the rationing of
advertisements, instructing that preference was given to

> those which appeal to women. Drapery advertisements are news
> to them and are so regarded by the American newspapers. Now
> that we have [temporarily] abolished the women's column,
> it is more than ever necessary not to neglect this important
> department.[26]

It was from Northcliffe's experiments with the format of the *Daily
Mail* that many of the features of the modern popular newspaper
were developed. But it was in the other newspaper that he launched,
the *Daily Mirror*, that pioneering steps were made to use photography
and create a more visually attractive publication. The first half-tone
newspaper photograph was printed in the *Daily Graphic* in 1891, but
it was only in 1904 that the *Daily Mirror* mastered the rapid rotary
printing of half-tone photographs, thereby making possible their
inclusion in cheap mass circulation papers.[27] Northcliffe recognized
the importance of paying close attention to these photographs,
and became increasingly convinced that 'that the public judge the
paper by the pictures, and the best paper can be marred by bad
pictures'.[28]

As photography was integrated into newspapers, a recognizably modern layout emerged. Columns of unbroken text in one typeface were replaced by a more fragmented and visually attractive format in which the reader was guided by prominent headlines and 'cross-headers', and articles were broken up by photographs, cartoons, and illustrated advertisements; there were countless different attempts to catch the reader's eye. The number of words per issue was reduced and editors filled space with striking photos and sketches. It was the production of these visually appealing papers that ensured that the practice of reading daily newspapers extended beyond the lower middle-classes and became a normal feature of working class life. By 1939 some two-thirds of all adults regularly saw a national daily paper, and almost everyone saw a Sunday paper. Circulations continued to rise during the Second World War, and reached a peak in 1950–51, with national dailies achieving a combined circulation of 16.6 million copies per day, and Sundays selling just over 30 million copies per week.[29] At mid-century the market was close to saturation point, with over 85 per cent of the adult population reading a paper every day.

After Northcliffe's death in 1922 the popular newspaper format was developed and extended by editors such as Arthur Christiansen at the *Daily Express* and Hugh Cudlipp at the *Sunday Pictorial* and *Daily Mirror*.[30] Generating interest among working-class readers, Christiansen admitted, was not always easy, because there was 'an immense reader-resistance to newspapers'. To counter this resistance, events sometimes had to be dressed up in rather more spectacular garb. He told his journalists to 'Make the news exciting, even when it was dull' and to 'Make the news palatable by lavish presentation'.[31] Christiansen judged the results by considering whether they would be read by 'the people in the back streets of Derby' or 'the man on the Rhyl promenade': 'Headlines, writing, thinking, phrasing, layout, recipes, fashion, all came under the ruthless test of whether they would be comprehensible to the people of Derby and Rhyl.'[32] Cudlipp had similar ideas. He did not want his papers to be devoid of serious material, but instead sought to lead readers on a path through the paper from the entertaining features to the 'heavier' articles. 'The general idea was to leave the reader gasping for breath, and then, leading him gently by the hand, to whisper in his ear: "Just a moment, friend. Before you take another look at that luscious Swedish blonde in the swimming pool on page 16, there's a piece on page 27 by the Foreign Editor of the *New York Times* analyzing the sources of Hitler's power."[33]

Such comments horrified critics like Q. D. Leavis who argued in her influential book *Fiction and the Reading Public* that the popular press was seducing readers away from wholesome and traditional forms of popular culture towards ones that relied on 'mechanical responses' and 'vicarious living'. The public had become so accustomed to the easy and superficial reading matter provided by the popular press that they were unable and unwilling to tackle anything more substantial or challenging: 'Northcliffe's interference with reading habits alone has effectively put literature out of the reach of the average man.' 'The reading capacity of the general public,' she contended, 'has never been so low as at the present time'; because it had become habituated to a diet of pre-packaged opinion, the reading public 'has no means of knowing what it really thinks and feels'. The cultural life of the majority, she concluded, was dangerously 'crude, impoverished, and narrow'.[34] Similar themes were developed twenty-five years later by Richard Hoggart in his widely-discussed work, *The Uses of Literacy*. Hoggart was also concerned that the press was undermining some of the best elements of working-class culture, encouraging acquisitiveness at the expense of inquisitiveness, and making it 'harder for people without an intellectual bent to become wise in their own way'.[35]

But what can be found about the newspaper reading experience if we move beyond polemical writing and examine readership surveys conducted by newspapers and advertisers, or by research organizations such as Mass Observation? We can see that many of the assumptions of Northcliffe and his successors were correct. Many people simply grabbed the opportunity to read when they had a spare moment, when commuting or taking a break from the housework. Most readers lacked the time or inclination to read everything in their newspapers, and they skipped over sections that did not interest them. A survey by the London Press Exchange in 1934 found that of ten prominent news items in national daily and London evening papers, the average person read four completely, two partly, and four not at all. Features were seen by about seventy per cent of readers.[36]

So what items did people select in the time that they spent reading their newspaper? Surveys throughout the period consistently found that human interest stories were the most popular type of news, and were enjoyed by all sections of the public. But this set of preferences was not restricted to readers of the popular press. Readers of elite newspapers also identified human interest stories as their favourite type of content, even though such material was not given the same amount of prominence as in the popular press.[37] Readers of all kinds were intrigued by the human dramas that unfolded around them, dramas which stimulated feelings of curiosity, pity and envy, and which could be enjoyably discussed with others.[38]

Investigating why people read newspapers, Mass Observation was generally given one of two, superficially contradictory, answers. Most respondents said that they read a paper so that they could be 'in touch' and 'up-to-date' with the events of the wider world. Some felt a sense of duty to be informed about political developments, while others just read whichever news stories sparked their curiosity, but all of these people wanted some knowledge of what was happening around them. The second, smaller group – consisting of more women than men – said that they regarded newspapers as a source of escapism and excitement.[39] A twenty-six year-old typist declared, for example, that in her paper she liked to find 'plenty of sensation' to take her 'away from this dull old place'; another woman suggested that features about 'film and dress' took her 'out of the rut'.[40] In many ways, however, these two reasons were not so very different. Newspapers gave both sets of respondents the opportunity to see beyond the narrow routines of their own lives and to glimpse the panorama of human existence, in all its forms. They offered drama and incident, fresh perspectives, a contrast with the everyday.

The replies also demonstrate that at the heart of the press's appeal was its value in providing a supply of material for everyday conversation. 'Whether it is politics or sport or the latest human story which interests them most,' noted Mass Observation, 'the newspaper enables them to talk to other people about it and to feel a sense of participation.'[41] This was true for both groups. The desire of some readers for escapism did not necessarily indicate absorption in a private world: fantasies of glamour or adventure could be shared just as much as opinions about the latest crime or scandal. Cinema and fashion, after all, provided the staple of many exchanges between young people.[42] This widespread reference to newspaper content in conversation was a testament to the skill of popular journalists in implementing the policies of Northcliffe and his imitators. Setting readers talking was one of Northcliffe's main priorities from the foundation of the *Daily Mail*, and the crusades, stunts, and opinionated columns that he included in the paper were specifically designed for this purpose.[43] It was widely accepted in Fleet Street that the effectiveness of these methods was one of the main reasons for the *Mail*'s success. Lord Beaverbrook, for one, ascribed the *Mail*'s 'immense popularity' to Northcliffe's ability to supply 'subject matter for discussion to countless thousands almost every day', with talking-points that were 'equally suitable for the suburbs and the luncheon tables of the West End'.[44] Northcliffe's tactics, which placed a premium on stimulating controversy, were copied by his rivals, and were perfected by the *Daily Mirror*. Hugh Cudlipp, perhaps the most successful practitioner of this form of popular journalism, observed that 'a popular newspaper has to be more than merely interesting: it must be alarmingly provocative in every issue'.[45]

Reading and talking about the stories in London-based newspapers seems to have fostered a feeling of engagement in a national, rather than merely local, society. Benedict Anderson has argued that the press played a major role in the emergence of what he described as a national 'imagined community'.[46] This argument is persuasive, and there is evidence to suggest both that national newspapers encouraged a wider sense of community and that this was one of the reasons behind their popularity. Several commentators in the late nineteenth and early twentieth centuries noted how parochial views were gradually challenged by the new habit of reading the national press. For example, the writer George Bourne, describing rural change in 1912, observed that the reader of a national newspaper was 'taken into the public confidence':

> Instead of a narrow village tradition, national opinions are at his disposal, and he is helped to see, as it were from the outside, the general aspect of questions which, but for the papers, he would only know by his individual experience from the inside.[47]

Robert Roberts, who grew up in Salford at the turn of the twentieth century, offered a similar assessment. 'Except in periods of national crisis or celebration', he argued, the Edwardian industrial labourer 'remained generally uninterested in any event beyond the local, horse racing excepted'; after 1918, however, the press built on the 'new awareness' created by the First World War, and helped to broaden the horizons of the working classes.[48]

Newspapers permeated British society to such an extent that they demanded attention. Anyone going about their normal business in towns and cities across the country would have found them very difficult to avoid. Vendors shouted the names of the papers they were trying to sell from street corners; pavements were furnished with branded sandwich boards offered tantalizing glimpses of the latest headlines; trains, buses, and trams were filled with people consuming that day's issue; countless sporting and cultural events were decorated with banners of newspapers that were sponsoring them; even those staying at home might be disturbed by the knock of canvassers selling subscriptions. There were innumerable invitations to participate in this shared experience, and it would have been easy to feel that not joining in would have been to forfeit something important. One did not even need to purchase a copy to be drawn in. Of those who did not buy a newspaper regularly, many must have been like the 'young Londoner' who told Mass Observation that when he passed a newsstand in the morning he would 'glance at all the papers displayed there [and] read the big headlines'; he also 'read bits' over the shoulders of passengers on the bus.[49] Hugh Cudlipp recognized that newspapers could make an impact on these passers-by: he used 'strong words and compelling type' to deliver the *Mirror*'s message 'not only to the millions who bought the paper regularly but to the millions who would catch a glimpse of the headlines on the shop counters, the railway bookstalls, the street corners, the trains and buses'.[50]

This sense of participation in a wider community also helps to explain the interest many readers had in the letters page. A 1933 survey by the London Press Exchange found letters to be the most popular feature in the mass circulation dailies, and Mass Observation agreed that 'Letters to the Editor are always popular, whether in *The Times* or the *Daily Mirror*, as the reader then feels that he is actively assisting the newspaper to present its (and his) view.' Another study in 1963 found that letters were the fourth most thoroughly read type of content, from a list of twenty-one categories.[51] Readers could find from the letters page whether others around the country shared their opinions: as one respondent commented, because so much of the *Mirror* was 'written by the readers, in the form of Viewpoint,

Live Letters, and Star letters, it gives a guide to what other people are thinking, if they are indeed thinking at all'.[52] The very fact that so many were moved to send in letters, and to inform the editor of their views, demonstrated the significance of newspapers to the lives of readers. Most correspondents must have recognized that their letter had a fairly small chance of being published, but nevertheless considered it a worthwhile exercise to send it. Editors equally placed great emphasis on the importance of replying to readers' letters.[53]

But readers by no means passively accepted everything they read: indeed, they were often fairly sceptical. A series of Mass Observation surveys just before and during the Second World War discovered fairly high levels of distrust of popular newspapers.[54] 'There is a common tendency to divide any news in the paper by half', one survey concluded in 1942, noting also that 'reading between the lines of the newspaper is becoming a national pastime'.[55] This scepticism was especially marked when newspapers were compared to BBC news broadcasts. In contrast to the highly opinionated journalism of the press, the apparent neutrality of the BBC's reports lent them a greater level of credibility to most listeners.[56] While the wartime context of censorship and information management probably increased doubts about the reliability of the news, later studies also revealed concerns about the trustworthiness of popular newspapers. A 1975 survey, for example, found that over thirty per cent of regular readers of the *Daily Mirror*, the *Sun* and the *Daily Record* felt that it was very or fairly true to say that their paper 'often gets its facts wrong'; only three per cent of the readers of *The Times*, the *Guardian* or the *Financial Times* said the same. Over sixty per cent of *Mirror*, *Sun* and *Record* readers also agreed that their papers exaggerated the sensational aspects of the news (compared to only five per cent of the readers of the elite papers).[57] A MORI poll in 1983 discovered that only nineteen per cent of respondents trusted journalists to tell the truth (the only consolation for Fleet Street was that government ministers scored even lower at sixteen per cent). In the final years of the century this low level of trust fell even further.[58]

It is possible to detect a certain amount of hypocrisy in many people's attitudes to their papers. On the one hand, circulation figures demonstrated the public's appetite for sensational stories about crime and scandal, and readership surveys repeatedly suggested that readers were fascinated by human interest and celebrity. On the other hand, many seemed to regard their consumption of this material as a guilty pleasure, and they did not necessarily have much respect for those who produced it. Lord Shawcross, the chairman of the Second Royal Commission on the Press, recognized this ambivalence in an article he wrote for the Press Council in the aftermath of the Profumo affair in 1963. Considering why public 'ill-favour' towards newspapers existed despite huge circulations, he suggested that

> although as individuals we may not be averse to wallowing vicariously in stories of sexual perversion and promiscuity, although we enjoy the spark of malice and listen curiously to the tongue of scandal, we do not approve of those who, for profit, purvey these things.[59]

The popular press's ever more vigorous pursuit of the celebrity agenda in the final decades of the century was often at the expense of the trust that had allowed journalists to educate and inform, rather than merely entertain, their readers.

One can make many justifiable criticisms of the triviality, cynicism and sensationalism of the popular press. But its readers were not, as Leavis and others suggested, passive dupes left uncritical by addiction to their daily newspaper fix. People bought newspapers because in the spectacular diversity of their content they found ways of connecting to a wider world. Readers were selective, sceptical and even hypocritical, and used newspapers for their own reasons. Newspapers may have provided some of the human drama traditionally supplied by novels – but there is little evidence that they put literature 'out of reach'.

Notes and references

1. For example, Mass Observation, File Report 2537, November 1947, 'Reading in Tottenham' (repr. Brighton: Harvester Press Microform Publications, 1983), p. 4.
2. Chris Baldick, *The Oxford English Literary History*, Vol. 10, *1910–40: The Modern Movement* (Oxford: Oxford University Press, 2004), p. 18.
3. Francis Williams, *Dangerous Estate: The Anatomy of Newspapers* (1957; London: Longmans, Green, 1958), pp. 1–2. See also Royal Commission on the Press 1974–77, *Final Report* (London: HMSO, 1977), Cmd. 6810, Appendix C, 105.

4. Q. D. Leavis, *Fiction and the Reading Public* (1932; London: Chatto & Windus, 1965), p. 117.
5. Virginia Berridge, 'Popular Sunday papers and mid-Victorian society', in *Newspaper History from the Seventeenth Century to the Present Day*, ed. George Boyce, James Curran and Pauline Wingate (London: Constable, 1978), pp. 247–64.
6. Lucy Brown, *Victorian News and Newspapers* (Oxford: Clarendon, 1985), chapters 5, 11.
7. Political and Economic Planning, *Report on the British Press* (London: PEP, 1938), p. 93.
8. Brown, *Victorian News*, pp. 30, 100.
9. Alfred Harmsworth (1865–1922), Viscount Northcliffe, launched *Answers to Correspondents* in 1888, the *Daily Mail* in 1896, and the *Daily Mirror* in 1903; he acquired control of the *Observer* in 1905, and *The Times* in 1908.
10. For more on the emergence of the *Daily Mail*, see Adrian Bingham, *Gender, Modernity and the Popular Press in Inter-War Britain* (Oxford: Oxford University Press, 2004), chapter 1.
11. Brown, *Victorian News*, p. 27.
12. Bodleian Library, Oxford, MS.Eng.hist d.303–5, Northcliffe Bulletins to the *Daily Mail*, 11 May 1920, 20 May 1920.
13. Northcliffe Bulletins, 28 January 1921.
14. For example, Northcliffe Bulletins, 13 November 1919; British Library, Northcliffe Papers Add MSS 62234, Northcliffe to Alexander Kenealy, 'The Ten Commandments', undated.
15. Kennedy Jones, *Fleet Street and Downing Street* (London: Hutchinson, 1920), p. 145.
16. Northcliffe Papers, Add MSS 62201, Northcliffe to W. G. Fish, 21 November 1910.
17. Norman Angell, *After All: The Autobiography of Norman Angell* (London: Hamish Hamilton, 1951), p. 128.
18. *Daily Mail*, 4 May 1896, p. 7.
19. Ibid.
20. Ibid.
21. Tom Clarke, *My Northcliffe Diary* (London: Hutchinson, 1931), p. 136.
22. Northcliffe Bulletins, 9 March 1918.
23. Northcliffe Bulletins, 21 February 1917.
24. Gillian Dyer, *Advertising as Communication* (London: Methuen, 1982), p. 42. See also Raymond Williams, *The Long Revolution* (Harmondsworth: Penguin, 1965), p. 225.
25. *Daily Mail*, 4 May 1896, p. 4.
26. Northcliffe Bulletins, 9 March 1918.
27. Eric Cheadle, 'Picture editing', in *The Kemsley Manual of Journalism*, ed. W. W. Hadley (London: Cassell, 1950), pp. 79, 81; *The Encyclopedia of the British Press, 1422–1992*, ed. Dennis Griffiths (London: Macmillan, 1992), p. 286. Rapid rotary printing of half-tone photographs was pioneered by Arkus Sapt for the *Daily Mirror*; see Hugh Cudlipp, *Publish and Be Damned!*

The Astonishing Story of the Daily Mirror (London: Andrew Dakers, 1953), p. 13; Bill Hagerty, *Read all about it! 100 Sensational Years of the Daily Mirror* (Lydney, Glos.: First Stone, 2003), p. 14.

28. Northcliffe Bulletins, 1 June 1920.
29. G. Harrison, F. Mitchell and M. Abrams, *The Home Market*, revised edn. (London: G. Allen & Unwin, 1939), chapter 21; A. P. Wadsworth, 'Newspaper circulations 1800–1954', *Manchester Statistical Society Transactions*, 4, Session 1954–55; Aled Jones, 'The British Press 1919–1945' in *The Encyclopedia of the British Press*, pp. 48–9; Jeremy Tunstall, *Newspaper Power: The New National Press in Britain* (Oxford: Clarendon Press, 1996), chapter 3; Colin Seymour-Ure, *The British Press and Broadcasting since 1945*, 2nd edn. (Blackwell, Oxford, 1996), chapter 3.
30. Arthur Christiansen (1904–63) edited the *Daily Express* from 1933 to 1957; Hugh Cudlipp (1913–1998) edited the *Sunday Pictorial* from 1937 to 1940 and 1946 to 1949; he was editorial director for both the *Mirror* and *Pictorial* from 1953 to 1968, and chairman of parent company IPC until his retirement in 1973.
31. Arthur Christiansen, *Headlines All My Life* (London: Heinemann, 1961), pp. 147, 150.
32. Ibid., pp. 2–3.
33. Hugh Cudlipp, *At Your Peril* (London: Weidenfeld & Nicolson, 1962), p. 51.
34. Leavis, *Fiction and the Reading Public*, pp. 74, 117, 182, 224, 244–5.
35. Richard Hoggart, *The Uses of Literacy* (1957; London: Penguin, 1962), pp. 338–9.
36. PEP, *Report on the British Press*, p. 249.
37. James Curran, Angus Douglas and Garry Whannel, 'The political economy of the human-interest story', in *Newspapers and Democracy: International Essays on a Changing Medium*, ed. Anthony Smith (Cambridge, MA: MIT Press, 1980), pp. 304, 338–40.
38. On the appeal of human interest stories, see D. L. LeMahieu, *A Culture for Democracy: Mass Communication and the Cultivated Mind in Britain Between the Wars* (Oxford: Clarendon Press, 1988), pp. 22–5.
39. Mass Observation File Report A11, December 1938, 'Motives and methods of newspaper reading'.
40. Ibid., pp. 10–11.
41. Ibid., p. 1.
42. Sally Alexander, 'Becoming a woman in London in the 1920s and 1930s', in idem, *Becoming a Woman and Other Essays* (New York: New York University Press, 1995).
43. On Northcliffe's interest in providing 'talking points', see Clarke, *My Northcliffe Diary*, pp. 195–205.
44. British Library, Add MSS 59544, Evelyn Wrench Papers, Beaverbrook to Wrench, 22 July 1935.
45. Cudlipp, *At Your Peril*, p. 47.
46. B. Anderson, *Imagined Communities: Reflections on the Origin and Spread of Nationalism*, revised edn. (London: Verso, 1991), chapter 2.

47. Cited in Jonathan Rose, *The Intellectual Life of the British Working Classes* (New Haven: Yale University Press, 2001), pp. 28–9; see also p. 10.

48. Robert Roberts, *The Classic Slum: Salford Life in the First Quarter of the Century* (Harmondsworth: Penguin, 1973), pp. 162–3, 228–9.

49. Mass Observation, *The Press and Its Readers: A Report Prepared By Mass Observation for the Advertising Service Guild* (London: Arts and Technics, 1949), p. 25.

50. Hugh Cudlipp, *Walking on Water* (London: Bodley Head, 1976), p. 96.

51. Curran et al, 'Political economy', pp. 318, 327; Mass Observation, File Report 2557, January 1948, 'Attitudes to newspapers'.

52. Mass Observation, File Report 2557, p. 31.

53. Gerald Barry, the editor of the *News Chronicle*, told the paper's board in the late 1930s that the practice of acknowledging letters could be discontinued 'at a considerable saving', but did not recommend the step because he believed the practice to be a valuable one: Gerald Barry Papers, BLPES, LSE, File 4, Undated memo (1938–39?), 'Economics in editorial expenditure'.

54. Mass Observation File Report 1,' The five channels of publicity', October 1939, p. 2; File Report 65A, p. 1; File Report 126, p. 13; File Report 1231, p. 5; File Report 1330A.

55. Mass Observation File Report, 1339, p. 23.

56. Mass Observation File Report 375, p. 158.

57. Royal Commission, *Attitudes to the Press*, p. 62.

58. Robert Worcester, 'Demographics and values', in *Sex, Lies and Democracy: The Press and the Public*, ed. Hugh Stephenson and Michael Bromley (London: Longman, 1998), p. 47.

59. Lord Shawcross, 'Curbs on the rights of disclosure', in *The Press and the People: The Tenth Annual Report of the Press Council* (London: Press Council, 1963), p. 10.

Part 4
Readers and Autodidacticism

9
James Lackington (1746–1815): Reading and Personal Development

Sophie Bankes

In his autobiography, *Memoirs of the First Forty-Five Years of the Life of James Lackington* (1791), Lackington tells us that he was born in Wellington in Somerset on 31 August 1746, the son of a wayward, impoverished shoemaker who provided him with little formal education.[1] Despite these disadvantages, he taught himself to read and write and eventually became a successful businessman, the owner of one of the largest bookshops in London.[2] He wrote his autobiography towards the end of his career, revising it considerably over several further editions, and followed it in his retirement with another volume, entitled *Confessions of J. Lackington* (1804).[3] In each of these works, Lackington chronicles his extensive reading, exhorting others to follow his example. His autobiographies offer a persuasive account of the power of reading to transform a life, but they need to be approached with caution as a source of evidence for the history of reading. *Memoirs*, in particular, mixes fiction, myth, gossip, tall tales and professional aspiration, and presents what seems an idealized record of reading experience. This chapter will examine Lackington's autobiographies to trace how he became a reader, what he may have read, and what influences motivated him to write and publish these extraordinary accounts of reading and personal development.

Given the importance of books in his life, it is rather disappointing to discover that no record of Lackington's personal collection of books has survived. In his will he simply packaged together 'household goods plate pictures books linen woollen household furniture casks & utensils'.[4] Despite the lack of specific evidence of the contents of his library, the sales catalogues he prepared for his bookshop indicate the thousands of titles to which he had access during his

Figure 9.1 James Lackington, by Edmund Scott, after John Keenan, stipple engraving, 1792 (© National Portrait Gallery, London)

working life. One of the incentives for setting up in business was, apparently, that it would bring him into contact with books:

> I farther observed, that I loved books, and that if I could but be a bookseller, I should then have plenty of books to read, which was the greatest motive I could conceive to induce me to make the attempt.[5]

This suggests that his ownership of books may have been fluid and transitory, particularly as he goes on to tell us that the stock with which he opened his new shop included his existing book collection or *'private library'*, odd magazines and 'a bagful of old books, chiefly divinity' which he purchased for a guinea from the estate of a recently deceased bookseller.[6]

In the absence of a catalogue of his personal book collection, Lackington's *Memoirs* and *Confessions* provide the primary source of information about the books he owned and read. The former was written when he was forty-five, the latter, dealing with more recent history, when he was fifty-seven or fifty-eight. The record of his reading experiences presented in *Memoirs* is illustrated by the many quotations which fill the work. Edward Marston noted with some irritation in his *Sketches of Booksellers of Other Days* that Lackington's *Memoirs* were 'brimful of poetical quotations', adding that the author 'had, or thought he had, the art of finding an apt quotation for every incident of life'.[7] Isaac Disraeli also commented on Lackington's remarkable ability to quote, writing that 'Mr Wakefield can recollect as great a number of quotations in Greek verse, as Mr Lackington seems to have known in English'.[8] The sheer number of Lackington's quotations from books seems to have been extraordinary, even in the eighteenth century. There are approximately 150 in the 344 octavo pages of the first edition of *Memoirs*, and in the longest of the subsequent editions this had risen to over 400 in 538 octavo pages. As we shall see, these quotations are used to lend authority to Lackington's writing, to embellish his account with the 'beauties' of (predominantly) English literature, and to advertise his learning.

The accounts in his *Memoirs* and his *Confessions* suggest that Lackington's reading life fell into three principal phases. In the first, he underwent an immersion in Protestant religious texts, mainly from the seventeenth century. In the second, he explored a broad spectrum of scholarly disciplines and writers, including freethinkers. In the third, he returned to works of religious devotion. He writes in his *Memoirs* of an incident which seems to throw light upon his early motivation for reading and can help to explain these phases. As a young apprentice to George and Mary Bowden, shoemakers of Taunton in Somerset, Lackington witnessed arguments between Mary Bowden and her elder son, who had recently become a Methodist. He was impressed by the ease with which they parried biblical references, and this created in him 'a desire for knowledge, that I might know who was right and who was wrong'. But to his 'great mortification' Lackington could not read.[9] He sought reading lessons from the younger Bowden son, John, surrendering his small weekly allowance in return for night-time letter learning, and followed the example of the older boy, George, by becoming a Methodist, a conversion experience sustained not only by the impassioned words of field preachers, but by his newfound skill in reading. This proved to be a significant development for Lackington since Methodist leaders actively encouraged daily reading of sermons and books of practical divinity. John Wesley himself produced devotional texts, pamphlets, books for children and books of hymns. His short religious tracts were priced between a penny and sixpence and were aimed at poorer members of society just like Lackington. This Methodist emphasis on the power of the printed word to transform the lives of readers undoubtedly left its mark on Lackington. In his *Memoirs* he stressed the enormous social, practical and spiritual advantages to be garnered from reading. He implicitly exhorted others to embrace print culture to better themselves socially, just as he had done.

Phase one: a 'very good library'[10]

The earliest books Lackington encountered were primarily religious and practical. During a short spell at a local dame school, he apparently impressed his teachers by memorizing chapters from the New Testament even before he could read. Forced to abandon his early education owing to the poverty of his parents, he sold almanacs, those essential practical guides to weights and measures, tides, county and town fairs, rates of interest, religious festivals, and so on. Later, whilst living with the Bowden family, he encountered their small collection of books, which included 'a school-size Bible, Watts's Psalms and Hymns, Foot's Tract on Baptism, Culpepper's Herbal, the History of the Gentle Craft, an old imperfect volume of Receipts in Physic, Surgery, &c. and the Ready Reckoner'.[11] Isaac Watts's *Hymns and Spiritual Songs*, first published in London in 1707 was a hugely popular book among Christians of all denominations. By contrast, William Foot's *A Practical Discourse Concerning Baptism*, first published in 1739 is a book that would appeal mainly to Baptists, as the Bowdens then were. It draws upon the example of Christ's baptism to advocate baptism of adults by total immersion. 'Culpepper's Herbal', the short title by which Nicholas Culpeper's *The English Physician or an Astologo-Physical Discourse of the Vulgar Herbs of this Nation* was known, offered instruction on curing common complaints using plants to be found in England. It was published widely from the mid-seventeenth century and throughout the eighteenth century. This, together with the 'Receipts in Physic, Surgery, &c' met the family's need for health advice, whilst Daniel Fenning's *The Ready Reckoner or Trader's Most Useful Assistant in Buying and Selling All Sorts of Commodities either Wholesale or Retail* (1757), provided tables showing the relative cost of different weights of goods, invaluable to the busy tradesman or merchant. Margaret Willes notes that the Bowden's library accords with evidence of the reading matter owned by other craftsmen and traders of the time.[12] However, looking back at his early encounter with this small collection of books, Lackington thought that 'the ideas of the family were as circumscribed as their library', a remark suggesting the importance he had come to place on a much more extensive access to books in nourishing the minds and ideas of individuals.[13]

The only work of no apparent practical value which Lackington recalls in the Bowden's library is Thomas Deloney's *The Gentle Craft* (first published at the end of the sixteenth century and frequently reprinted in a variety of formats), a very popular work which celebrated the shoemaker's craft. George Bowden's only 'light' reading thus concerned the lore of his trade. The book included the story of Simon Eyre, a shoemaker's apprentice who became Lord Mayor of London. This story of rags-to-riches resonates with the account the *Memoirs* presents of Lackington's own rise from humble origins to a position of wealth, ending up with a vignette of him and his wife strolling along the esplanade at Weymouth in the company of their Majesties and the four princesses.[14]

Whilst living with the Bowdens, Lackington used every opportunity to practise his new skill of reading. Later, he moved to Bristol, to earn a living as a journeyman shoemaker, sharing lodgings with fellow shoemaker, John Jones, who soon became a friend with whom to explore reading and religion. At this time, he tells us, 'I had only read a few enthusiastic [i.e. religious] authors, and Pomfret's poems; this last I could almost repeat by memory; however I made the most of my little stock of literature, and strongly recommended the purchasing of books to Mr. Jones.'[15] The two young men, although initially daunted by the task of choosing books for themselves in bookshops, eventually bought Hobbes's translation of Homer and 'Walker's Poetical paraphrase of Epictetus's morals' at a book stall at an annual fair in and around St James's churchyard in Bristol.[16]

Homer was to prove a disappointment 'owing to the obscurity of the translation . . . together with the indifferent language and the want of poetical merit in the translator'.[17] Epictetus's 'morals', however, proved a more popular purchase. Ellis Walker produced his translation of Epictetus at the end of the seventeenth century, under the title *Epicteti Enchiridion made English in a Poetical Paraphrase*, and five editions were published between 1692 and 1699. Walker's translation becomes a talisman for Lackington on his path to maturity and independence: 'the principles of the *Stoic* charmed me so much, that I made the book my companion wherever I went, and read it over and over in raptures, thinking that my mind was secured against all the smiles or frowns of fortune'.[18]

This strong sense of possession over the texts he read was to be characteristic of Lackington. There is evidence in *Memoirs* that he had indeed, as he claimed, absorbed 'Pomfret's poems'. John Pomfret (1667–1702) was one of the most popular poets throughout the eighteenth century. There are eight or nine quotations from his poems in the longer editions of *Memoirs*, mainly from 'Reason: a Poem' and 'Love Triumphant over Reason'. Letter XXXVIII of the 1794 edition opens with fourteen lines from 'Reason' emphasizing the effort which must be expended in order to acquire knowledge. Lackington is free with Pomfret's words, altering the line order by adding six lines near the opening of the poem to eight later lines. The extract introduces a chapter describing Lackington's own efforts to expand his education and he is clearly drawing from Pomfret what he needed, adapting the poem with the confidence of ownership to endorse his own life writing.

Lackington and Jones's first foray into shopping for books had involved relatively old volumes. They seem to have felt more comfortable browsing amongst bookstalls and in shops selling old books, and in time they acquired what Lackington described as a 'very good library'. He had managed to persuade Jones's brother and sister, who were also then living with him, to embrace Methodism too, and describes how each member of the household took turns to read aloud from religious works as they worked.[19] He lists their book collection in some detail:

> This choice collection consisted of Polhil on precious Faith; Polhil on the Decrees; Shepherd's sound Believer; Bunyan's Pilgrim's

Progress; Bunyan's Good News for the vilest of Sinners; Bunyan's
Heavenly Footman; his Grace abounding to the chief of Sinners;
his Life and Death of Mr *Badman*; his Holy War in the town
of *Mansoul*; Hervey's Meditations; Hervey's Dialogues; Rogers's
Seven Helps to Heaven; Hall's Jacob's Ladder; Divine Breathings
of a devout Soul; Adams on the second epistle of Peter; Adams's
Sermon on the *black* Devil, the *white* Devil, &c, &c, Collings's
Divine Cordial for the Soul; Pearse's Soul's Espousal to Christ;
Erskine's Gospel Sonnets; The Death of Abel; The Faith of God's
Elect; Manton on the epistle of St. James; Pamble's Works; Baxter's
Shove for a *heavy-arsed* Christian; his Call to the Unconverted;
Mary Magdalen's Funeral Tears; Mrs Moore's Evidences for
Heaven; Mead's Almost a Christian; The Three Steps to Heaven;
Brooks on Assurance; God's Revenge against Murder; Heaven
upon Earth; The Pathway to Heaven; Wilcox's Guide to eternal
Glory; Derham's Unsearchable Riches of Christ; his Exposition
of Revelations; Alleine's Sure guide to Heaven; The Sincere
Convert; Watson's Heaven taken by Storm; Heaven's Vengeance;
Wall's None but Christ; Aristotle's Masterpiece; Coles on God's
Sovereignty; Charnock on Providence; Young's Short and sure
Guide to Salvation; Wesley's Sermons, Journals, Tracts, &c. and
others of the same description.

We had indeed a few of a better sort, as Gay's Fables; Pomfret's
Poems; Milton's Paradise Lost; besides Hobbes's Homer, and
Walker's Epictetus.[20]

Most of the books in this collection are of a religious nature and
mainly date from the sixteenth or seventeenth centuries. Some were
written by nonconformists such as John Bunyan, but most were
by Anglican clergymen with Presbyterian leanings, many of whom
had been ejected from the Church of England after the Restoration.
These included Joseph Alleine (1634–68), Richard Baxter (1615–91),
Matthew Mead (1629–99), Edward Pearse (1633–73), Edward Polhill
(1622–94) and Thomas Watson (d.1686). A notable exception in
this company is the Jesuit martyr Robert Southwell, the author of
Marie Magdalens Funeral Teares (1591). Many of the books listed
here were best sellers, in particular the works of John Bunyan and
Richard Baxter, Arthur Dent's *The Plaine Mans Path Way to Heaven*
(1601), Elisha Coles's *A Practical Discourse of God's Sovereignty* (1673),

Salomon Gessner's *The Death of Abel*, translated from German by Mary Collyer (1761), Ralph Erskine's *Gospel Sonnets* (1726), James Hervey's *Meditations Among the Tombs* (1746) and *Theron and Aspasio a Series of Dialogues* (1755), and John Gay's *Fables* (1727). It is puzzling to find *Aristotle's Masterpiece* (1690), a practical guide to matters sexual and procreative, listed amongst a collection of religious books. Perhaps easy availability and a cheap price determined its inclusion in this library. The fact that Lackington was able to build up such an extensive collection of religious books would seem to support the claim made by C. John Sommerville, that religious interest rather than wealth determined the readership of such books, which were 'cheap enough and circulated sufficiently for almost anyone to have access to them'.[21]

For the most part, Lackington and Jones bought books by Protestant writers, and particularly by nonconformists. Their choice of literature is likely, in turn, to have fuelled further reading, for many of the selected writers emphasize the importance of reading within an active Christian life. Richard Baxter, for example, exhorts readers to 'go now and then to their Ignorant Neighbours, and read this or some other Book to them of this subject'.[22] N. H. Keeble notes that such writers were 'heirs to a literate, literary and bookish religious tradition'.[23] Indeed for many nonconformists, banned from preaching during the Restoration period, writing had been the only means to spread their message. Bunyan, who was confined in prison in the 1670s, and Thomas Shepard, who addressed *The Sound Believer* to those he left behind when he emigrated to America in 1635, relied upon the printed word to speak for them in their absence. Something of their evangelizing vigour is reflected in Lackington's *Memoirs*, even though he is not promoting religion but embodying his business values and eliciting a personal response from potential customers.

After a period of intense immersion in religious texts, Lackington began to broaden his reading, perhaps laying foundations for his move towards freethinking later in his life:

> At an old Book-shop I purchased Plato on the Immortality of the Soul, Plutarch's Morals, the Morals of Confucius the Chinese Philosopher, and a few others. I now can scarce help thinking that I received more real benefit from reading and studying them and

Epictetus than from all other Books that I had read before, or have read since that time.[24]

The works he referred to here may have been *Plato his Apology of Socrates, and Phaedo or Dialogues Concerning the Immortality of Mans Soul and Manner of Socrates his Death* (London: James Magnes and Richard Bentley, 1675); one of the volumes of Plutarch's morals published by Gellibrand in the late seventeenth century, such as *Plutarch's Morals translated from the Greek by Several Hands* (London: Gellibrand, 1684); and *The Morals of Confucius a Chinese Philosopher* (London: Taylor, 1691). Once again, Lackington seems to have drawn upon seventeenth-century books, no doubt because these were cheaper.

His life was to change once again when he sought work with John Taylor of Kingsbridge who encouraged him to learn to write. Some time between 1768 and 1770, he married Nancy Smith, a dairy maid, and after struggling to make a living in the south-west, the couple moved to London. Lackington kept up his book-buying habits: 'Nor did I forget the old book-shops: but frequently added an old book to my small collection.'[25] His collection now included:

Fletcher's Checks to Antinomianism, &c. 5 volumes; Watts's Improvement of the Mind; Young's Night Thoughts; Wake's Translation of the Apostolical Epistles; Fleetwood's Life of Christ; the first twenty numbers of Hinton's Dictionary of the Arts and Sciences; some of Wesley's Journals, and some of the pious lives, published by him; and about a dozen other volumes of the latter sort, besides odd magazines, &c.[26]

This collection of books is strikingly more up to date than his previous libraries. John Fletcher's series of 'Checks' to Antinomianism were published in the 1770s; Isaac Watts's *The Improvement of the Mind* was first published in 1741; John Fleetwood's *The Life of our Blessed Lord and Saviour Jesus Christ* was first published in 1766; John Barrow's *New and Universal Dictionary of Arts and Sciences* was published by John Hinton in 1751; and Wesley's 'Journals' were published throughout the century as were his various short lives of the faithful. Only William Wake's *The Genuine Epistles of the Apostolical Fathers* dates to the seventeenth century, having been published in 1693. It was with this stock that Lackington set up business on Midsummer day in 1775, as a bookseller.

Phase two: 'intellectual light and pleasure'[27]

The second phase of his reading life opened in 1776 after Lackington's second marriage. His new wife, Dorcas Turton, a former school mistress, was 'immoderately fond of books'.[28] Dorcas seems to have inspired her husband to read more broadly, and at about this time Lackington's friend, Ralph Tinley, a shoemaker and amateur entomologist, advised him to read Thomas Amory's *The Life of John Buncle*. This remarkable work, volume one of which was first published in 1756 and volume two in 1766, touches upon philosophy, religious ideas, scientific discoveries, mathematics, travels and voyages within the framework of an account of the life of the eponymous hero. William Hazlitt was later to describe it as a 'Unitarian romance' and it is no coincidence that around this time Lackington's Methodist beliefs were shaken, and he became an enthusiast for *John Buncle*, regarding it as an antidote to excessive piety and religion: 'I know not of any work more proper to be put into the hands of a poor ignorant bigoted superstitious Methodist.'[29] He would later come to regret this lapse from piety, and would return to Methodism, changing his mind about *Buncle* as a consequence. In his *Confessions*, he describes it as a 'pernicious work' which 'not only eradicated the remains of Methodism, but also nearly the whole of Christianity'.[30]

The curiosity sparked by Amory's novel, and his marriage to book-loving Dorcas clearly prompted Lackington to diversify in his reading still further: 'I now also began to read with great pleasure the rational and moderate divines of all denominations: and a year or two after I began with metaphysics, in the intricate though pleasing labyrinths of which I have occasionally wandered ever since.'[31] He went on to describe his programme of self education:

> In the beginning I attached myself very closely to the study of divinity and moral philosophy . . . I next read the works of Lord Herbert, Tindal, Chubb, Morgan, Collins, Woolston, Annet, Mandeville, Shaftesbury, Bolingbroke, Williams, Voltaire, and many other Free-thinkers. I have also read most of our English poets, and the best translations of the Greek, Latin, Italian and

French poets; nor did I omit History, Voyages, Travels, Natural History, Biography, &c.[32]

It is an indication of how far Lackington had moved from his Methodist past that this list includes some of the most notorious deists and freethinkers of the eighteenth century. He also now included in his reading plays and novels:

I have . . . read most of our best plays, and am so fond of the Theatre, that in the winter season I have often been at Drury-lane or Covent-garden four or five evenings in a week. Another great source of amusement as well as knowledge, I have met with in reading almost all the best novels; by the *best*, I mean those written by Cervantes, Fielding, Smollet, Richardson, Miss Burney, Voltaire, Sterne, Le Sage, Goldsmith, and others.[33]

There are few further references to specific titles which he might have read during this period of intellectual expansion. Quotations, however, help to provide a more detailed picture of the poetry and drama with which he was familiar. That 'the best poets' includes popular writers such as Pope, Cowper, Dryden, Gray, Blair, Young, Thomson, Goldsmith, Milton and Shakespeare is not surprising, and indeed there are eighteen quotations from Pope and seventeen from Dryden in the 1794 edition of *Memoirs*. He also quotes extensively from Samuel Butler's satirical poem *Hudibras* (1663–78), a famous Restoration attack on the Puritans, using it in his own attacks upon the 'enthusiastic' Methodist groups he had belonged to as a young man. Quotations are also drawn from works which are perhaps less well known today, such as James Grainger's *The Sugar Cane: a Poem,* published by Dodsley in 1764; *Seldeniana: or the Table Talk of John Selden*, published in 1789; and fellow bookseller, publisher, and auto-didact Robert Dodsley's *Art of Preaching*, first published in 1739.[34] Among the other poets represented were James Beattie, John Bidlake, Ralph Broome, Charles Churchill, Abraham Cowley, Sneyd Davis, Matthew Green, Soame Jenyns, Samuel Rogers, James Smith and William Somerville. Poet and philosopher James Beattie's *The Minstrel* (1771) was particularly popular at the end of the eighteenth century, as was Samuel Rogers's *The Pleasures of Memory* (1792).[35] This list also includes well known humorists such as John Wolcot (1738–1819), better known as Peter Pindar, from whom Lackington drew numerous quotations; author and politician Soame Jenyns (1704–87); and James Smith (1775–1839).[36] Christopher Anstey's much reprinted *New Bath Guide* (1766) presents a satiric view of fashionable life in verse through the letters of his protagonist Simkin.[37] Anstey spawned numerous imitators including Ralph Broome whose highly topical *Letters from Simpkin the Second to his Dear Brother in Wales; Containing an Humble Description of the Trial of Warren Hastings Esq.* gives an account of the trial of Warren Hastings. This poem went through eleven editions between 1788 and 1796 and Lackington clearly enjoyed it since he included nine quotations from it in the later editions of *Memoirs*.[38]

The quotations in his *Memoirs* sometimes provide evidence of the editions and translations which Lackington must have read. He used quotations from Thomas Cooke's *The Works of Hesiod*; Philip Francis's translations of the works of Horace; Thomas Francklin's translations of the tragedies of Sophocles; Grainger's Tibullus; Owen's Juvenal; Pope's Odyssey; and Gilbert West's *Odes of Pindar*. We know, too, that he read Thomas Creech's translation of Lucretius' *De Rerum Natura* (first published in 1682), as can be seen by his reference to 'CREECH's Lucretius' on page 283 of the 1794 *Memoirs*. What is not clear, however, is whether further references to Lucretius are taken directly from Creech. The lines quoted on page 287 of the 1794 edition of *Memoirs* – 'Such impious use was of religion made, / Such dev'lish acts religion could persuade' – appear not to have been taken from Creech, but are to be found in identical poetic and typographical form in Montaigne's essay, 'An Apology for Raimond de Sebonde', on page 260 of the second volume of *The Essays of Michael Seigneur de Montaigne* (London: S. and E. Ballard and others, 1759). This volume is also the likely source of a quotation from Horace's Ode XVII which can be found on page 126, where, again, the wording is almost the same as that found in the 1794 edition of *Memoirs* on page 36. Volume I likewise provides the source for lines from Terence, 'Things to the owners minds, their merit square, / Good if well used; if ill, they evils are'.[39]

This example raises an interesting question as to the source of other quotations, and the extent to which Lackington may have drawn upon reference books such as Thomas Hayward's *The British Muse or a Collection of Thoughts Moral Natural and Sublime of our English Poets who flourished in the Sixteenth and Seventeenth Centuries* (London: F. Cogan and J. Nourse, 1738); Edward Bysshe's *Art of*

English Poetry (London: R. Knaplock, E. Castle, B. Tooke, 1702); a work of unknown authorship, the *Thesaurus Dramaticus* (London: Thomas Butler, 1724) which was republished as *The Beauties of the English Stage* in 1737 and as *The Beauties of the English Drama* in 1777; and a work, also of unknown authorship, entitled *A Poetical Dictionary* (London: J. Newbery and others, 1761). These works resemble modern dictionaries of quotations. Each arranged 'beauties' from selected texts – pithy couplets and apposite phrasing – under headings arranged alphabetically, for easy reference.

Evidence of Lackington's use of these reference works can be found in oddities of phrasing, typography and word or line omissions, of which there are many examples in his *Memoirs*. One of the most convincing is a long quotation in the 1791 edition, beginning 'Set *Woman* in his eye, and in his walk', which Lackington records as being taken from 'Milton's Samson's [*sic*] Agonistes'.[40] The 1794 edition of *Memoirs* also uses the same quotation but does not state its source. In fact it comes from Milton's *Paradise Regained*, Book II, line 153. A slightly extended version of this passage is included in *A Poetical Dictionary* (London: J. Newbery and others, 1761), volume IV, p. 249, under the heading 'Woman', followed by the accreditation 'Milton's Samp. Agonistes'. *The Beauties of English Drama* (London: G. Robinson, 1777) similarly misattributes the same lines to 'MILTON's Sampson Agonistes' (Vol. IV, p. 210). Given that he follows them in the misattribution, it seems certain that Lackington drew upon one or other of these works of reference, and not on an edition of Milton, when copying out the quotation.

Phase three: 'divine subjects'[41]

The final phase of Lackington's reading life is chronicled in his *Confessions*. He explains in his preface that he is now seeking to undo the harm caused by some of the scurrilous stories ridiculing Methodists that he had included in his earlier *Memoirs* and to bring others back to religion: 'Several of my friends have thought that, if the following Letters were made public they might prove useful as a warning to others not to fall into those errors which had nearly proved fatal to me.'[42] This final volume of autobiography recants many of the ideas the author had embraced with such enthusiasm in his *Memoirs*, but reading is as important in recapturing his religious faith as it had been in his earlier lapse into freethinking, and in his social and intellectual advancement more generally.

The book was written in Lackington's retirement and it reflects his retreat into conservatism following reports of the horrors of the French revolution and a perceived threat to English security. The advantages which he had accrued from his own education now seemed menacing to him when he saw 'Paine's Age of Reason' being passed from cottage to cottage.[43] Voltaire, whom he had quoted so freely, now became for him 'that arch infidel', Rousseau was an 'inconsistent infidel', and freethinking was no longer a cause for intellectual excitement but something that would lead to social unrest.[44] His aim now is to promote religion shorn of fanaticism, and he tries to ameliorate the effect of his earlier works on readers by suggesting that his target had been 'enthusiastic' elements within the Methodist movement, not Methodism as such.[45]

Lackington's arguments might have been somewhat slippery but his return to Methodism appears heartfelt and urgent. He describes how he changed his reading habits as he began to contemplate the state of his soul:

> We had, some time before this, given up novels, romances, and books of a trifling nature. Now we even neglected history, voyages and travels, &c. not that we thought it wrong to read them, but because we found more pleasure and satisfaction while engaged with those that treated of divine truths and religious duties.[46]

He duly sent orders for books to his old firm, now named Lackington and Allen, for what would constitute an intensive course of sermons, tracts and treatises to read with his third wife, Mary:

> I sent to my late partners for Secker's Lectures on the Catechism, Gilpin's Lectures on the same, Wilson's Sermons, 4 vols. and Gilpin's Sermons . . . I also sent for Bishop Watson's Apology for the Bible, in Letters to T. Paine; Bishop Porteus's Compendium of the Evidences of Christianity, Butler's Divine Analogy, Paley's Evidences of Christianity, Pilgrim's Good Intent, Pascal's Thoughts, Addison's Evidences of Christianity, Conibeare on Revealed Religion, Madam de Genlis's Religion the only Basis of Happiness and sound Philosophy, with Observations on pretended modern

Philosophers, 2 vols. Jenkin's Reasonableness and Certainty of Christianity, and several others of the same tendency . . . I sent for Bishop Horne's Sermons, 4 vols. Carr's Sermons, Blair's Sermons, 5 vols. Scott's Christian Life, 5 vols. several learned and sensible expositions of the Bible; Calmet's Dictionary of the Bible, with the Fragments; Josephus's Works, Prideaux's Connections, 4 vols. Mrs. H. More's Works, and various other excellent Works.[47]

Many of the quotations which fill *Confessions* are drawn from this reading list. They include passages from Addison's *The Evidences of the Christian Religion* (1730), Joseph Butler's *The Analogy of Religion* (1736), Robert Jenkin's *The Reasonableness and Certainty of the Christian Religion* (1698), George Horne's *Discourses on Several Subjects and Occasions* (1779), and many extracts from Wesley's hymns. Whilst Lackington revisited some seventeenth-century writers such as Jenkin, he also included a large number from the eighteenth century. This is the reading list of man who knew his subject and selected material with deliberation and care.

In view of the subject of the book, it is perhaps not surprising that many of the works quoted are sermons and hymns, but Lackington also turned to the poetry of Robert Blair, Dryden, Pope, Shakespeare and Pomfret, and to works such as Richard Cumberland's *Calvary: or, The Death of Christ* (first published in 1792). More than any other work, however, it is Edward Young's *Night Thoughts*, a lengthy didactic poem published in 1742–45 which seems to have fed his imagination, and to which he refers most often. He had described in *Memoirs* how he had used savings intended for a Christmas dinner to buy this book, reasoning that the nourishment he would gain from it would last much longer than food.[48] There are approximately nine quotations from *Night Thoughts* in the longer editions of *Memoirs* but around thirty in *Confessions*. Lackington credits the poem with preventing him from 'settling in unbelief' and it recurs with totemic echoes throughout the work.[49]

By comparison with his use of them in his *Memoirs*, Lackington's quotations fulfil a more urgent role in *Confessions*, as the import of his subject weighed on him. He had begun to preach and to build Methodist chapels, and he used his religious reading to instruct as well as to embellish. There is a marked didacticism in *Confessions* as he urges readers to refer to works by Butler or Jenkin. He gives specific volume and page references to direct the reader to the passages he recommends. There are considerably more quotations in prose than in *Memoirs*, and Lackington now analysed the texts of the authors who inspired him, rather than simply offering them as decorative trimmings to his own text. He reinforced this proselytizing in print by sending to Lackington and Allen for cheap books to distribute to the local poor. These included large numbers of tracts, together with famous books such as Richard Allestree's *The Whole Duty of Man* (1658) and Richard Baxter's *A Call to the Unconverted* (1658), but he also included *Robinson Crusoe*, evidently believing that this too might provide religious instruction as well as entertainment.

Conclusion

Lackington clearly drew intellectual and spiritual nourishment from what he read. Indeed, his *Memoirs* reveal how reading changed his life and led eventually to the acquisition of riches and social status. His frequent use of quotations is a striking feature of his writing, not only because it provides information about his reading, but also because it suggests that his early belief in the power of the written word to confer authority and convey 'truth' remained with him throughout his life. His use of reference books to source quotations shows how he sought to enhance his own thoughts, actions and opinions with well-chosen lines. His account of his reading throughout his life is clearly intended to persuade, but this very partiality – illustrated in his advocacy of freethinking and the rewards of reading *John Buncle* in *Memoirs* as much as in his urgent call to follow a path of Christian reading in *Confessions* – reveals it to be central to Lackington's personal development. It was the foundation upon which he built his business and sought salvation for his soul.

Notes and references

1. James Lackington, *Memoirs of the First Forty-Five Years of the Life of James Lackington* (London: Lackington, [1791]). Lackington added considerably to this first edition in further editions of his *Memoirs*. Further references will be to the first edition or to the longest of the subsequent editions, that of 1794, and the date will be specified.
2. On Lackington's career as bookseller, see James Raven, 'Selling one's life: James Lackington, eighteenth-century booksellers and the design of

autobiography', in *Writers, Books and Trade: An Eighteenth-Century English Miscellany*, ed. O. M. Brack, Jr. (New York: AMS Press, 1994), pp. 1–23, and idem, *The Business of Books: Booksellers and the English Book Trade* (New Haven: Yale University Press, 2007).

3. James Lackington, *The Confessions of J. Lackington* (London: Richard Edwards for the author, 1804). Further references will be to this edition.
4. National Archive, prob 11/1578.
5. Lackington, *Memoirs* (1794), p. 216.
6. Ibid., p. 217.
7. E. Marston, *Sketches of Booksellers of Other Days* (London: Sampson Low, 1901), p. 156.
8. Isaac Disraeli, *Vaurien: or Sketches of the Times*, Vol. VI (London: Cadell, Davies, Murray, Highley, 1797), p. 143.
9. Lackington, *Memoirs* (1794), p. 84.
10. Ibid. (1791), p. 91.
11. Ibid. (1794), p. 76.
12. Margaret Willes, *Reading Matters: Five Centuries of Discovering Books* (New Haven: Yale University Press, 2008), p. 196.
13. Lackington, *Memoirs* (1791), p. 76.
14. Ibid., p. 338.
15. Ibid., p. 83.
16. Ibid., p. 85.
17. Ibid. The volumes in question may have been *The Travels of Ulysses* (London: Crook, 1673), *Homer's Odyssey* (London: Crook, 1675), *Homer's Iliads in English* (London: Crook, 1676), or one of the two editions of *The Iliads and Odysses of Homer Translated out of Greek into English by Tho. Hobbes of Malmesbury*, printed in 1677 and in 1686.
18. Lackington, *Memoirs* (1791), p. 86.
19. Ibid., p. 94.
20. Ibid., pp. 91–3. Spelling discrepancies such as 'Pamble' for 'Pemble' and apparent errors such as 'Baxter's Shove for a *heavy-arsed* Christian' mean that some works in this list are difficult to trace. *An Effectual Shove to the Heavy-Arse Christian* (London: J. Roson, 1768) was in fact written by William Bunyan, not Baxter as here.
21. C. John Sommerville, *Popular Religion in Restoration England* (Gainesville: University of Florida Monographs, 1977), p. 24.
22. Richard Baxter, *A Call to the Unconverted* (London: Booksellers of London and Westminster, 1704), preface.
23. N. H. Keeble, *The Literary Culture of Nonconformity in Lateer Seventeenth-Century England* (Leicester: Leicester University Press, 1987), p. 83.
24. Lackington, *Memoirs* (1791), p. 97.
25. Ibid., p. 134.
26. Ibid., p. 137.
27. Ibid., p. 165.
28. Ibid., p. 162.
29. William Hazlitt, 'The Round Table: No. 20. Sunday September 17, 1815', *The Examiner*, 17 September, 1815; Lackington, *Memoirs* (1791), p. 166.

30. Lackington, *Confessions* (1804), p. 4. Further references are to this edition.
31. Lackington, *Memoirs* (1791), p. 167.
32. Ibid., p. 237.
33. Ibid., p. 239.
34. Ibid., *Memoirs* (1794), pp. 504, 360, 446, 73, 74.
35. Ibid., pp. 105, 199, 475 for examples of quotations from *The Minstrel*, and pp. 398, 410, 500, 512 for quotations from *The Pleasures of Memory*.
36. Ibid., pp. 85, 158, 237, 254, 262, 267, 278, 302, 317 for examples of quotations by Peter Pindar; pp. 85, 89, 408 for quotations from Soame Jenyns; and pp. 132, 249 for quotations from James Smith.
37. Ibid., pp. 236, 243 for quotations from *New Bath Guide*.
38. Ibid., pp. 75, 78, 180, 227, 228, 245, 264, 277, 306.
39. Ibid., p. 431.
40. Ibid. (1791), p. 309.
41. Lackington, *Confessions*, p. 166.
42. Ibid., p. v.
43. Ibid., p. 78.
44. Ibid., pp. 82, 138.
45. Ibid., p. 138.
46. Ibid., p. 166.
47. Ibid., p. 52.
48. Lackington, *Memoirs* (1791), pp. 134–6.
49. Lackington, *Confessions*, p. 125.

10
Henry Head (1861–1940) as a Reader of Literature

Stephen Jacyna

This chapter deals with the reading habits of the neurologist Henry Head (1861–1940).[1] Head was born into a prosperous Quaker family and spent his early years living in a variety of houses in north London. His relatives included the surgeon, Joseph Lister and the author Edward Verrall Lucas.

In an autobiographical fragment written in 1926, Head recalled his early encounters with imaginative literature. Henry was the eldest of the Head children and often found the bustle of the household vexatious. He remembered 'creeping under the sofa to read the Arabian Nights in order to escape the annoyances of the riotous younger children'.[2] These distractions notwithstanding, Head was brought up in a household that encouraged literary interests. 'At home', he recalled, 'I had been accustomed to become daily acquainted with fine literature, for my Mother would read aloud to us by the hour both poetry and prose, thus awakening in me a real enthusiasm for the world of letters.'[3] Hester Head may also have instilled in her son an enjoyment for communal reading that he was to carry into adulthood.

When at the age of thirteen Henry was sent to continue his formal education at Charterhouse, he moved from this cultured environment to one characterized by philistinism, chronic disorder and casual brutality. Head developed a precocious interest in natural science – a subject in which he excelled. He also took an active part in school athletics. But he still found time for reading fiction. In one letter, after recounting the beatings being handed out to some of his fellow pupils, he told his mother that 'Jules Verne's books are very interesting[.] I have read "Journey into the interior of the Earth"[.] I am reading the other.'[4]

Figure 10.1   Henry Head (photograph by Theodore C. Marceau, 1859–1922, New York)

Walter Scott's novels were another favourite. Henry reported that he had 'finished the Talisman in bed whilst stopping out this morning there'. So voracious was his appetite for reading that it outstripped the available supply. Because there were 'so few books I can . . . read in the library . . . I read the same one over again'.[5] He was thus obliged to beg his mother to lend him some of her books. Despite the evident satisfaction the teenage Head took from this reading, he was oddly reluctant to see the practice become disseminated among the masses. Unlike the majority of cultural commentators of his period, he felt that it was a 'waste of time teaching the Board School children English Literature'.[6] This was perhaps an early intimation of the cultural elitism that was a marked feature of the adult Head.

After Charterhouse, Head was to proceed to read Natural Sciences at Trinity College, Cambridge. But first he embarked on an excursion to the European continent that he was to describe in his autobiography as 'one of the most important events in my life'.[7] In view of his interest in pursuing a medical and scientific career, he was advised that it would be advantageous to spend some time in Germany, and in particular at 'one of the smaller and less known universities, pointing out the advantage of associating with Germans only'.[8] In April 1880, he therefore set off for the University of Halle.

The ostensible purpose for Head's trip was for him to pursue courses in the medical school while undertaking intensive training in the German language. The relatively obscure University of Halle had been chosen largely on the grounds that it offered the advantage of 'associating with Germans only and avoiding the temptation of meeting my fellow-countrymen, which would occur at Berlin or Heidelberg'.[9] Head's time in Halle was, however, to spark in him an enthusiasm for all aspects of German culture that was to last until 1914. In particular, during this sojourn, the young Head fell in love with German literature.

This was in part the result of the accident that he was lodged with the Niemeyer family. Herr Niemeyer was 'the University Bookseller and a man of wide culture'.[10] Head thus found himself living above a bookshop. His hosts, moreover, were happy to guide him through his early exploration of German letters. Head soon found himself reading fairy stories to the Niemeyer children. He still read English works – on 22 April 1880 he recorded that 'I bought an Aurora Leigh from Mr Niemeyer & am now beginning at the beginning again'[11] – but soon he also ventured to essay works in his new tongue. A former master at Charterhouse assisted by sending Head a book of German verse, and he told his mother that 'I now translate, some Goethe to Mrs Niemeyer at her suggestion and learn the pieces – two a week'.[12]

Social meetings with fellow students also allowed Head to engage in acts of communal reading. While taking coffee with a visiting American student named Bahnson, the students

> began to read a few sentences of a play by Schiller called 'Turandot'. It is a sort of extravaganza but I cannot find out when it was written. We set about taking parts and as it was easy I could

understand all of it nearly; what I could not Bahnson translated. We read 20 pages at coffee – on Monday. So also at coffee yesterday 60 and today we had only ten more. We are now going to read Faust in the same way though of course at nothing like the pace.

Head boasted to his mother, 'My reading also has wonderfully improved', and confided to her that 'We hope to get through Faust before Bahnson leaves.'[13]

This immersion in Continental literature, on Head's own account, effected an irreversible transformation in his nature. On returning to England he commenced his Cambridge career 'steeped in "Peer Gynt" and similar poems'. This conversion did not, however, impress the 'cold quiet dons' who were obliged to read essays 'filled with execrable Teutonisms', and who 'thought I was mad'.[14]

While at Cambridge, Head was tempted to devote himself to a career in laboratory science. Ultimately, however, he resolved to pursue his original design of a career in clinical medicine. As well as working as a physician at the London Hospital in Whitechapel, he maintained a private practice in Harley Street. He was to develop a special interest in diseases of the nervous system. Head nonetheless continued to consider himself as a physiologist who used the neurological cases that he encountered as material from which to draw inferences about the workings of the nervous system. His special areas of interest were in the physiology of sensation and in the cerebral mechanisms underlying language.[15]

He found time amid his hectic professional activities to pursue his literary and other artistic interests. He kept company with poets as well as with men of science. Head moreover wrote verse of his own, some of which was eventually published.[16] His appetite for fiction remained voracious; according to Ruth Mayhew, 'your book bill exceeded even your shirt-bill and Heaven knew how long that was'.[17] Mayhew was a long-time friend who shared many of Head's literary interests. She was herself to write two novels. After a lengthy courtship Mayhew and Head married in 1904. The two exchanged letters at least once a week during the early years of the relationship. Before their marriage, the two also had regular meetings, usually at weekends. Often these revolved around the communal reading of works that Mayhew and Head found especially alluring or fascinating.

Their correspondence was full of lively discussion about their current reading. Thus in November 1898, Mayhew wrote to tell Head:

> I have been profoundly interested by [Paul] Bourget's new novel 'La Duchesse Bleue'. It is, in parts, too nasty for me to lend you, I think, but the preface is masterly and the whole idea is one which, I know, will interest you. It is working out a theory which I fancy I have heard you maintain, that a man may, and will, produce work which does not represent his own life or feelings or ideals in the least; and that the work may be very excellent apart from the man's life.[18]

Bourget's use of current psychological theories – particularly those dealing with the possibility of 'dual personality' within the same individual – piqued Head's interest. He declared that:

> It is not necessary to call in that idea of dual personality. For if a man has a dual personality he experiences that which he describes in one or other and the problem is only shoved one step further back. I have always felt (and in my humble way have always experienced) that an artist can lead an entirely imaginary life.

Head spoke from personal experience: 'Since I was a boy I have always known characters that I have never met – It is true that they were founded and shaped on persons I had known – But once formed they acted coherently and moved in paths different from anything I had ever experienced.'[19]

At a later date Head and Mayhew sought another literary form for such exchange of views. They started to keep a set of 'Rag Books' into which they copied extracts from favourite works along with critical comments and remarks upon the personal significance of these writings. As with the observations on Bourget, the end was as much to gain insight into their own personalities as to analyse the works under discussion. According to his friend and former patient, the poet and playwright Robert Nichols, Head had planned eventually to publish the Rag Books in order to make available to a wider readership 'a book that should resemble a patch quilt in being composed of a multitude of notes on the arts & on human character'.[20]

Reading fiction was for Head no mere recreational activity. He engaged intellectually and emotionally with the works of the authors he most esteemed. Moreover, he drew no sharp distinction between these literary interests and his clinical and scientific concerns. On the contrary, he maintained that the kind of psychological insights and analytic skills that were of use to him in the consulting room could also be applied in reading works of fiction. Indeed, these skills might even be honed to a higher degree of perfection through reading authors who were themselves accomplished 'psychologists'.

Reading could exert a mysterious effect upon Head's mental states, he believed. Whereas 'when the old practitioners of magic wished to raise a spirit they drew pentagons and other sedate patterns upon the ground [and] placing themselves within this unromantic enclosure were at once surrounded by supernatural sounds sights and scents', he had only to open a favourite volume to be similarly transported. Surely, he told Mayhew, 'one of the secrets of books is only known to those who use them as the materials for such white magic'.[21]

Head was especially alert to the emotional effects that certain works could invoke. These results could be extreme. He recalled that the first time he had read Ibsen's *The Wild Duck* 'was on a summer evening in a little Beergarden where I frequently supped in Prag'. He had gone out about 7.00 p.m. with the newly translated play in his pocket to peruse it over his customary Vienna schnitzel and glass of beer:

> When I rose to go home I thought I was drunk. But the two round mats told me that I had only drunk two glasses of beer in more than three hours. Moreover when I rose next morning I was still drunk. The daily world around me seemed unreal. I felt as if I had gone through some colossal personal experience of which the memory could only end with death.[22]

Head had 'experienced this condition more than once and twice' when reading other books.

Literature could also serve to salve a troubled psyche. In 1903 Head wrote of a distressing incident that had occurred during his work at the London Hospital. 'A letter of complaint to the Hospital had made me very angry and I wrote a too vehement reply which

upset all the Sentimentalists and brought me into unpleasant collision with the powers.' The parties involved were 'mixed up in a coil
from which there seemed no way out except by the humiliation of
somebody'. During 'this extremely unpleasant period' Head found
that he had 'received the greatest comfort from Hotspur's apology'.
He wrote out an extended quotation from *Henry IV, Part 1*, Act One,
Scene 3, to illustrate his point, adding that 'Such comfort comes to
me frequently from the expression of my thoughts or feelings in
some character or in great & beautiful words.'[23]

Head invested the large library of books he had accumulated with
great sentimental value; indeed, like so many readers, he personified
these possessions as friends. He wrote in August 1899 of how he was
trying to 'get my books onto my new shelves'. This endeavour was,
however, continually thwarted: 'I start with much energy and then
some old friend, some forgotten marker or scarcely remembered note
catch my eye and all progress ceases.'[24]

Head's taste in writers of fiction was catholic. He was sufficiently fascinated by the work of William Makepeace Thackeray,
for example, to spend part of a holiday in September 1903 cycling
around Cambridgeshire in an attempt to discover 'the scene of
the early chapters of Pendennis'. He concluded that 'Peterboro
which Thackeray probably knew well would do excellently for the
Cathedral town, the name for which might have been taken from
a small neighbouring town.'[25] There were, however, certain authors
with whom he found he could not engage. He informed Mayhew
that 'I am afraid I suffer from certain limitations that prevent my
enjoying the novels of Disraeli.' Head found it impossible to con-
nect with 'a series of characters who all assume that it costs more
than 5000 a year to live comfortably. Don't laugh at me for my
limitations.'[26]

His bias was, however, towards novelists who sought to describe
and explicate the mental processes of their characters. He was
thus drawn to writers who were also accomplished 'psychological'
observers. The accuracy or otherwise of such observations became
a criterion by which to judge the value of a novel. Thus in the Rag
Book that he kept with Mayhew, Head noted that '"The house on
the Sands" by Charles Marriott is a failure. But some of the characteristics of the two women are well observed.' For example, Marriott
succeeded in accurately depicting what went through the mind of

one of his female characters when she received a letter announcing the imminent arrival of her lover.[27]

Sometimes even a mediocre novelist would betray psychological truths inadvertently. This was true of Elizabeth von Arnim's novels. Head considered *The Solitary Summer* a better book than *Elizabeth and her German Garden* because 'as long as she is gossiping about her garden and telling stories about her children and the man of wrath, she is charming; but as soon as she describes her commerce with another woman she at once sinks to a lower level'. This trait drew attention to the 'curious paradox that a woman may look upon her husband and her children with sufficient objectivity to talk of them wittily and well but is incapable of looking at another woman without emotion destroying the clearness of her vision'. Head had observed the same phenomenon in the women of his own acquaintance. Ruth Mayhew's 'description of [her] talks with my mother exactly bear out the same idea. She can be clear and original in her observation but when she talks to or of you and Hester her conversation at once drops to that of any other woman.'[28]

A great psychological novelist could, however, capture aspects of the human mind better than any other. Such a writer could create a representative character – a 'complete figure' – that could 'reveal our state better than any individual outpourings'. The Rag Books were in large part to be composed of extracts from works of fiction chosen by Head and Mayhew that exemplified such 'complete figures'. This exercise would, Head maintained, provide him and Mayhew with insights into their own characters. Indeed, 'the Rag Book becomes a double diary without the crudity of attempt at mutual analysis'.[29]

Head regarded Joseph Conrad as a master in the exploration of character and motivation. According to Robert Nichols, at their initial clinical encounter, Head's first question was to ask 'me if I liked Conrad'.[30] Nichols had been invalided from the army in 1915 suffering from shell shock. Head was for a time his physician and the two were to become lifelong friends. After Head's death, Nichols tried to recreate one of the conversations the patient and doctor had conducted on the subject of Conrad's writings. The discussion had evidently focused upon the question of: 'why in Conrad's <u>Lord Jim</u>, did Jim leave the bridge of the refugee ship <u>Patna</u> in that disgraceful fashion?' Head tried to steer Nichols towards the conclusion that Conrad had provided the reader with 'a perfectly sound & particularly psychological reason' for Jim's decision, even 'tho' never, as I remember, openly declared'. The reason was thus left implicit, Head suggested, 'Because Jim would be ashamed to declare it. Yet it exists & can be inferred.' Head eventually revealed that the 'reason' that finally overcame Jim's reluctance to join 'the disgraceful & all too busy group' that was preparing to abandon ship was the death of one of their number from a heart attack. This created a sudden vacancy in the lifeboat: 'This is the last straw–& Lord Jim jumps.'[31]

Gustave Flaubert was another writer to whom Head ascribed this kind of quasi-clinical insight.[32] In particular, *Madame Bovary* was a novel for which he felt a special fascination. 'Emma Bovary', he declared, 'is the portrait of an egoistic hedonist painted by a supreme constructive artist.'[33] In the Rag Book, Head observed that 'When I think of "Madame Bovary" I have an impression that the book is of immense length. I see upon my table the small volume in its worn boards and wonder that so small a compass can contain so much that I have learnt from life.' He was lost in admiration for Flaubert's skill as a writer, noting that 'No metaphor in this book fails to add to the vividness of the picture.' Head carefully copied into the Rag Book several examples from the novel illustrating this gift. But what most impressed Head was the expertise with which Flaubert knew how to employ his literary technology to achieve striking psychological effects and insights.

Head shared his admiration for Flaubert with Mayhew; they read *Madame Bovary* together on at least two occasions. Mayhew was also an avid reader of Flaubert's correspondence. But her special passion was for the work of Henry James. Head remarked that 'As Flaubert to H. so HJ to R'.[34] Although he had read some of James's work before he met Mayhew, it was she who persuaded Head to become more fully acquainted with the work of this author. As he wrote in October 1903, 'Your account of the "Ambassadors" makes me itch to read it. But for you I should never have read any H. James more recent than the Daisy Miller set. What a number we have now read together.'[35] (Head met James on at least two occasions – on the second of which in a professional capacity after James had suffered a stroke.)

Head's emotional response to some of James's stories was extreme. When Mayhew lent him her copy of *The Aspern Papers*, Head claimed that 'You had I suspect little conception of how it would affect me.'

On reading James's account of the narrator's doomed attempt to gain access to the dead poet's letters, Head

> almost cried and felt as if I had suffered an analogous loss. For Henry James has described with consummate accuracy what all investigators feel when a research is baulked – I have been made miserable for days by the loss of an opportunity of versifying or placing the coping stone on a series of observations and I was made equally miserable by living through this loss of opportunity even though fictitious.[36]

The impact of the story thus derived from James's success in representing the psychology of the archetypal 'investigator', a category central to Head's understanding of his own self.

In his sixties Head developed Parkinson's Disease. This infirmity obliged him to retire from practice and to abandon his scientific researches. He and Ruth left London to live in the country, residing first in Forston in Dorset – a location chosen in part so that the Heads could be near Max Gate, Thomas Hardy's home. After Hardy's death, the Heads moved to Reading so as to be nearer their other friends. Because of Head's increasing frailty, in retirement he and Ruth were obliged to live the life of virtual recluses. Reading was one of the few occupations still open to the invalid Head. However this became increasingly physically taxing. He became too feeble even to hold a book. A lectern had to be set up in front of him and a servant assigned the task of turning the pages. Eventually however this also proved too tiring and Head was obliged to rely on others – and above all, Ruth – to read to him. During his enforced retirement, Head had developed a taste for 'modern' novels. The works of Virginia Woolf gave him particular pleasure. Ruth confided to Siegfried Sassoon that 'We too think The Lighthouse more perfect than Mrs Dalloway and are so glad to have our opinion reinforced by Lytton Strachey. It is the most wonderful book and we talked of little else all the time I was reading aloud.'[37]

Despite the growing physical impediments to reading, Head persisted because books provided one of the few sources of stimulation still available to him. Indeed, reading seemed to serve a therapeutic function warding off the depressions to which he became increasingly prone. Some of his author friends sought to contribute to this therapy by forwarding drafts of their works for Henry and Ruth to peruse and comment upon. For instance, Siegfried Sassoon sent the manuscript of the various volumes of his fictionalized *Memoirs* for the Heads' scrutiny.

In April 1929, Ruth gave Sassoon an account of one such session:

> a man of great discretion was staying with us and we gave him the honour of reading it to us, a fact for which I had cause to be thankful as I could not have done it: it was too poignant and a choking voice tho' a tribute to your powers, would have annoyed H.H. who was listening with the open-eyed attention of a two-year old child joined to the critical mind of a Professor hearing a thesis from a candidate for the membership of the Royal Society.

Head had only minor criticisms to make of Sassoon's text. But he did question Sassoon's use of the word 'visualize' in various parts of the book.[38] He was however much taken by one of Sassoon's characters. Ruth told Sassoon that:

> He chuckles every time he thinks of 'Whincop' – 'General Sir Archibald Whincop K.C.B.' he repeats, having spent his waking moments for several nights thinking out a suitable Christian name. We both like Archibald, for his wife who is a nagging woman says 'Archie' in a voice that makes the General tremble.[39]

'Whincop' was a thinly disguised version of General Reginald Pinney who had been Sassoon's divisional commander in France. Pinney had married Head's sister Harriet – a match that her brother heartily detested.

Head demonstrated a kind of blindness when it came to distinguishing between fiction and non-fiction. In particular, he saw the prime interest of the novel to lie in the insightful depiction of personality. To achieve these effects the best novelist had to be a 'psychologist': that is, had to be equipped with the same skills that a clinician might need in diagnosing and treating patients. The demonstration of such skills became a critical criterion by which to judge the value of a piece of fictional writing. Good fiction thus gave direct access to *truth* in the same way as sound science.

The association between fiction and psychological medicine is further strengthened by the therapeutic role that Head assigned to literature. This is evinced in his use of Conrad's *Lord Jim* in his treatment of the shell-shocked Robert Nichols. The fact that the novel dealt with the issues of the conflict between a sense of duty and the instinct for self-preservation made it a particularly fitting choice when dealing with an officer who had left the front physically intact but psychologically damaged. During his long twilight as an invalid, books played a therapeutic, or at least a palliative, role in Head's own life.

Literature moreover played a central role in the processes of self-formation in which Head, in conjunction with Ruth Mayhew, engaged. In particular the 'Rag Books' that they compiled and annotated over a period of several years were supposed to be as much revelatory of their own personalities as of the characteristics of the various works of fiction that were excerpted in these volumes.

Unusually rich materials exist to document the place that reading played in the life of Henry Head. A study of this material provides a number of insights into the relations of scientific and literary culture at the turn of the twentieth century. In particular, Head's case shows how complex the interactions between these 'Two Cultures' was.

Head's insistence that the value of some works of fiction lay in their capacity to reveal objective psychological truths might be seen to signal a positivist affirmation of the primacy of scientific discourse. But at the same time Head insisted that aspects of the fictional form – and of the novel in particular – were better adapted to penetrating certain aspects of the human psyche than could scientific enquiry. Moreover, the personality was no stable entity waiting to be discovered, whether by scientific or literary technologies. Certain exceptional works could effect a dramatic transformation in the self – an experience that verged on the mystical.

Despite his fervent devotion to the ethic of natural science, Head's attitude to modernity was ambivalent. He found the urban environment in which he was obliged to spend most of his time deeply alienating and sought to escape to more idyllic settings whenever he could. Books provided a further means of escape from the vulgarity and ugliness of his mundane life. An ability to appreciate their true existential value moreover provided a criterion for distinguishing between persons. A just appreciation of the life-enhancing potential of literary works was the mark of a truly refined kindred spirit. The most important relationship of Head's life – that with Ruth Mayhew – was thus one founded upon and shaped by a shared appreciation of the joys and insights that the practices of reading could yield.

Notes and references

1. For an account of Head's life, see L. S. Jacyna, *Medicine and Modernism: A Biography of Sir Henry Head* (London: Chatto & Pickering, 2008).
2. Henry Head, 'Autobiography', Head Papers, Wellcome Trust Library for the History of Medicine, CMAC, PP/HEA, A1, p. 3.
3. Ibid., p. 15.
4. Henry Head to his mother, undated, PP/HEA/D1–D2/2.
5. Henry Head to his mother (undated), ibid.
6. Henry Head to his mother, 17 November 1878, ibid. For a discussion of prevailing attitudes towards reading in the Board Schools, see Anna Vaninskaya's commentary in Chapter 4 of this volume.
7. Head, 'Autobiography', p. 18.
8. Ibid.
9. Ibid.
10. Ibid., p. 19.
11. 'Halle Journal', Head Papers, CMAC, PP/HEA, Box 3, 21–2 August 1880.
12. Henry Head to Hester Head [31 May 1880], PP/HEA BOX 3.
13. Henry Head to Hester Head, 1 August 1880, ibid.
14. Henry Head to Ruth Mayhew, 21 July 1899, PP/HEA/ D4/5.
15. Henry Head, *Studies in Neurology* (London: Henry Frowde, 1920); idem, *Aphasia and Kindred Disorders* (Cambridge: Cambridge University Press, 1926).
16. Henry Head, *Destroyers and Other Verses* (London: Humphrey Milford, Oxford University Press, 1919).
17. Ruth Mayhew to Henry Head, 20 July 1899, CMAC/PP/HEA/D4/5.
18. Ruth Mayhew to Henry Head, 17 November 1898, CMAC/PP/HEA/ D4/3.
19. Henry Head to Ruth Mayhew, 20 November 1898, CMAC/PP/HEA/D4/3.
20. 'Notes on Henry Head', Robert Nichols Papers, British Library, uncatalogued.
21. Henry Head to Ruth Mayhew, 5 August 1899, CMAC/PP/HEA/D4/5.
22. Rag Book, vol. iii A. CMAC/PP/HEA/E3/5, p. 28.
23. Rag Book vol. ii B. PP HEA E3/41, pp. 35–6.
24. Henry Head to Ruth Mayhew, 18 August 1899, CMAC/PP/HEA/D4/5.
25. Rag Book, vol. iii A. CMAC/PP/HEA/E3/5, p. 28.
26. Henry Head to Ruth Mayhew, 6 March 1901, CMAC/PP/HEA/D4/13.
27. Rag Book, vol. lii A. CMAC/PP/HEA/E3/5, p. 1.
28. Henry Head to Ruth Mayhew, 21 July 1899, CMAC/PP/HEA/D4/5.
29. Henry Head to Ruth Mayhew, 9 January 1902, CMAC/PP/HEA/D4/13.
30. Robert Nichols to Henry Head, 26 June 1925, Nichols Papers, British Library, uncatalogued.

31. Robert Nichols, 'Notes on Henry Head'.
32. See Lawrence Rothfield, *Vital Signs: Medical Realism in Nineteenth-Century Fiction* (Princeton: Princeton University Press, 1992), chapter 2.
33. Rag Book vol. ii A. CMAC/PP/HEA/E3/3, p. 13.
34. Ibid., p. 28.
35. Henry Head to Ruth Mayhew, 30 October 1903, CMAC/PP/HEA/D4/16. Head met James socially at least once: Henry Head to Ruth Mayhew, 23 February 1900, CMAC/PP/HEA/D4/6. After James suffered a stroke, Head also saw him professionally.
36. Henry Head to Ruth Mayhew, 22 February 1998, CMAC/PP/HEA, unclassified.
37. Ruth Head to Siegfried Sassoon, 24 May [1927], Sassoon Papers, Cambridge University Library, Add 9375/369.
38. Ruth Head to Siegfried Sassoon, 7 April 1929, ibid., 371.
39. Ibid.

11
In a Class of their Own: The Autodidact Impulse and Working-Class Readers in Twentieth-Century Scotland

Linda Fleming, David Finkelstein and Alistair McCleery

The twentieth century is commonly perceived as the era when the lofty pursuit of 'learning for learning's sake' began declining as an aspiration amongst British working classes. It is a perception strongly informing, for example, one of the most recent and influential studies on the subject, Jonathan Rose's *The Intellectual Life of the British Working Classes*.[1] From the perspective of histories of readership, this certainly amounts to a bleak indictment of working-class ambitions and the place of educational self-improvement in contemporary society. Such assumptions are particularly problematic in the context of Scotland, given this country's predominant working-class identity and reputation for high levels of literacy.[2] An assault on the reputation of Scots certainly raises questions about areas of national identity that inform the writing of Scottish history, and regularly surface in the popular image of the Scot at home and abroad.[3] More lately too, elaborations on what constitutes a newly robust Scottish national identity have invoked aspects of Scotland's historical traditions of intellectualism, and called attention to the supposed widespread respect for learning found at all levels of Scottish society. In the run up to the establishment of a devolved Scottish Parliament, for example, such rhetoric underpinned a political discussion that envisaged a reinvigoration of the Scottish national identity separate from, and not in thrall to, concepts of Britishness. Within the devolved institution that is the Scottish Parliament, inaugurated in 1997, this notion of fairness and equity is often referred to, as comments from the following Scottish parliamentary debate in 2008 make clear:

> One main underpinning of the Scottish education system's reputation throughout the world is the inherent honesty in our approach, which has led to the insistence that it is the abilities of the individual that matter, not their place in society. That is a prime support of the Scottish education system and I am glad that we have it. . . .
>
> [W]e in Scotland are exceptionally good – better than most other countries in the world – at 'formal equity'. . . .
>
> [A]lthough we may not have our independence as a country we at least have it for our education system.[4]

It is apparent from such publicly stated remarks that equality in educational opportunity and the maintenance of high levels of literacy, whether real or imagined in Scottish society in both the past and present, do exercise a powerful hold over the collective Scottish self-image.[5] This chapter sets such a fashioned image within a historical context also informed by recent research. We begin by examining the confused legacy of a twentieth-century Scottish working-class identity inherited from the nineteenth century. This is followed by an analysis of twentieth-century Scottish working class formations as reflected in attitudes to literacy, learning and reading, the purpose of which is to interrogate class and the relationship that developed between reading and the Scottish working classes within the timeframe of the last century. Thirdly, this discussion focuses on the separate social and educational traditions that persisted in Scotland and which it could be argued have encouraged the continued survival of reading as an act of self-improvement in twentieth-century Scotland. We will cover certain aspects of autodidactic behaviour in twentieth-century Scotland, using evidence from personal testimony in three areas: library use, newspaper and magazine reading choices, and lastly, the simple will to read and to continue to read, over other media that deliver education and leisure activity. Much of the oral evidence that will be cited comes from the reading reception project, *Scottish Readers Remember*, an initiative of the Scottish Archive of Print and Publishing History Records (SAPPHIRE).[6] This study has collected oral testimony from Scots born before 1945. The oral histories take a life course format, but have the implicit themes of reading done, and reading practices engaged in, across the course of the subjects' lifetimes – from child-hood to the present. In this type of research, social class cannot be avoided as a key influence on both personal reading tastes and behav-iours, and on the circumstances that created a social relationship with print culture.[7] We end with some reflections on how we might view the autodidactic tradition within a specifically Scottish context.

The nineteenth century

Any definition of class is always open to interpretation, more usu-ally through the prisms of varying levels of industrialization and urbanization, and from the viewpoint of the temporal relationships between social groupings and their moment in history. During the nineteenth century, Scotland became the most intensely industrial-ized and urbanized country in Europe. One of the results was the development of a keenly felt sense of class distinctions in its over-populated urban areas, and it is certainly fair to say that in the great industrial ferment of Glasgow, for example, there was not a single working class. Instead, one found a conglomerate of *working classes* wherein a hierarchy existed, with distinctions between unskilled workers and what labour historians have termed the skilled, gener-ally literate 'labour aristocracy'.[8] Working-class life varied so widely, grew so constantly and in growing so outnumbered all other classes, that it was probably inevitable that distinctions between working people would quickly come to be a part of the commerce of everyday life in Scotland. This in turn created a cultural hierarchy in terms of everyday practices in work, education and leisure.

One way of observing how class distinctions operated is through studying those who transgressed them; indeed a positive effect of such rapid social change was that upward class mobility often was more easily facilitated; but a downward economic trajectory was equally common in such a voracious capitalist age. Education and literacy were certainly implicated in supporting social movement upwards. Literacy, as the historian W. Knox notes, alongside drink and the elaborate rituals of traditional craft associations, was a key element of culture for this skilled stratum of the working class.[9] Conversely, a taste for learning could also be found in sectors where, on the face of things, unskilled workers were unlikely to achieve a higher social status. Willie Gallacher, for example, who was Scotland's only communist MP in the interwar period, was born into an Irish Catholic family in Paisley in 1881. His education ended even earlier than most at age twelve when he started work as a delivery boy. Gallacher relates that by the time he was sixteen he 'was going round the bookshops'. His favourite author was Dickens, bought in cheap editions, but from there 'it was an easy transition, a few years later, to socialist literature'.[10] Gallacher was the classic autodidact in the sense that he was a teetotaller and political thinker who saw learning as means of salvation from some of the less admirable features of proletarian life. However, it is fair to say that his political trajectory did distinguish him from the mainstream of working-class socialist allegiance in Scotland. He is untypical too in that his high profile political career prompted him to leave a written record of his life.

The working-class autodidact, nurtured by Scottish traditions in education and self-improvement, was often seen as an admirable feature of working-class life north of the border. Yet the many changes that occurred, which either sent artisans rapidly upward into the realms of the lower middle classes, or equally, destroyed the social status of many with previously sought after skills, have meant that the Scottish autodidact is often misidentified as working class, or missed altogether because of a lack of surviving written evidence for what is sometimes called the underclass. The rapid and transforming pace of industrialization, together with Scotland's place in the Union, created a rather different set of class relationships. It is fair to say for example, that unlike its English neighbour, Scotland had no relevant upper class to speak of in the age of empire, or at least not one that was wholly Scottish in terms of an identity.[11]

The twentieth century

By the twentieth century, the problem of understanding class relations in Scotland becomes more acute. The rapid unravelling of Scotland's key industries in engineering and manufacturing undoubtedly created downward social mobility for many families. In those industries where there was relative safety for the skilled until later in the century, there was conversely a great deal of inter-generational upward mobility into what has been coined 'a state-sector middle class'.[12] It is usually assumed that the major events of the early twentieth century bolstered working-class identity in Scotland. Economic depression, two World Wars and the rise of large-scale trades unionism all served to sharpen working-class distinctiveness, creating a less fractured class – of itself and for itself – that was internationalist in outlook rather than parochially Scottish. Within this twentieth-century Scottish working-class mentality, the stereotypical figure of *Lad o Pairts* came to be scorned alongside other aspects of the late-nineteenth-century Scottish Kailyard as nothing more than myth, and moreover, a device that operated as an antiquated sop to the proper advancement of the working classes.

The notion that there had ever been equality of opportunity in education for anything more than a select few has been a common argument in recent Scottish labour history, with the result that previously revered ideals about nineteenth-century traditions of meritocracy have been damned.[13] By this way of thinking, the post-war educational reforms enacted in Scotland during the 1940s did nothing to undermine meritocracy and promote democracy in opportunity.[14] The extension of the school leaving age to fifteen and the enshrinement of the filtering eleven-plus examination – popularly known in Scotland as the 'Quallie' – cemented a system wherein the educational futures of entire generations of children were cast in a narrow and mostly prejudicial way.[15] Moreover, increasingly limited opportunities to obtain secure skilled employment did much to ensure that many in the Scottish working classes knew their place and the small to non-existent likelihood of ever escaping it, except on a boat going across the Atlantic. Indeed, emigration and its social effects, is another key component of contemporary Scottish identity and is deeply written into the modern Scottish psyche. The drain on Scotland's population through emigration was a nineteenth-century pattern that continued well into the twentieth century.[16]

Assumptions have been made suggesting that the twentieth century saw the disappearance of the autodidactic tradition.[17] It is commonly concluded by many that it was a tradition that died a much-lamented death with free secondary education, welfare rights, the 'you've never had it so good' ethos of the post-austerity 1960s and the exclusion of the masses from an intellectual life. It can be argued that this is a case where the 'north' of Britain differs markedly from the south in this respect from an economic, social and cultural standpoint. Just who the working classes have been is no clearer in the twentieth century than it was in the previous century. Indeed, if the *Lad o Pairts* really was a mythical figure, so too perhaps is his late-twentieth-century opposite – the feckless, idle and drunken urban working-class Scot – seen most famously in recent popular culture in the figure of Rab C. Nesbitt.[18] The Nesbitts of Scotland vividly portray a twentieth-century working-class culture wherein a lack of education has produced the antithesis of the sober, well-read autodidact from a humble Scottish background. Yet one can question such anti-intellectual stereotypes in the face of recently gathered research, which suggests that the traditions of self-improvement through reading and learning remained manifest in significant sections of the Scottish working class.

Although many families in Scotland have become accustomed in the twentieth century to long cycles of unemployment and material poverty in terms of income, housing conditions and health expectations, many did, and still do, transcend such circumstances. It may be that the unusually broad Scottish education system has encouraged this, but not for the reasons that politicians imagine. In this period, the working-class autodidact can be found, but not in the places inhabited by the Nesbitts of the world. They are to be encountered amongst the employed, the skilled and the intellectually aspiring that have left written accounts of their lives.[19] There is continuity between the two centuries from an economic and social perspective in this respect.

Perhaps more surprisingly, there is also continuity from the point of view of the trajectory of education across the two centuries. As the Scottish Historiographer Royal, T. C. Smout, has commented on the history of Scottish education, 'The more it changes the more it stays the same.'[20] Such cynicism about the true effects of the democratic principle in education continues to be common in Scottish history. Nevertheless, this should not detract from the fact that a positive attitude towards learning is one of the core elements upon which the modern Scottish identity is pinned. Personal testimony obtained through the *Scottish Readers Remember* project confirms that changes that came about in Scottish education at the start of the twentieth century did perpetuate a meritocratic rather than a democratic system in education. As the Labour politician Ramsay MacDonald stated on the eve of World War 1, what this amounted to was '[a]scheme for helping a few individuals to rise from one class into another . . . nothing to do with the improvement of national education'.[21]

This much-mythologized democratic system of education was, for a fortunate minority, a means of obtaining a ticket out of their class through higher education. In addition, those who did rise up the ladder were more likely to have been male and the children of skilled workers. Yet since free, secondary education was available only up to age fourteen before 1944, and age fifteen until the early 1970s, the inquisitive, literate working-class person was generally channelled not into further education or university studies but into seeking a trade. Such social engineering ran aground as shifts in industry in face of international competition took their toll, along with the economic slumps that were longer lasting and harder to shake off than those experienced in the south of Britain.[22] Yet to have a trade was liberty enough for most of the respectable Scottish working classes, even in the post-war years. For it meant, if nothing else, that one had mobility. However, the types of new industries introduced in post-war Scotland often led to rampant de-skilling.[23] In speaking with many Scots born in the earlier part of the century, it would appear that the will to read, to improve one's mind through reading, and to seek out new ideas through reading, persisted in spite of such pressures. The majority of the urban Scottish working classes were likely never to have considered university and could not have afforded university. In remote areas, there may have been even more of a disincentive in terms of expense and cultural dislocation; however, across Scotland, most could visit the public library.

Reading, learning and libraries

The introduction of free public libraries, at the start of the twentieth century, was undoubtedly an offshoot of the sensibility surrounding a democratic tradition of learning in Scotland. In Glasgow, for example, the first publicly funded neighbourhood library was established in 1901 in the Gorbals. This area would shortly become notorious, and remain infamous for most of the twentieth century because of its slum conditions.[24]

Nevertheless, it produced its fair share of autodidacts. These included the late Ralph Glasser who famously became 'the Gorbals boy at Oxford' and who commented in memoirs of his early life in Glasgow that, '[T]he library drew me like a magnet, after work of an evening in the busy time, and for whole days in the slack season.'[25] Glasser's employment in the garment making industry, which flourished in the city centre area, was one that commonly entailed long periods of irregular working hours and seasonal variations. Thousands of workers in Scottish manufacturing were familiar with this pattern of employment and the economic insecurity that it produced. The library was one place where free heat and light as well as reading could be had; and in a country where by mid-century more than half the population lived in homes of two rooms or less, the library was a refuge from endemic overcrowding.[26] Glasser took shelter in a number of reading facilities, including the free reading room of the Jewish Workers' Circle.[27]

His favoured place for learning however, was Glasgow's famous Mitchell Library, at that time the largest reference library in Europe to provide free public access. One of the notions that abound about public libraries in Scotland is that they did indeed encourage reading as a means of intellectual enquiry and moral improvement – not as a place of light entertainment. Thus in only one example of thousands, the Corporation of Glasgow's Library Committee in 1920 freely approved titles such as *Bibliography and Methods of English Literary History* and *Introduction to the Study of Beowulf*, which were requested by enthusiastic readers. But in the same year, they declined requests for *The Man of the Forest* by Zane Grey and Max Beer's *A History of British Socialism*, titles which had been requested for inclusion in the industrial, northern fringes of Glasgow at Springburn Public Library.[28]

The Depression years in Scotland further cemented class loyalties and a turn to socialist and labour politics in Scotland.[29] It is pertinent that it was at this time that the use of public libraries increased hugely. In 1932 for example, proposed budget restrictions on Glasgow's libraries prompted this curt assessment from the senior Librarian: 'Unemployment has materially increased demands upon libraries and added largely to the numbers of readers.'[30] Indeed by the early 1930s, Glasgow had expanded its network of branch libraries from eight to twenty-six in number – most of which were situated in working-class, or mixed social class localities. Also recognized was the fact that many Glaswegians were using the libraries as a place of study; free lecture series were instigated from the mid 1920s onwards – always accompanied in publicity with suggested preparatory reading. Even in Calvinist Scotland, or perhaps *because this was* Calvinist Scotland, Sunday opening was briefly tried in deference to the working man.[31] The poet Tom Leonard was born in the industrial west of Scotland in 1944. He has commented on the central role played by these municipal institutions:

> The public library to me – to my generation, I would say – was crucial because of the freedom it gave to choose what you wanted to read, and the freedom it gave you to make up your own mind what you thought about what you had read . . . Public libraries are crucial to democracy.[32]

Such usage of public libraries is borne out in oral testimony. The oral history study, *Scottish Readers Remember*, includes an interview with Mr Todd, whose father was injured in a mining accident and following this became an unskilled worker in the local steel works. This interviewee, who grew up in a two-roomed house, is articulate on the subject of the influence of the libraries. In the industrial towns of Lanarkshire, there was little demand for the purchase of books because there was little money to buy them:

> I always was brought up with books and I haunted Wishaw Library . . . we plundered the library. We were there twice a week sometimes, I'm sure, and my reading such as it was, was also influenced by the fact it was a time of scarcity. . . . We couldnae buy them and nobody, I mean they just weren't, there was no book shops in Wishaw, except the Co-op had a wee stock o' books.[33]

Recollections such as this of public libraries are replicated many times in the oral testimony produced by the *Scottish Readers* study. Moreover, the tone of testimony in these memories echoes Tom Leonard's view; although requests for certain texts that did not meet the city fathers' dictates on what constituted self-improvement could be dismissed, there was still scope to choose from a vast array of literature that was not passively consumed. From the popular to the trenchantly intellectual, the Scottish library user was able to exercise personal judgement about what to read, and given the eclectic tastes sometimes evident in individual reading histories, Scottish readers did indeed feel the freedom that comes with making up their own minds. This preference may be seen in the fact that despite a huge demand for extra-mural education for workers, the Workers'

Educational Association was slow to take off in Scotland. In part, this was due to a lack of institutional support from Scottish universities and municipal authorities, but it also was a result of widespread fear that the WEA was a representative of bourgeois control and did not encourage freethinking.[34]

Continuity of this independent spirit can still be seen in the post-Second World War period, when the working-class autodidact is supposed to have become a near extinct species. One interviewee, born in 1945, reported reading over the summer of 1961, several works by Oscar Wilde, Dickens, Conrad, Tolstoy, Lewis Grassic Gibbon and Vera Brittain, alongside Margaret Mitchell's *Gone With the Wind* and a classic of popular self-help – *The Power of Positive Thinking* by Norman Vincent Peale.[35] As with a minority of her contemporaries, this woman from a working-class background did manage to attend university. However, her reading history shows that a will to become well read, often indiscriminately exercised, started long before she became an undergraduate. The bounty of the library encouraged such eclectic tastes.

Reading choices

Mr Todd relates that there was little money for books when he was growing up, but what little there was, would sometimes be used to buy newspapers, magazines and comics – all of which cemented a domestic culture of reading in many working-class homes. By the bounty of a slightly better off uncle with socialist leanings, Mr Todd was gifted the twelve-volume *Book of Knowledge*, bought by subscription from a travelling sales outfit, and as he describes it, both he and later his brother 'pored over' these books. Glasgow Corporation boasted in 1932 that not more than ten per cent of its stock was works of fiction – but they were likely preaching to a converted audience. Indeed, in examining readers' requests in the period, the great numbers of self-help books asked for is notable.

Inescapable too is the conservative nature of many of the works, but maybe these readers knew what they were dealing with in the attitudes of municipal library committees. For example, one request was made in 1929 for work by D. H. Lawrence: predictably, it was turned down.[36] Where popular reading matter is concerned, there was, as Mr Todd describes, frequently a queue for new titles in fiction at the library. He also recalls that the purchase of books was revolutionized in such towns with the coming of the Penguin paperbacks, just about affordable, and available to buy in the local Co-op. Mr Todd's first purchase of one of these, still in his possession at the time of his interview, was a title by Ford Madox Ford – not exactly a new work and not one that specially reflected any parochially Scottish flavour. The reading memories of this man, like many others in his age group demonstrates that the tastes of Scots were eclectic and wide, and tended to look outwards, rather than simply at their own traditional literary heritage.

Moreover, in parts of Scotland even more remote from metropolitan tastes, the working classes were often still inclined to loftier reading than that associated with their station. As a young man Mr Moncrieff, who grew up in Shetland, cut his intellectual teeth on the *Manchester Guardian* for example, whilst still making time for a bit of Zane Grey, which he recalls the public library in Lerwick did supply:

> We could go to the library and get these Western books. And the older men there in the building . . . they were a bright bunch – they would descend on you and try to encourage you to throw away these Westerns and read something more serious; and I remember being told that we had to get a paper and really try and follow it. And the papers they were recommending were *The Times*, *the Manchester Guardian*, *The Yorkshire Post* and *The Scotsman* and I don't remember if the *Glasgow Herald* was included in that.[37]

The variety and number of newspaper and magazine publications available to the working classes through libraries, subscription and the ubiquity of corner shop newsagents was phenomenal, and these were devoured avidly.[38] In February 1928, Glasgow Corporation Library Committee reviewed those periodicals that were regularly gifted to the city libraries; these totalled 594 copies of 164 different journals and magazines.[39] These gifts were in addition to the plethora of daily and weekly items on regular purchase. In respect of these, available figures for the year 1931–32 indicate that the number of current periodicals and newspapers was 3,989. This report further remarks on the extensive use made of these.[40] Moreover, unlikely popular texts might stir up unusual intellectual questions. George

Rountree, born in 1930s Glasgow for example, found a love of astronomy as a teenager after reading a sensationalist science fiction magazine – an interest he then nurtured at his local library in the Clydeside shipbuilding district of Govan.[41]

The love of reading

Lack of money and lack of availability did not necessarily block an individual love of books, in fact quite the opposite; oral testimony includes strong and fond memories of the purchase of books second-hand. Mrs Reid, born in 1932, was raised by her grandparents in the east end of Glasgow. Her grandfather and his brother were union activists and, as she says, 'they always sort of used their brains'.[42] In this locality, second-hand books were available cheaply at the *Barras* – a well-known Glasgow street market – and Mrs Reid recalls the family favourites as being the works of Dickens. Second-hand book purchase was indeed extensive amongst the Scottish working classes, and has even been reported in the oral testimony of western islanders who were often seasonal migrants to lowland towns and cities.[43] In both urban and rural areas, the second-hand principle was endemic; books, newspapers and magazines might be read by countless members of extended families and neighbours. Mrs Murphy, as another example, who was also a child of Glasgow's east end, had an even more ingenious way of nurturing a love of reading: as she put it, they used to 'rake the middens' or go through rubbish left for collection at the rear of tenement dwellings. The bounty of the 'middens' was not high-class literature, but it meant children otherwise deprived of reading matter were able to read. Mrs Murphy recognized the influence of Conan Doyle in the cache of out of print *Thriller* comics discarded in a nearby but more salubrious neighbourhood than her own and memorably raked from what she described as this 'snobby midden'.[44] It was the sheer love of reading that flourished in this way.

Conclusion

By looking more locally at reading practices, and through this prism, more keenly examining class identity and its relationship with culture, we can conclude that the autodidact tradition is not lost in Scotland, but has assumed new guises. Autodidactic practices likely did change in response to mass culture and mass literacy during the twentieth century. However, the materiality of many Scottish lives meant that access to elite culture through higher education and upward social mobility continued to be a minority pursuit until relatively recently. Yet the notion that Scots had respect for learning, and a love of the democratic principle where reading and intellectual enquiry are concerned, is not built on foundations of straw. Rather than seeing mass culture as functioning in opposition to the autodidact impulse, it makes much more sense to see the two as functioning together. The spread of public libraries and the popular reading material available during the twentieth century provided new inroads in leisure and learning for Scots who continued to perceive themselves as working class. Many Scots did what they had always done, that is to read, make up their own minds about what to read, and about what to think about their reading. Jonathan Rose memorably states that his work on British working-class autodidacts is about 'a success story with a downbeat ending'.[45] But there is much that can be identified about Scotland that diverges from the general UK experience he chronicles. A distinct pattern in education and literacy is certainly one area, but so too is the growth throughout the twentieth century of a particularly Scottish working-class identity. In the last century, working-class Scots (that is most Scots) left school at the statutory leaving age for both material and ideological reasons.[46] The supposed tradition of egalitarian access to education meant little to them, but the notion that an educated mind was open to all meant much. It is bound up with how Scots see themselves, both in terms of class and national identities. At the end of the twentieth century, Scotland famously surpassed other parts of the UK in obtaining a 'mass higher education system' that sends over half its school leavers on into tertiary education.[47] Sadly though, an unskilled working-class background remains a significant factor affecting non-entrants.[48] Perhaps the Scottish autodidacts of the future will come from this group.

Notes and references

1. Jonathan Rose, *The Intellectual Life of the British Working Classes* (New Haven: Yale University Press, 2001).
2. Discussion of the distinctiveness of class relations in Scotland can be found in John Foster, 'A proletarian nation? Occupation and class since

1914', in *People and Society in Scotland*, Vol. III, 1914–1990, ed. A. Dickson and J. H. Treble (Edinburgh: John Donald Publishers and The Economic and Social History Society of Scotland, 1992), pp. 201–40; for literacy levels, see David Finkelstein, 'Readers and reading', in *The Edinburgh History of the Book in Scotland*, Vol. 4, ed. David Finkelstein and Alistair McCleery (Edinburgh: Edinburgh University Press, 2007), pp. 431–2.

3. Richard J. Finlay, 'Scotland in the twentieth century: in defence of oligarchy?', *The Scottish Historical Review*, 73 (1994), 103–12.

4. The Scottish Parliament – Official Report 16 January 2008, Cols. 5035–5102, http://www.scottish.parliament.uk/business/officialReports/meetings Parliament/or-08/sor0116-02.htm#Col5104 [Accessed 8 December 2008].

5. Robert Anderson, 'In search of the "lad of parts": the mythical history of Scottish Education', *History Workshop Journal*, 19 (1985), 82–104.

6. *Scottish Readers Remember* has been funded by the Arts and Humanities Research Council. As described, this study is collecting recorded interviews with Scots, which will be archived by SAPPHIRE; the project is the first sustained attempt to understand reading practices within twentieth-century Scotland. The SAPPHIRE initiative is a partnership between Edinburgh Napier University and Queen Margaret University, Edinburgh, with Napier as the lead institution. Recordings are held in the Edward Clark Collection at Napier's Merchiston Campus.

7. See Christine Pawley, 'Seeking "significance": actual readers, specific reading communities', *Book History*, 5 (2002), 143–60.

8. See for example Robert O. Gray, *The Labour Aristocracy in Victorian Edinburgh* (Oxford: Oxford University Press, 1976), and Robert Gray, *The Aristocracy of Labour in Nineteenth-Century Britain, 1850–1914* (London: Macmillan, 1981).

9. W. Knox, 'The political and workplace culture of the Scottish working class, 1832–1914', in *People and Society in Scotland 1830–1914*, ed. W. Hamish Fraser and R. J. Morris (Edinburgh: John Donald, 1990), p. 145.

10. William Gallacher, *The Last Memoirs of William Gallacher* (London: Lawrence & Wishart, 1966), p. 25.

11. David McCrone, 'Towards a principled society: Scottish elites in the twentieth century', in *People and Society in Scotland*, ed. Fraser and Morris, pp. 176–7.

12. Christopher Harvie, *No Gods and Precious Few Heroes: Twentieth-Century Scotland* (Edinburgh: Edinburgh University Press), p. 87.

13. H. M. Paterson, 'Incubus and ideology: the development of secondary schooling in Scotland, 1900–1939', in *Scottish Culture and Scottish Education 1800–1980*, ed. Walter M. Humes and Hamish M. Paterson (Edinburgh: John Donald, 1983), pp. 197–215.

14. Andrew McPherson, 'Schooling', in *People and Society in Scotland*, ed. Fraser and Morris, pp. 80–107.

15. T. C. Smout, *A Century of the Scottish People, 1830–1950* (London: HarperCollins, 1997), pp. 227–8.

16. M. Flinn, *Scottish Population History* (Cambridge: Cambridge University Press, 1977), p. 448.

17. See for example, Guglielmo Cavallo and Roger Chartier, *A History of Reading in the West* (Oxford: Polity, 2003).

18. The comedy series, *Rab C. Nesbitt* (1990) was created by Ian Pattison and broadcast by the BBC, its protagonist being described thus: 'the string vest-wearing, permanently sozzled Rab C. Nesbitt is an armchair philosopher, living a life of near poverty in Glasgow's Govan'. The original ran for fifty-two episodes but a new series has recently been recommissioned. See: http://www.bbc.co.uk/comedy/rabcnesbitt & http://www.imdb.com/title/tt0129709/

19. See Martyn Lyons, 'Working-class autobiographers in nineteenth-century Europe: some Franco-British comparisons', *History of European Ideas*, 20 (1995), 236.

20. Smout, *Century of the Scottish People*, p. 230.

21. Ramsay MacDonald in 1914, quoted in Smout, *Century of the Scottish People*, pp. 226–7.

22. Foster, 'A Proletarian Nation', pp. 208–9.

23. Knox, 'Class, work and trade unionism in Scotland', in *People and Society in Scotland, 1914–1990*, ed. A. Dickson and J. H. Treble (Edinburgh: John Donald, 1992), pp. 116–21.

24. Despite its notoriety, there has been little scholarly work done on the culture of the Gorbals as a community. Discussion of discourses surrounding the reputation of the locality can be found in Linda Fleming, 'Gender, ethnicity and experience: Jewish women in Glasgow c.1880–1950' (unpublished doctoral thesis, University of Glasgow, 2005), Chapter 3, 'Gender, ethnicity and the Gorbals story', pp. 91–148; for a general history see E. Eunson, *The Gorbals: An Illustrated History* (Ochiltree, Ayrshire: Stenlake Publishers, 1996).

25. Ralph Glasser, *Growing Up in the Gorbals* (London: Chatto & Windus, 1986), p. 118.

26. See Lynn Abrams and Linda Fleming, 'From scullery to conservatory: everyday life in the Scottish home', in *A History of Everyday Life in Twentieth-Century Scotland*, ed. L. Abrams and C. Brown (Edinburgh: Edinburgh University Press, 2010), pp. 48–75.

27. Linda Fleming, 'Ralph Glasser', in *The Edinburgh History of the Book in Scotland*, ed. Finkelstein and McCleery, p. 440.

28. Glasgow City Archives (GCA), 'Suggestions by Readers submitted to the Committee on Libraries', 20 September 1920, uncatalogued library papers, box file ref no: D-TC 8/22.

29. This is a contested area in Scottish political history; a summary may be found in Smout, *Century of Scottish People*, pp. 252–75.

30. GCA, 'Report on the request by the Special Committee on estimates for reduction of libraries estimates for 1932–33 by £5000', Mitchell Library Correspondence, ref no. DLB4.4.

31. The experiment ran from December 1918 to May 1919. GCA, 'Meeting of the Committee on Libraries, 17 June', para. 1534(a) in *Minutes of the Corporation of Glasgow, April to November 1919.*

32. Attila Dosa, 'Interview with Tom Leonard', *Scottish Studies Review*, 5 (2004), 69–83 (p. 75).

33. SAPPHIRE, Scottish Readers Remember Collection (SRR), accession no. 2007/9 interview with Bob Todd (b.1932); interviewed by Linda Fleming 25 January 2007.
34. Rob Duncan, 'Ideology and provision: the WEA and the politics of workers' education in early twentieth-century Scotland', in *A Ministry of Enthusiasm: Centenary Essays on the Workers' Educational Association,* ed. Stephen K. Roberts (London: Pluto Press, 2003), pp. 176–97.
35. SRR, Bibliography of Margot Alexander (b.1945), accession no. 2008/46.
36. GCA, 'Suggestions by Readers submitted to the Committee on Libraries'; request for *Pansies* at Anderson Library, August, 1929. Uncatalogued library papers, box file ref. D-TC 8/22.
37. SRR, accession no. 2007/68 interview with Edward Moncrieff (b.1922); interviewed by Linda Fleming 24 April 2007.
38. Harvie, *No Gods*, pp. 122–3.
39. GCA, uncatalogued library papers, box file ref. D-TC8/22.
40. GCA, 'Summary of Facilities, Use and Cost of the Department', Mitchell Library Correspondence Vol. 4 (Dec. 1931–Mar. 1936), ref. DLB4.4.
41. SRR, accession no. 2007/ 154, interview with George Rountree (b.1935), interviewed by Linda Fleming 11 November 2007.
42. SRR, accession no. 2007/1, interview with May Reid (b.1932), interviewed by Linda Fleming 11 January 2007.
43. SRR, accession no. 2007/127, interview with Mary Sinclair (b.1936), interviewed by David Finkelstein 22 July 2007.
44. SRR, accession no. 2007/153, interview with Janet Murphy (b.1941), interviewed by Linda Fleming 21 November 2007.
45. Rose, *Intellectual Life*, p. 11.
46. Smout, *Century of Scottish People*, p. 228, quotes figures for school leavers (1951) as 87 per cent of twenty to twenty-four year olds leaving school at the statutory leaving age of fifteen years.
47. Teresa Tinklin and David Raffe, *Scottish School Leavers Entering Higher Education*, http://www.scotland.gov.uk/edru/Pdf/ers/ssls_specialreport_ 1.pdf (p. 2 of 12) [Accessed 24 January 2010].
48. Ibid., pp. 6–7.

Further Reading and Weblinks

Selected books

Altick, Richard, *The English Common Reader: A Social History of the Mass Reading Public* (Chicago: University of Chicago Press, 1957)

Clayton Windscheffel, Ruth, *Reading Gladstone* (Basingstoke: Palgrave Macmillan, 2008)

Colclough, Stephen, *Consuming Texts: Readers and Reading Communities, 1695–1870* (Basingstoke: Palgrave Macmillan, 2007)

Crone, Rosalind, Katie Halsey and Shafquat Towheed (eds), *The History of Reading* (London: Routledge, 2010)

Hammond, Mary, *Reading, Publishing and the Formation of Literary Taste in England, 1880–1914* (Aldershot: Ashgate, 2006)

Jackson, H. J., *Marginalia: Readers Writing in Books* (New Haven: Yale University Press, 2001)

—— *Romantic Readers: The Evidence of Marginalia* (New Haven: Yale University Press, 2005)

Jajdelska, Elspeth, *Silent Reading and the Birth of the Narrator* (Toronto: University of Toronto Press, 2007)

Klancher, Jon, *The Making of English Reading Audiences, 1790–1832* (Madison, WI: University of Wisconsin Press, 1987)

Murphy, Andrew, *Shakespeare for the People: Working Class Readers, 1800–1900* (Cambridge: Cambridge University Press, 2008)

Patten, Robert L. and John O. Jordan (eds), *Literature in the Marketplace: Nineteenth-Century Publishing and Reading Practices* (Cambridge: Cambridge University Press, 1995)

Pearson, Jacqueline, *Women's Reading in Britain, 1750–1835* (Cambridge: Cambridge University Press, 1999)

Raven, James, Helen Small and Naomi Tadmor (eds), *The Practice and Representation of Reading* (Cambridge: Cambridge University Press, 1996)

Rose, Jonathan, *The Intellectual Life of the British Working Classes* (New Haven: Yale University Press, 2001)

Secord, James, *Victorian Sensation: The Extraordinary Publication, Reception, and Secret Authorship of Vestiges of the Natural History of Creation* (Chicago: University of Chicago Press, 2000)

St Clair, William, *The Reading Nation in the Romantic Period* (Cambridge: Cambridge University Press, 2004)

Vincent, David, *Literacy and Popular Culture: England, 1750–1914* (Cambridge: Cambridge University Press, 1989)

Waller, P. J., *Writers, Readers and Reputations: Literary life in Britain, 1870–1918* (Oxford: Oxford University Press, 2006)

Willes, Margaret, *Reading Matters: Five Centuries of Discovering Books* (New Haven: Yale University Press, 2008)

Wright, Thomas, *Oscar's Books* (London: Chatto & Windus, 2008)

Selected articles

Bradley, Matthew, 'The Reading Experience Database', *Journal of Victorian Culture*, 15: 1 (2010), 151–3

Crone, Rosalind, 'Reappraising Victorian literacy through prison records', *Journal of Victorian Culture*, 15: 1 (2010), 3–37.

Darnton, Robert, 'First steps towards a history of reading', *Australian Journal of French Studies*, 23 (1986), 5–30

Dobraszczyk, Paul, 'Useful reading? Designing information for London's Victorian cab passengers', *Journal of Design History*, 21 (2008)

Dow, Gillian and Katie Halsey, 'Jane Austen's reading: the Chawton years', *Persuasions Online*, 30: 2 (Spring 2010)

Esbester, Mike, 'Nineteenth-century timetables and the history of reading', *Book History*, 12 (2009), 156–85

Grafton, Anthony and Lisa Jardine, '"Studied for action": how Gabriel Harvey read his Livy', *Past and Present*, 129 (Nov. 1990), 30–78.

Halsey, Katie, '"Folk stylistics" and the history of reading: a discussion of method', *Language and Literature*, 18: 3 (2009), 231–46

—— 'Reading the evidence of reading', *Popular Narrative Media*, 2 (2008), 123–37

Jajdelska, Elspeth, 'Pepys in the history of reading', *Historical Journal*, 50: 3 (2007), 549–69.

McDowell, Kathleen, 'Toward a history of children as readers, 1890–1930', *Book History*, 12 (2009), 240–65

Navest, Karlijn, 'Marginalia as evidence: the unidentified hands in Lowth's *Short Introduction to English Grammar* (1762)', *Historiographia Linguistica*, 34: 1 (2007), 1–18

Owens, W. R., 'John Bunyan and the Bible', in *The Cambridge Companion to Bunyan*, ed. Anne Dunan-Page (Cambridge University Press, 2010), 39–50

Price, Leah, 'Reading: the state of the discipline', *Book History*, 7 (2004), 303–20

Stimpson, Felicity, '"I have spent my morning reading Greek": the marginalia of Sir George Otto Trevelyan', *Library History*, 23: 3, (2007), 239–50.

Towheed, Shafquat, 'Reading history and nation: Robert Louis Stevenson's reading of William Forbes-Mitchell's *Reminiscences of the Great Mutiny 1857–9*', *Nineteenth-Century Contexts*, 31: 1 (2009), 3–17

Towsey, Mark, '"An infant son to truth engage": virtue, responsibility and self-improvement in the reading of Elizabeth Rose of Kilravock, 1747–1815', *Journal of the Edinburgh Bibliographical Society*, 2 (2007), 69–92

Watson, Alex, 'Byron's marginalia to *English Bards and Scotch Reviewers*', *Byron Journal*, 37: 2 (2009), 131–9

Selected weblinks

British Fiction Database, 1800–1829: http://www.british-fiction.cf.ac.uk
British Library Newspapers Online: http://newspapers.bl.uk/blcs/
History of the Book Online: http://www.english.ox.ac.uk/hobo/
The Library History Database: http://www.r-alston.co.uk/content/libraryhistory/
Mass Observation Online: http://www.massobservation.amdigital.co.uk/
The National Archives (UK) Research Guide to Newspapers and the Press: http://www.nationalarchives.gov.uk/records/research-guides/newspapers.htm
Old Bailey Proceedings Online: http://www.oldbaileyonline.org/
Oxford Dictionary of National Biography: http://www.oxforddnb.com/
The Reading Experience Database, 1450–1945: www.open.ac.uk/Arts/RED/
Scottish Readers Remember: http://www.sapphire.ac.uk/readers.htm
Society for the History of Authorship, Reading and Publishing: http://www.sharpweb.org/

Index

Page numbers for illustrations are given in bold. References to tables are indicated in brackets.

government propaganda
materials, 91
and reading newspapers, 145, 150
non-fiction read during, 94, 95,
96, 97 (5.1)
affecting production quality of
books, 86, 91
reading preferences during, 84–5,
92–4
and having time to read, 87–8, 95
second-hand books, 58, 130, 200
security censorship (Second World
War), 85–6, 150
self-improvement *see*
autodidacticism
Shakespeare, William, 68, 69, 70, 90
Sharpe, Kevin, 16
Shawcross, Lord, 151
Shepard, Thomas, 164
Sherman, William, 16
Shirley (1849), 32
Shoemaker, Robert, 105
Sinclair, George, 24
Sketches of Booksellers of Other Days,
159
slavery, Christian attitudes to, 40, 41
Smillie, Robert, 68
Smith, Nancy, 165
Smout, T. C., 194
social/class mobility, 191–2, 192–3,
195
socialist ideology/politics
in inter-war Scotland, 196
and literature, 48–9, 50, 53–4
publications disseminating
socialist principles/ideals, 50,
52–3, 57
nineteenth century revival of
(Britain), 49, 50–1, 52, 62 n16
Socialist League, the, 52
socialist organizations, 52
see also under individual entries
Sommerville, C. John, 164
Southwell, Robert, 163
Spalding, Hilary, 88–92
books bought by, 88–90
diary, 88, **89**, 90, 91

use of libraries, 88, 90
reading list, 88, **89**, 90
Spencer, Herbert, 56
St Peter's Young Men's Club,
Preston, 126–7
Stamper, Joseph, 75–6
Stanley, Arthur Penrhyn, 41
Stanton, Elizabeth Cady, 43
Stead, W. T., *Library of Penny Poets,
Novels, and Prose Classics* (1895)
76
Story of an African Farm, The (1883),
49, 50, 51–2, 53, 56–7, 60 n5
featuring in the *Prophet* reading
lists, 56–7, 60 n5
Strahan, Alexander, 72, 73
Styles, John, 104
Sun, the, 150
Sunday newspapers, 140, 145
Sunday Pictorial, the, 145, 153 n30

Taylor, John, 165
Temperance Hall, Preston, 127
Tennyson, Alfred (Lord), 69, 76
Thackeray, William Makepeace, 68,
74, 75, 181
Thom, John Hamilton, 40
Thompson, Flora, 69, 70, 71
Times, The, 149, 150, 152 n9, 199
Tinley, Ralph, 166
Trevor, John, 4, 53, 55, 57, 58,
59–60, 62 n21
Labour Prophet, the, 4–5, 50, 53,
54, 55–6, 57, 59, 62 n21
Turton, Dorcas, 166

Urquhart family, 20, 21, 22, 24
Urquhart, Mary, 21, 22, 25
Uses of Literacy, The (1957), 146

Vincent, David, 75
Voltaire, 170

Walker, Ellis, 162
*Epicteti Enchiridion made English
in a Poetical Paraphrase* (1692),
162